Stained Glass
in England

An angel musician, fifteenth century. St Peter Hungate, Norwich

Stained Glass
in England

June Osborne

Foreword by Myfanwy Piper

SUTTON PUBLISHING

First published by Frederick Müller in 1981

This revised edition first published in the United Kingdom in 1993
by Alan Sutton Publishing Ltd, an imprint of Sutton Publishing Limited
Phoenix Mill · Thrupp · Stroud · Gloucestershire

Paperback edition with corrections first published by Sutton Publishing Limited in 1997

British Library Cataloguing in Publication Data

A catalogue record for this book is available from the British Library

ISBN 0–7509–1613–3

Title page illustration: a man scaring birds. 14th-century roundel at Stanton St John, Oxfordshire.

 ALAN SUTTON™ and SUTTON™ are the
trade marks of Sutton Publishing Limited

Typeset in 10/15 Times.
Typesetting and origination by
Alan Sutton Publishing Limited.
Printed in Great Britain by
WBC Limited, Bridgend.

Contents

Foreword

When *Stained Glass in England* was published in 1981 it was the first general study of the subject for more than seventy years. It was hailed with delight by those who were already knowledgeable about glass and those who knew little or nothing were inspired to know more.

June Osborne had written a lucid, learned, perceptive history of the subject without overloading her text with self-important scholarship. She also included (which no one had done before in a book on stained glass) a gazetteer, organized under counties and so turned an elegant monograph into a brilliant guidebook. There were eighty-eight illustrations in colour showing glass from the Saxon Age to the present day.

All these riches have been updated in the new edition and what already seemed to be a more than adequate gazetteer greatly expanded. The format is a little bigger and there are now over a hundred illustrations, half in black and white so that some of the coloured ones have been lost. But the choice and disposition is so visually sensitive that one does not feel deprived. It is a book that manages to combine information and passion with a natural ease. No dedicated church crawler should be without it and no beginner either.

I should like to thank June Osborne for asking me to write this short foreword to a book that John so much admired and that he would have written about so much more adequately.

MYFANWY PIPER

Preface and Acknowledgements

In the parish church of Fladbury near Evesham there is a small but particularly fine panel of Virgin and Child, dating from the fourteenth century; and it was in this village that I spent the first four years of my life. It may perhaps be an exaggeration to say that this lovely piece of stained glass exerted a subliminal influence on me; but the fact remains that I cannot put any date to the arousing of my interest in the subject.

As to how I came to write the first edition of this book (published by Frederick Müller in 1981), here I am on firmer ground. A few years before, I had been invited by London University Extra-Mural Department to be the tutor for the Applied Arts year of their Visual Arts Diploma. In conducting this course, I was allowed to specialize to some extent, and the field I chose in particular was stained glass. That was for these reasons: that the art is very closely linked to the periods and circumstances in which it was made; that it spans many centuries and often survives remarkably the ravages of time; and that, unlike many of the applied arts, it has the extra dimension of iconography. Added to which, by illustrating the lectures with colour-slides, one achieves near-perfection in visual aids – a transparency depicting a transparency.

The only problem was that in preparing this course I found there were few useful books available, and those few largely outdated. None of them had a regional index to show where the most interesting glass in the country was to be found. So I became aware that here was a gap to be filled. Meeting a fellow-writer (Nigel Foxell) at a private view, he asked me what book I had in mind to undertake next. I replied that I had long felt that there was a need for something about stained glass. 'You're right', he said, and immediately introduced me to Robin Garton, who became my agent for the first edition.

As I was to a large extent breaking new ground, it was not altogether easy to write. But I was greatly assisted by many knowledgeable people, and owed

ix

much to the help of, for instance, Peter Gibson of the York Glaziers' Trust (especially in the chapter on Conservation), F.W. Cole (then at Canterbury Cathedral), Dennis King of Norwich, Paul San Casciani of Oxford (for help in preparing the chapter on techniques), Peter Burman of the Council for the Care of Churches, Jill Kerr of the *Corpus Vitrearum Medii Aevi*, and the late Dr Peter Newton (then at the Centre for Medieval Studies at York). I owed much too to Philip Shenton's and John North's photography, to the co-operative attitude of my children (Ian, Elizabeth, Patrick and Jane), as well as an immeasurable debt to Pevsner's *Buildings of England* series.

The book met with considerable critical acclaim, from such distinguished people as Sir John Betjeman, Sir Ernst Gombrich, John Piper and Alec Clifton-Taylor. However, if one is attempting to do something for the very first time, as I was with the regional index, it is inevitable that there should be mistakes and omissions. Rare is the opportunity of a second chance, a new and revised edition where such things might be put right. I am extremely grateful to Alan Sutton for giving me this, and also to my discerning editor, Roger Thorp. During the twelve years since the first edition, other books had been published, and I had acquired some skill in photography. Moreover, and most valuably, I had been able to see a great deal more glass at first-hand. This last would not have been possible if it had not been for the generous help given me by Leyland Shawe, who has driven me on numerous stained glass explorations. My son Patrick has from time to time drawn my attention to glass I might otherwise have missed, and my daughter Jane kindly made it possible for me to become acquainted with some very important glass in Dorset.

In preparing the text for this new edition (now extensively revised) and in obtaining permission to photograph, I drew on the assistance of a large number of people. To all, my thanks. They are listed here in alphabetical order:

Hester Agate (St Edmundsbury-Ipswich Diocesan Advisory Committee)
Revd John Barnes of the Norwich Diocesan Committee for the Care of Churches
John Beaumont of Southwell
Mervyn Blatch of Pyrford (who inherited and passed on to me the late Alec Clifton-Taylor's notes on the first edition)
Revd Canon Denis Boyling, Chairman of the Hereford Diocesan Advisory Committee

PREFACE AND ACKNOWLEDGEMENTS

Canon Brian Brindley, Chichester Diocesan Advisory Committee

The British Society of Master Glass-Painters

Michael Brown, Secretary, Diocesan Advisory Committee

Sarah Brown of the Royal Commission for Historical Monuments

Lt Cdr D.W. Crampton-Thomas, Bath & Wells Diocesan Advisory Committee

Joan Denne, Administrative Secretary, Council for the Care of Churches

Edward Evans, Dean's Verger, Christ Church Cathedral, Oxford

David Hugh Farmer, author of *The Oxford Dictionary of Saints* (for information on Robert of Knaresborough and other saints)

Peter Gibson of the York Glaziers' Trust (for allowing us to use photographs of conservation taken in his workshop)

C.B. Gorton, Diocesan Secretary, Truro

Rachel Grant of Shipton-under-Wychwood

Michael Harvey, Chairman, Worcester Diocesan Advisory Committee

Sue Haydock, Administrator, Rochester Diocesan Advisory Committee

John Hayward, stained glass artist (for extensive help in revising the regional index)

Dr Martin Henig of the Institute of Archaeology, Oxford

R.M. Hubbuck of Petersfield (for extensive help with sorting out stained glass in Hampshire)

J.P. MacKechnie-Jarvis, Assistant Diocesan Secretary, Gloucester

W.A. McLelland of the Cathedral Hall, Bradford

Dr Elizabeth Maxwell

Miss S.A. Mills & staff of the Bede Monastery Museum, Jarrow

David O'Connor, History of Art Department, Manchester University

David Palfreyman, Bursar, New College, Oxford

Glyn Royal, Hon. Sec., Ripon Diocesan Advisory Committee

John Rutherford, Canon, St Edmundsbury (and brother of the late Rosemary Rutherford, stained glass artist)

Mary Saunders of the Oxford Diocesan Advisory Committee

Paul Sharpling of Kettering (for much help in sorting out stained glass in the Diocese of Peterborough)

The Revd George and Mrs Betty Stokes of Charlbury

The Master & Fellows of Trinity College, Cambridge (for giving permission to reproduce the photograph of the window of Trinity College Library)

STAINED GLASS IN ENGLAND

Elisabeth Vinty, daughter of Philip Shenton, for allowing me to reproduce his photograph of Adam Delving (Canterbury Cathedral)

Mrs Joan Western of Dalbury Lees, Derbyshire (for much help on the ancient St Michael window in Dalbury Church)

Glennys Wild, Keeper, Applied Art Department, Birmingham Museums & Art Gallery

John Winter of Rugby School

Ralph Wood of Rye (in connection with stained glass in the Diocese of Chichester)

Christine Zwart, Editor of the *Door* (Oxford Diocesan magazine)

My thanks are also due to the libraries of Oxford, and to my 'Stained Glass in England' class at the University's Department of Continuing Education, for their fund of encouragement and suggestions. In addition, I am most grateful to the chaplains and bursars of Oxford colleges for allowing me to photograph their glass, and to the many vicars, vergers, churchwardens and key-holders who have welcomed me into their churches. Finally, I should like to thank Myfanwy Piper for writing the Foreword to this book.

JUNE OSBORNE

1993

'What I tell you three times is true' declared Lewis Carroll's Bellman (*The Hunting of the Snark*).

I was delighted to have the opportunity for this third edition of my book, and to be given the chance of making, within the limits of the format, various amendments and additions, in particular to the Gazetteer. It would be rash now to promise absolute veracity, but at least I can claim that this third version is true to the best of my knowledge and belief.

I am happy too that the book appears this time in softback, which should enable it to reach a wider readership.

JUNE OSBORNE

1997

CHAPTER ONE

The Qualities of Stained Glass

> and immediately
> Rather than words comes the thought of high windows
> The sun-comprehending glass
> And beyond it, the deep blue air, that shows
> Nothing, and is nowhere, and is endless.
>
> Philip Larkin, *High Windows*

If in the mind of a modern writer glass may be associated with ecstacy, in the medieval mind it had power to inspire visions. Even in earlier periods, as Aldous Huxley reminds us [1], it had been thought of as the very stuff of paradise. The Celtic name for the land of the blessed was *Ynisvitrin* (the Island of Glass) and the Teutons spoke of the kingdom of their dead as *Glasberg*.

Although not a natural substance, glass was regarded as magical, and even divine during the Middle Ages. Indeed, to take a base material such as sand and by an irreversible process purify it into a new and nobler form was like alchemy but demonstrably more successful. Glass-makers, firing their wood-burning furnaces, could turn the lowest of the elements, earth, into a durable and 'sun-comprehending' substance. It was its ability to transmit light which made glass so special. In religious terms, light was a symbol of vital import-ance, used to describe the quality of Spirit Itself. Glass was a medium closely linked with light and which was as much to be looked through as looked at. It allowed both man's creation in its structure and design and God's creation in the sky beyond. Clearly this medium was ideally suited to the interpretation of spiritual themes. Small wonder that they said it could induce visions.

Glass has parallels in nature both in obsidian and in alabaster, both of which were used to make windows. But neither material had the same extraordinary quality of near transparency and in consequence they could not have the same transcendental overtones.

Even if the finest glass is technically imperfect, full of bubbles, striations and impurities, to this it owes its character. It is not entirely transparent, it is translucent and reveals its images through a modification of the sun's radiance.

Today glass is so familiar a material that we treat it with scant respect. Many of us throw away our non-returnable bottles without a second thought. But to appreciate the stained glass of the Middle Ages we have to realize that all glass was precious and that coloured glass was especially so. In general, it was only to be found in the church and was much too difficult to obtain for domestic use.

The colouring of glass was a secret guarded with particular care. Theophilus (writing in the first half of the twelfth century) in his treatise *On Divers Arts*[2] (extracts from which will be quoted in the next two chapters), goes into considerable detail about the making of windows, but the chapters which would have given precise instructions for the colouring of glass with copper, lead and salt are missing. This was probably no accident: these recipes were too secret to be put into writing. It was only by word of mouth, from master to trusted apprentice that they might be divulged. And while, from a purely functional point of view, a church could have been lit more cheaply and effectively by using plain glass, stained glass had a profounder purpose. Not only would it expound the teachings of the Church, but both symbol and halation[3] could be used to fill the congregation with the sense of mystery and vision. Glass also had the spiritual function of glorifying God for His own sake. Some windows were placed so high that no mortal eye could appreciate them. The twelfth-century genealogical windows at Canterbury cannot have been easily visible in their original setting in the clerestory. Likewise the content of the 'Dean's Eye' at Lincoln must have been as difficult to decipher when it was placed, as it is today.

Naturally when the medium was used in a secular context it could not have the same force. But from as early as the thirteenth century stained glass was used to depict heraldry and certain types of portraiture, mainly in the form of full-length figures. Even so, these are more often to be found in a church than in a castle or a guildhall. The changes in religious belief and observance in the sixteenth century meant that there were fewer commissions for religious works but the demand for secular glass continued steadily until in the seventeenth century

Arms of Henry III, mid-thirteenth century, one of the earliest examples of heraldic glass. Chetwode, Buckinghamshire

when, under Puritan rule, the art was threatened with total annihilation.

Throughout the two centuries that followed, it survived, broadly speaking, as one of the lesser arts, and was frequently secular in content. The Victorian age saw a revival of the art – at least the opportunities were there, even if the resulting windows varied from the superb to the deplorable. In the twentieth century, two world wars brought their aftermath of memorials, and windows were commissioned to replace those destroyed by aerial bombardment. Today with few ecclesiastical commissions, several artists and craftsmen are turning to designing stained glass for domestic settings. So secular glass continues, mainly as a secondary use of the medium.

An important aspect of stained glass is its architectural setting. More than fresco or mosaic, glass can be used as an integral part of church architecture. As well as being an embellishment, it also forms part of the building itself. Obviously it has a practical function in admitting light and affording protection against the elements, but it also has a visual relationship to architecture. When we see glass in its original setting, its impact is far stronger than the glass displayed with the artificial light of a museum. This is not to disparage the thoughtful and imaginative displays in, say, the Victoria and Albert Museum, where the problems have been overcome as well as they can be under the circumstances. But tracery lights make little sense without tracery. And to recreate in the museum the atmosphere of a church, not any church but *the* church the glass was intended for, is obviously impossible. Even though the museum may place together works of the same period, say English and French glass of the thirteenth century, if we see part of a Jesse tree next to a panel from a Miracle window next to a fragment from an Annunciation (the examples are hypothetical), none of them can move us in the same way as if we had come across them in their original setting.

STAINED GLASS IN ENGLAND

The character of glass in fact depended much on its setting. For example Romanesque churches tended to be rather dark with thick walls, admitting few and small windows. Without the counterbalance of flying buttresses the structure could not in any case support large apertures. In consequence where glass was used, its brilliance was intensified by the atmosphere of darkness and mystery. But in the fourteenth century, and to a greater extent in the fifteenth century, church structure and fenestration were revolutionized by the new understanding of both arch and buttress. Nowhere was the Gothic mind more dramatically expressed than in the great traceried window. Such vast windows might occupy almost the whole of the east and west elevations, and they were in general effect paler, with more white glass surrounding panels of coloured.

Equally the stained glass artist today has to be especially sensitive to the setting of his work. On the whole we do not destroy in order to rebuild, we have a respect for antiquity which would have puzzled our forebears. So it often happens that a modern window is set in an ancient church; this sets the artist an interesting problem. He will, one hopes, treat it with sympathy and yet avoid archaism. He is unlikely to design quite the same window as he would if it were a new building. If it *is* a new building, he may decide to use thick slab glass embedded in concrete, in which case the window becomes an essential part of the structure, the stained glass indissolubly blended with the architecture.

The subject of this book is stained glass in England; this is not precisely the same as English stained glass. The first artist-craftsman may have come from France or, later, from Flanders. It is quite possible that the same glaziers worked at Canterbury as at Chartres. Or, again later, a panel of glass may have been bought abroad, shipped to this country and set up in the local parish church. It is certainly true that the raw material, the coloured glass itself, was, for centuries, imported. Yet there are few countries more rich in stained glass. It is interesting that this art so prospered here, and in Northern Europe more than in Italy, for instance, normally in the forefront of all artistic developments. The most obvious reason is the difference in the quality of light; the medium is better suited to our greyer skies. Brilliant sunshine dazzles and does not enhance stained glass as well as a diffuse light. Under the infinitely variable conditions of the northern sky, hues intensify or merge, faces and figures come into prominence or fade and scenes are created or lost.

QUALITIES

NOTES

1 *Heaven and Hell.*
2 See Bibliography.
3 *Halation* is used in this context to describe the effect of putting opposing colours next to each other in a pattern. The effect is a fusing, rather than a merging of the colour. For example red and blue do not become mauve but red and blue together at the same time.

CHAPTER TWO

Techniques

If we are to appreciate windows, we must have some inkling of how they were made. This is not a technical handbook (there are many excellent works on the 'how to do it' principle) but with some knowledge of the possibilities and limitations of the craft comes a greater understanding, and appreciation.

To begin then with the basic material. What is glass, and how is it made? It is found in nature in the form of obsidian, a blackish-grey somewhat translucent substance which breaks conchoidally and has very much the same properties as man-made glass. But leaving obsidian on one side, three things are needed for making glass: silica, alkali and heat. Pliny, writing in the first century AD[1], tells a somewhat incredible story of how it was first invented. Certain Syrian merchants, transporting a load of natron, camped for the night on the sandy shores of Lake Belus. They lit a fire and placed their cooking-pots next to it, supporting them on the cakes of natron. In the morning they were surprised to find that with the heat of the fire the natron and sand had fused to form glass. This can scarcely be credited because although the basic components of the material figure in the story, it is hardly possible that the merchants could have left burning overnight a fire anywhere near hot enough to effect the transformation. This would require a temperature of about 1200 °C. Their breakfast would have been burnt and their cooking-pots melted long before the heat would have reached this intensity.

The art of making glass, which in the first place was coloured and virtually opaque, seems to have begun in Egypt in about 4000 BC, and was a development of the glazes used for pottery. The Egyptians used the material for making beads, and later small vessels, generally built up on a sand core. The glass was coloured with metallic oxides, such as copper, iron and cobalt. As far as is known, no window glass was made before the time of the Romans; the emperor Caligula, we are told, had glass windows in his palace. One speaks of 'Roman' glass, but much that comes under this general heading was actually made in Syria. It was in Syria that the technique of glass-blowing developed during the first century BC, and from there spread to the rest of the Roman empire, and ultimately Britain. The technique of blowing is basic not only to the making of vessels, but often to the making of window glass also. The earliest window glass (first century AD) was made by one of two methods, either by casting into a shallow mould, or by blowing an elongated bubble, cutting off one end, splitting down the length of the cylinder thus made and opening it out to form a flat sheet. In its essentials, this method of making 'antique' glass is still used, and is one of the types suitable for stained glass windows.

'Muff' glass is made by placing the molten glass bubble into an iron cylinder or muff and blowing again. The cylinder determines the shape and finished size, usually about 24 x 14 inches. The glass is often cut by touching it with a wet stick. Then it is flattened in a spreading kiln with a wooden tool like a bat, or rubbed down with charcoal blocks. Finally it is cooled or 'annealed', a gradual process taking some seventy hours.

The other method used by the Romans, generally called 'pressed' glass where molten glass is run into a mould, is also used for modern stained glass where it is to be set in concrete, and so thicker pieces are required.

There is also 'slab' or 'bottle' glass, sometimes referred to as 'Norman slab' – the technique seems to have been developed in Normandy. A bubble of glass is blown into a square mould, making a glass box. When this has cooled it is cut at the corners and makes five rectangular slabs. These will be smaller than pieces of glass made by the 'antique' method, not larger than 10 x 7 inches. They will tend to be thicker and darker in the centre, thinner towards the edges. This very irregularity helps to give it character, and makes it very suitable for stained glass windows.

Modern manufacturing methods have produced 'sheet' glass. Molten glass is run through mechanical rollers; this makes large sheets of glass cheaply, but with less interesting texture. Although it is sometimes used for stained glass, it is hardly to be preferred.

Finally there is 'crown' glass. This begins by being blown, but the bubble produced is opened up and spun until it flattens out into a plate. This is cracked off the blowing iron and placed in an annealing oven. The glass produced is thick in the centre and has a whorl pattern. Rectangular pieces, probably eleven in number, are cut from the disc. The centre one has the most pronounced whorl pattern and is less suitable for stained glass than the others.

When admiring the colour in stained glass, it is important to realize that the artist has probably chosen the glass pieces from a selection and not coloured them himself. The colouring is in general part of the process of manufacture, and is obtained by adding metallic oxides: cobalt for blue, copper or chromium for green, ferric oxide or uranium for yellow, manganese for purple, copper again or silenium or gold will obtain red, nickel added to lime glass will make brown, and added to potash lead glass will make violet. Red glass made from copper, however, presents a particular problem. If it is solid 'pot-metal', that is to say if it is coloured all the way through, it tends to be opaque. Therefore it has to be 'flashed'; a bubble of white (clear) glass is blown first, and then this is dipped into a crucible of red. In the early Middle Ages red glass seems, sometimes at least, to have been made with many laminations, a multiple sandwich of red and white. In general this is difficult to appreciate because one does not often see a piece of medieval glass edge-on.

It was soon realized that the technique of flashing, evolved through necessity, made further decorative effects possible. A single piece of glass could be made in two colours, or in one colour and white, at the same time. Part of the upper layer could be etched away with acid to reveal the lower. Abrading (scraping away) of flashed glass could be used with great dramatic effect, as in the red devil of the west window of Fairford, Gloucestershire (colour plate 33).

Unless one counts enamelling, almost the only glass that is stained, in the sense that the colour is applied after the piece of glass is manufactured, is that made yellow by silver nitrate. This technique will be discussed in a little more detail in Chapter Five, dealing with the fourteenth century.

When the artist chooses his glass, he will often prefer lime-glass which contains striations or 'reams' and perhaps some bubbles and impurities, rather than glass which is technically perfect. This will help give his work greater richness and character. The glass is fixed together with lead in the form of calms (pronounced 'cams'); (the transatlantic version of the word seems to be 'cames'). Lead has qualities which make it especially suitable for the purpose: it is flexible, relatively durable, easily cut and soldered. The calms are made in an H-shaped section and the glass is fitted into the flanges thus produced. The traditional way of making these calms was to sand cast them in a box. This cumbersome method has now been superseded, and calms are now cast in moulds. Some glass-workers prefer to make their own calms in the studio, using a small lead-mill. The leading can be a vital part of the design; the medieval glazier would sometimes vary the width of the calms in order to emphasize salient features of his composition.

In order for the window to be weatherproof, however, it is necessary to apply a special kind of cement or putty. The constituents of this are equal parts of powdered whitening and plaster of Paris. Lampblack is added with a small quantity of red lead; then this is mixed with boiled oil and turpentine.

If the window is more than about three feet high it has to be supported horizontally with saddle-bars; these are set into the stonework on either side, about twelve inches apart. Traditionally they are made of iron; the early ones were made of charcoal iron – iron ore placed in a charcoal fire – which was malleable and virtualy rustproof. Now other non-rusting metals are sometimes used. As the size of windows increased it became necessary to support them vertically as well. Visually the result of this gave rise to a grid of squares, then variations were introduced by alternating the squares with circles, then all manner of patterns were developed. Thus the practical necessity of supporting windows had a considerable influence on their design.

The leaded glass was generally fixed to the saddle-bar with copper wire ties, each one about four inches long, soldered appropriately to the panel. Other methods were sometimes used: at Canterbury they had a system of loops and wedges; at Tudeley in Kent the modern Chagall windows are fixed with coils of lead.

We tend to think of leading as an essential part of stained glass, but some modern windows are made with no lead at all. They are constructed by embedding slab glass in concrete or epoxy resins. Slab glass, sometimes referred to as *dalle-de-verre*, is far thicker than the glass normally used for leaded windows. In this kind of window the tendency is to show much less glass in proportion to its setting; for structural reasons the apertures must be limited in size. The tendency also is towards abstract, or at least not pictorial, design. The Piper-Reyntiens lantern in the Cathedral of Christ the King, Liverpool, is a superb example of this technique. Whole curtain-walls of embedded stained glass are possible as long as they do not have to be load bearing; it is hard to say what is structure and what is decoration. The window becomes very much part of the architecture.

Traditional stained glass windows, however, have the advantage of being resilient. Because they are slightly flexible, they are considerably tougher than a

Modern glass in the *dalle-de-verre* technique.
Prinknash Abbey, Gloucestershire

single sheet of glass of comparable thickness. The force that would shatter a plate-glass window might leave a leaded one only slightly warped.

Before the glass is cut and the window assembled, the whole process of design will have taken place. First of all the site will have been assessed and measurements taken. Then usually a small sketch is prepared, to scale, so that it may be enlarged into a full-sized cartoon. The cartoon is traced on to transparent paper or linen to make a 'cut-line'. On the cut-line will be shown the placing of saddle-bars, the divisions of the glass necessary if the window is at all large, and the pattern of the leading. The pattern will be dictated by the lines of the design and the placing of the colours, bearing in mind that allowance must be made for the thickness of the core of the calms.

Then the glass is cut piece by piece, the selection of the colours being vitally important; they are placed on the cartoon so that the main drawing-lines may be traced on to them, using special brushes called riggers, and the drawing is often fired at this stage. The pieces are then laid over the cut-line on a glass easel, and stuck together with beeswax or Plasticine. After this the half-tones or textures are put on. The paints used are iron oxide with powered glass, and are blackish-brown in their finished effect. They are used for defining the details of faces, hands, drapery and so forth, and for 'matting' so as to modify the colour. Matting is done by applying a layer of glass-paint with a large brush called a flat or a mop, and then smoothing the wet paint with a badger brush. Highlights or patterns are removed with stiff brushes known as 'scrubs', or with a stick, or for very fine work, with a quill or a needle. Modern techniques also use sponges, fingers, or splashes of oil or water to give texture. The pieces are then fired again, at a temperature of about 620 °C. The process of firing fixes the paint permanently.

If any of the glass is to be stained yellow, this is done last. The grains of silver that will produce this effect are ground up with madder, and applied usually to the back of the glass. Unlike paint, which remains on the surface, stain will actually penetrate the glass once it is fired. This firing is done at a lower temperature, about 520 °C. Then the glass is taken from the easel, set in plaster in flat trays, paint side uppermost, and placed in the kiln. The glass is cooled very gradually, otherwise it would crack, and re-assembled on the easel. Then it is leaded, soldered and cemented; the leads are blacked and brushed as a dark lead-line enchances the design and enriches the colour.

The technique of making stained glass has long been known. It is described thus by the German monk who called himself Theophilus – his dates have been placed variously between the tenth and twelfth centuries; John Harvey holds that he wrote between 1100 and 1140:

When you wish to compose glass windows, first make yourself a flat wooden table, of such breadth and length that you can work upon it two portions of the same window (lay every window field double on it); and taking chalk, and scraping it with a knife over all the table, sprinkle water everywhere, and rub it with a cloth over the whole. And when it is dry, take the dimensions of one portion of the window in length and breadth, marking it upon the table with rule and compass with the lead or tin; and if you wish to have a border in it, portray it with the breadth which may please you, and in the pattern you may wish. Which done, draw whatever figures you will, first with the lead or tin, then with a red or black colour, making all the outlines with study, because it will be necessary, when you have painted the glass, that you join together the shadows and lights according to the [drawing on the] table. Then arranging the different tints of draperies, note down the colour of each one in its place; and of any other thing which you may wish to paint you will mark the colour with a letter. After this take a leaden cup, and put chalk, ground with water, into it; make two or three pencils[2] for yourself from hair, either from the tail of a marten or badger, or squirrel, or cat, or the mane of an ass, and take a piece of glass of whatever kind you like, which is in every way larger than the place upon which it is superimposed, and fixing it in the ground of this place, so that you can perceive the drawing upon the table through the glass, so portray with the chalk the outlines upon the glass. And if the glass should be so thick (opaque) that you cannot perceive the lines which are upon the table, taking white glass, draw upon it, and when it is dry place the thick glass on the white, raising it against the light, and as you look through it, so portray it. In the same manner you will mark out all kinds of glass, whether for the face, or in the draperies, in hands, in feet, in the border, or in what ever place you intend to place the colours.[3]

The technique that Theophilus describes would seem fairly reasonable to a stained glass artist working today. He would make minor differences. Now, instead of having to construct himself a table, he would have a glass-topped bench, usually with a mirror placed at an angle beneath; in Theophilus's day glass was too precious to be used in this way, nor had they the technique to make it in such large sheets. Theophilus goes on to describe the cutting of glass by drawing a red-hot iron across it.[4] Now the artist uses a glass-cutter, but still nibbles off any extraneous bits with a much older tool, the special type of pliers known as a grozing iron. His kiln is unlikely to be wood-fired as Theophilus's was, but heated with gas or electricity; his soldering iron likewise.

In its essentials, though, the craft has not changed much, and nor has the artist's intention. Granted that Theophilus's method in designing windows is sometimes a little quaint – it is doubtful whether many artists nowadays would pause midway in order to make brushes from the tail of a cat – it has a commendably clear and constant purpose. He never forgets the medium he is working in, and at no stage is the designing divorced from it.

'Like a diligent enquirer', wrote Theophilus, 'I have laboured to inform myself, by all methods, what invention of art and variety of colour may beautify a structure and not repel the light of day and the rays of sun.'

TECHNIQUES

NOTES

1 *Historia Naturalis* XXXVI.
2 brushes.
3 *Diversarum Artium Schedula*, Book II, Chapter XVII, Of Composing Windows.
4 The discovery that diamonds could be used for cutting glass does not seem to have been made before the sixteenth century. Therefore if a window is taken apart, the nature of the edges of the pieces, whether they appear 'nibbled' or clean-cut, is an aid to determining their age.

CHAPTER THREE

From the Beginnings to the Twelfth Century

In AD 680, according to Bede, who had been his pupil, Benedict Biscop (*c.* 628–90) 'sent messengers into Gaul, to fetch makers of glass thence, that by a craft until then unknown in Britain, they might glaze the windows of the church, and the cloister, and the refectory. They came and this was done, and they not only did the work required but also taught English folk their mystery, which was suited to the enclosing of lanterns of churches and to the making of useful vessels.' The glass was installed at St Peters's, Monkwearmouth, where building had begun in 674, and at St Paul's, Jarrow, founded in 681–2.

Benedict Biscop was a well-travelled man – he journeyed from England to Rome no less than five times – and singularly aware of foreign styles and techniques. He was greatly impressed by the classical architecture he had seen, and had sought out masons in France who would build him a fine stone church in the Roman manner. The structure completed, he sent for the glaziers. 'They do arrive,' continued Bede, 'and not only execute their commission, the glass of the windows of the porticos and principal parts of the church, but likewise communicate to the natives the mystery of their trade, and an endless variety of useful and commercial articles are formed with wonderful beauty and facility.' For about a century, glass-making flourished. At York, for instance, Wilfrid, Bishop of the Northumbrians (we are told by his biographer, Eddius), had the church embellished with foreign glass. But by AD 764 the art seems to have been in decline; we find the Abbot Cuthbert writing to the Abbot of Mainz: 'If there be any man in your diocese who can make vessels of glass well, that you will deign to send him to me, because we are ignorant and destitute of that art.'

The documentary evidence provided by these contemporary sources remained unsupported until excavations at the monastic sites of Jarrow and Monkwearmouth (under Dr Rosemary Cramp) revealed numerous specimens of coloured glass dating from the seventh and early eighth centuries.[1] Other fragments of this period have been found at Winchester, Brixworth, Repton and Escomb; but the Jarrow and Monkwearmouth finds are especially impressive. Not only have some hundreds of pieces of window glass been discovered, but also parts of vessels and decorative pieces such as *millefiori* glass. Varying considerably in thickness and texture, they are of soda-glass, cylinder-blown, and of a fine range of colour: golden yellow, jade green, different shades of blue, red derived from copper and generally 'flashed', and glass with a marbled effect. Pieces from Monkwearmouth have been leaded up into a rectangular panel, which is on display in Sunderland Museum. Meanwhile at Jarrow, significantly, fragments of lead calms have been found alongside the glass. The presence of these, together with careful note being taken of the exact location of the finds, have made it possible to make conjectural reconstructions. A number of small square quarries have been found, suggesting patterned rather than figurative glass in these cases. But the most interesting finds are carefully shaped fragments which (while no traces of paint are on them) together appear to make up a standing figure; they have now been leaded up as such, and set on display at the Bede Monastery Museum at Jarrow (colour plate 1). There is also a tiny roundel in the Saxon chancel of St Paul's Church nearby; it is non-representational, but assuming that the reconstruction is correct, has a claim to be the earliest window in Europe.

The art of stained glass probably originated in the Middle East, and perhaps first took the form of the infilling of small holes pierced in walls. Slabs of window glass were found at Pompeii and Herculaneum, and Roman muff glass at Silchester. Pieces of greenish window glass, which seem to have been moulded, have recently been found on the site of a Roman villa at Hartfield in East Sussex. The Romans sometimes set their glass in metal frames, of bronze or copper or lead. It also seems probable that the origins of the art are

The oldest known stained-glass window in Europe. This window was made in AD 681 for the refectory at Jarrow Monastery (*reproduced by kind permission of Bede's World/St Paul's Church, Jarrow*)

linked with enamelling. Although obviously on a very different scale, it has something in common with *cloisonné* work. And it is known that there were Venetian glass-makers working in Limoges, the centre of the art of enamelling, as early as 959. The glass at Augsburg Cathedral is said to date from 1065 – its design strongly influenced, one feels, by the Byzantine tradition of Ravenna; and in 1066 the first Benedictine monastery at Monte Cassino had stained glass windows in its chapel. The 'Ascension' window in the Cathedral of Le Mans dates from about 1081, the early glass at St Denis from *c.* 1144.

By the twelfth century, then, the technique of stained glass was fairly widely known. But it was a point of controversy whether this art should be used to embellish churches or not. St Bernard of Clairvaux (1091–1153) maintained[2] that too much ornament in the church distracted men's minds from spiritual things:

> Their eyes are feasted with relics cased in gold, and their purse-strings are loosed. They are shown a most comely image of some saint, whom they think all the more saintly that he is the more gaudily painted. Men run to kiss him, and are invited to give; there is more admiration for his comeliness than veneration for his sanctity. Hence the church is adorned with gemmed crowns of light – nay, with lustres like cart-wheels, girt all round with lamps, but no less brilliant with the precious stones that stud them. The church is resplendent in her walls, beggarly in her poor; she clothes her stones in gold, and leaves her sons naked . . . The rich man's eye is fed at the expense of the indigent. The curious find their delight here, yet the needy find no relief.

St Bernard belonged to the order of Cistercians, or White Monks, and gave new vigour to it. The Cistercians followed the rule of St Benedict, and laid great emphasis on purity and simplicity of faith. The monks wore habits of natural undyed wool and lived lives of austerity and solitude. In architecture they sought to achieve the pure and harmonious lines which are still to be seen, even amid the ruins, at the abbeys of Fountains and Rievaulx in this country. Stained glass was never used; that would have been against the tenets of the Order.

On the subject of decoration, the Abbot Suger (1081–1151) (see p. 171) took the opposite view. A contemporary of St Bernard, he enjoyed the patronage of

King Louis VI of France and was responsible for rebuilding the Abbey of St Denis, on the outskirts of Paris. He considered it spiritually elevating for a man to find delight in observing the house of God filled with beautiful things:

> The loveliness of the many-coloured gems has called me away from exter-
> nal cares, and worthy meditation has induced me to reflect, transferring
> what is material to that which is immaterial, on the diversity of the sacred
> virtues: then it seems to me that I see myself dwelling, as it were, in some
> strange region of the universe which neither exists entirely in the slime of
> the earth nor entirely in the purity of heaven; and that, by the grace of God,
> can be transported from this inferior to that higher world . . . to me, I con-
> fess, one thing has always seemed pre-eminently fitting: that every costlier
> or costliest thing should serve, first and foremost, for the admission of the
> Holy Eucharist.[3]

This is the alternative view: that all man's best endeavours should be to embellish the House of God. The Abbot Suger did not belittle the importance of spiritual things, a saintly mind and a pure heart, but held that the enriching of the church was in itself an expression of worship. God should be served, he advocated, 'with all inner purity and with all outward splendour'.

Theophilus wrote similarly, 'God delights in embellishment of this kind.' 'Through the spirit of counsel,' he instructed the artist, 'make sure you do not hide away the talent given to you by God, but, working and teaching openly and with humility, you faithfully reveal it to those who desire to learn.'

In adorning the House of God, Theophilus maintained, you have shown the beholders a likeness of Paradise, 'you have caused them to praise God the Creator in this creation and to proclaim Him marvellous in His works. A human eye cannot decide on which work it should first fix its attention; if it looks at the ceiling panels, they bloom like tapestries; if it surveys the walls, the likeness of paradise is there; if it gazes at the abundance of light from the windows, it marvels at the in-estimable beauty of the glass and the variety of this most precious workmanship.'

From such beliefs as the Abbot Suger held, the patronage of stained glass fol-lowed. In the Cathedral of St Denis is a Jesse tree window, restored in part, which survives as a testimony of the encouragement he gave to the art. From this we can only dimly imagine the richness of the whole original scheme.

Moreover we caused to be painted, by the exquisite hands of many masters
from different regions, a splendid variety of new windows, both below and
above; from that first one which begins the series with the Tree of Jesse in
the apse of the church to that which is installed above the principal door in
the church's entrance.[4]

After discussing the iconography of the windows, Suger turns to the measures taken for the conservation of the glass:

Now because these windows are very valuable on account of their wonderful execution and the profuse expenditure of painted glass and sapphire
glass, we appointed an official master craftsman for their protection and
repair, and also a goldsmith skilled in gold and silver ornament, who would
receive their allowances and what was adjudged to them in addition, viz.,
coins from the altar and flour from the common storehouse of the brethren,
and who would never neglect their duty to look after these works of art.

It is interesting that Suger employed artists from different parts of France, possibly from other countries too, just as, four hundred years earlier, Benedict
Biscop had found it necessary to summon glaziers all the way from Gaul.

Glass had been made in England during the Roman occupation, although
there is no evidence of coloured glass being made here. Nor is it certain that the
knowledge of the technique survived here throughout the Dark Ages. In France,
however, it is much more likely that there was an unbroken tradition of glass-
making. It may be significant that in 1147 the Normans conquered Corinth;
Corinth had at that time two glass factories of her own and was an important
trading post between the rest of Europe and the countries of the Near East
where the craft seems to have originated. It is possible that the Normans carried
off some of the glass-workers, or at least absorbed some of their secrets.
Certainly the art of glass-making prospered in Normandy, and coloured glass as
well as white glass was produced. The glass used in early coloured windows in
this country was almost always French.

It seems probable that it was a common practice to import the craftsman along
with his material. After all, he was likely to have good understanding of it, and
was no great expense compared with the cost of the glass itself. It was also easier

This remarkable figure has been reconstructed from late seventh-century glass excavated from beneath the guest-house of the Saxon monastery at Jarrow, Tyne and Wear. The lower portion of the drapery and the main background are conjectural *(reproduced by kind permission of Bede's World/St Paul's Church, Jarrow)*

An early twelfth-century window from Dalbury, Derbyshire. The wings suggest that the figure represents St Michael

A twelfth-century patterned window preserved in its original setting high up on the north wall of Brabourne Church, Kent

'Adam Delving', originally the first of eighty-four figures tracing the genealogy of Christ set high in the clerestory of Canterbury Cathedral in the late twelfth century *(photo: Philip Shenton)*

Above
A thirteenth-century window, uniquely set in a Saxon tombstone, at White Notley Church, Essex. It has been suggested that the figure represents St Etheldreda, to whom the church is dedicated; it might alternatively show an unidentified king

Left
A beardless saint, or possibly Christ, depicted in late twelfth-century French glass at Wilton, Wiltshire

Two examples, one biblical and
one relating to the miracles of
Becket, of thirteenth-century
narrative glass from
Canterbury Cathedral: Jonah
and the whale (prefiguring the
Resurrection) *(left)*, and fear of
plague in the house of Sir
Jordan Fitzeisulf *(below)*

The 'Six Ages of Man', thirteenth century, from Canterbury Cathedral

The dove returns to Noah in the Ark, thirteenth century, from Canterbury Cathedral

11

Left
A detail from the early thirteenth-century rose window in Lincoln Cathedral known as the 'Dean's Eye'. The lower left portion depicts the body of the recently canonized St Hugh of Lincoln being carried into the city

Below
The Becket window in the Chapel of St Lucy at Christ Church Cathedral, Oxford, is a rare example of early fourteenth-century glass *in situ*. This detail shows, besides St Thomas's martyrdom *(lower centre)*, various fabulous beasts, the coats of arms of France and England, a kneeling canon (depicted twice), St Augustine preaching *(lower left)* and St Martin dividing his cloak *(lower right)*

12

This detail from the east window at Eaton Bishop, Hereford and Worcester, showing the Virgin and Child, exemplifies the delicate and rhythmic Decorated style of the fourteenth century

14

The dramatic use of one predominant colour, combined with white glass, which is here and there stained yellow (a technique newly developed in the fourteenth century), is shown in these two further examples of the Decorated style. *Above:* Virgin and Child, from Fladbury, Hereford and Worcester; *below:* St Catherine, from Deerhurst, Gloucestershire

15

Hugh Despencer *(left)* and Robert Fitzhamon *(right)*, two of the Lords of the Manor of Tewkesbury depicted in fourteenth-century glass at Tewkesbury Abbey, Gloucestershire. Eleanor de Clare, the wife of the first-named knight, was the donor of the window

This fourteenth-century glass from Chinnor, Oxfordshire, shows St Lawrence holding the gridiron upon which he was martyred and a book of the Gospels

The 'Lily Crucifix' panel, fourteenth/fifteenth century, from Long Melford, Suffolk. The lily symbolizes both purity and the Resurrection

The base of the Jesse window, *c.* 1340, at St Mary's Church, Shrewsbury. From the sleeping Jesse sprouts the genealogical tree of Christ

The Great East Window in York Minster, made between 1405 and 1408, was the work of John Thornton of Coventry and was donated by Walter Skirlaw, Bishop of Durham. This detail, showing the creation of the birds and the fishes, is just one of 127 panels depicting the beginning and end of the world, which, along with 161 compartments of tracery, take up 1,680 square feet

The 'Prykke of Conscience' window from All Saints' Church, North Street, York, was made in approximately 1410 and depicts from left to right and bottom to top the last fifteen days before the end of the world. The window is based on a poem by Richard Rolle linking the end of the world with the Old Testament flood *(reproduced by kind permission of RCHME)*

Four examples showing the variety of figural depiction in fifteenth-century glass. *Above:* two kings; that on the left, of around 1400, is from Oxborough Hall, Norfolk, while that on the right, from Canterbury Cathedral, was made slightly later and is thought to depict Edward the Confessor; *below left:* an angel, from Yarnton, Oxfordshire; *below right:* St Alban, from the east window (1440–62) of the Beauchamp Chapel, St Mary's Church, Warwick, an example of the very rich glass made by John Prudde, the King's Glazier

here layth robert plesoro wyth the

Above left
Visiting prisoners in the stocks; a detail from the early fifteenth-century 'Corporate Acts of Mercy' window in All Saints' Church, North Street, York

Above right
St Robert of Knaresborough ploughing his land with deer; glass of 1482, from Morley, Derbyshire

Left
God promising Abraham a son, fifteenth century, from Malvern Priory, Hereford and Worcester

for the glazier to work on the site. For one thing, he could ensure that the window he was making would fit the aperture for which it was intended. It would have been much more difficult to achieve this at a distance, especially at a time when measurements were not properly standardized. It was also easier to transport pieces of glass than finished windows, and the risk of breakage was less. Then there was a question of secrecy. If a French craftsman possessed the rare knowledge of how to make coloured glass, he would have guarded it jealously, to the extent of insisting that he should be the one responsible for its setting.

The result is that with early glass it is difficult to define any regional or even national style. Three twelfth-century panels of stained glass depict figures from Jesse trees. One is that at St Denis mentioned by Abbot Suger, one is at Chartres, and the third is at York Minster. In all three the kings sit centrally but not quite symmetrically in the oval space (suggestive of a *mandorla*) formed by the curving branches of the tree. The resemblance between them is remarkable; and it is quite credible that they should be by the same hand or at least from the same workshop. As has already been mentioned, the twelfth-century glass at Canterbury, too, could well have been made by the same artists who worked at Chartres.* After all, the architect at Canterbury, William of Sens, was a Frenchman; it is quite possible that while he was importing the coloured glass to fill the windows, he also imported his countrymen to carry out the scheme.

In discussing glass of this age, we have to consider the power the Church wielded over the community. The Church's function was to promote the faith, not to explain it. For most people, it was something to be accepted and swallowed whole. There were few who disputed it; Abelard was exceptional in encouraging others to argue in defence of their beliefs. The Church saw the function of stained glass to illustrate its teachings. The images on the window were not necessarily to explain the texts precisely, for, implicit in them, there was a sense of mystery that was deemed more important than the rendering of facts. In consequence, scenes in twelfth-century windows were not naturalistic but symbolic. In 'Adam delving' at Canterbury (colour plate 4), for instance, a garden is represented by a single, stalky tree. The glass not only related stories – the life of Christ, the acts of the apostles, the miracles of saints – but frequently dealt in images; and it was particularly concerned with the ancestry of Christ.

---

* For further evidence of this, see page 35, note 4.

This could be displayed in two ways: first by depicting the prophets and fathers of the Old Testament – usually these were shown as impressive single figures, such as Methuselah, Noah, Enoch, Hezekiah (all these are at Canterbury). These were generally set high up in the church, therefore their design is such as would tell at a distance. They are bold and majestic, and their features are strongly marked, even exaggerated, to allow for the steep angle of view from the congregation.

The other way in which the genealogy of Christ was depicted was the Jesse tree, an image derived from the Book of Isaiah 11: 1–2:

And there shall come forth a rod out of the stem of Jesse, and a Branch shall grow out of his roots:

And the spirit of the Lord shall rest upon him, the spirit of wisdom and understanding, the spirit of counsel and might, the spirit of knowledge and of the fear of the Lord.

In 1 Samuel 16, the words of Isaiah's prophecy are recalled:

And the Lord said unto Samuel . . . fill thine horn with oil, and go, I will send thee to Jesse the Bethlehemite: for I have provided me a king among his sons.

Samuel brings a heifer to sacrifice at Bethlehem. Jesse attends the rite, and brings his seven elder sons before Samuel, but they are all dismissed in favour of the youngest son, David, a shepherd, who is chosen and anointed by Samuel. Thus begins the lineage of David from which Christ was born.

The stem of Jesse is pictorially represented as something between a vine and a candlestick. In later medieval windows this often sprouts from the side of the reclining Jesse, who may be asleep (colour plate 19). He is nearly always on a large scale compared with the figures of the kings dispersed among the branches; in the Jesse window at Selby Abbey, for example, he is a giant figure who extends across all three lights. The Virgin enthroned, sometimes holding a rod or a rosebush, sits with the Child at the top of the Jesse tree.

An early example of a king from a Jesse tree is that in York Minster. It used to be inscribed 'Oldest Stained Glass in England', and was installed in the second window from the west in the north wall; it has now been moved to a light-box in the museum below, and no longer bears this label. It is, nevertheless, a fine example of twelfth-century glass, even if not quite as ancient as was once thought, dating from the latter part rather than from the middle of the century. In recent years other, even earlier examples have come to light.

Twelfth-century king from a Jesse tree, York Minster

In the tiny church of All Saints, Dalbury, about six miles to the west of Derby, there is a small panel of a standing figure, which probably represents St Michael. He is shown frontally, looking straight ahead, his wings folded behind him and his hands raised in prayer (colour plate 2). In recent years cleaning by the York Glaziers' Trust has revealed that it is clearly very old, similar in style (though simpler) to the hieratic figures in Augsburg Cathedral. Whether the glass has always been in Dalbury is not absolutely certain, but there appears to be no record of its being brought in from elsewhere. With the lack of much to compare it with, it is difficult to date; however, the early twelfth century seems probable.

An early window still in its original setting is at Brabourne, Kent (colour plate 3). High up in the north wall, where it escaped damage for centuries, this twelfth-century glass bears a near-abstract image – incorporating semi-circles with yellow-centred, white-petalled flowers; in the spaces between are formalized flowers with four yellow petals and rose-pink centres. One hesitates to describe as abstract a design made in an age when every element of pattern contained a symbol. Yet it would be interesting to know how typical the Brabourne window is of its time, and if so, whether *grisaille*, into which category it falls, was ever used for an entire glazing scheme, or whether it was restricted to windows set high up where pictorial glass would have had little impact. *Grisaille* is the name for a design in glass composed in muted colours, sometimes grey, as the term implies, which is devoid of pictorial theme; thus it fulfills the requirement of the Cistercians, under whose influence it was probably developed as an alternative to pictorial glass, for decorative pattern subordinate to the architecture. Also from the twelfth century, a tiny Virgin and Child panel survives at Compton in Surrey, in the East window of the lower chancel, very dark and difficult to date.

Many of the pieces of very ancient glass to be seen in this country are in fact of French origin, and were not brought in until about the time of the French Revolution. The earliest tend to come from St Denis, just outside Paris, and date from 1140–5. Examples are to be found at Wilton (Wiltshire), Twycross (Leicestershire) and Raby Castle (Co. Durham). At Wilton are panels of the Flight into Egypt, the Return of the Prodigal Son, and a figure from a Jesse tree, all of this date, as well as a very impressive beardless half-figure with folded arms, also from St Denis, if slightly later (colour plate 5). At Twycross, ancient panels from St Denis include a Presentation in the Temple (where the Child is almost taking flight over the altar), a devil with stones to throw, and a St Benedict casting a devil out of a monk, also a kneeling figure which may possibly represent the Abbot Suger who commissioned the glass. At Raby Castle, more early glass

Presentation in the Temple; French glass of 1140–5, originally at St Denis near Paris, now at Twycross, Leicestershire

from the same source, including the Angel appearing to the Three Magi, and a robed, seated and tonsured figure with lectern and halo – like some of the Twycross panels, this came from a window dedicated to St Benedict.

There is twelfth-century glass at Rivenhall, Essex, which is also French; it was purchased from the *curé* of Chénu-sur-Sarthe, near Tours, in 1839 by the Revd B.D. Hawkins, who installed it in his parish church (see p. 136). The four central medallions of the East window at Rivenhall date from about 1145[5]; the knight in the bottom right-hand corner is of a later date. The top halves of the two archbishops on either side of the medallions are also specimens of ancient glass.

Of the unparalleled windows at Canterbury, the earliest sections must date from the rebuilding of the cathedral after the fire of 1174. When this disaster occurred, the monks consulted various experts, there being no builder among their own number (and very likely no glazier either). Some said the fabric could be repaired, some that it could not.

However, amongst the other workmen there had come a certain William of Sens, a man active and ready, and as a workman most skillful both in wood and stone. Him, therefore, they retained, on account of his lively genius and good reputation, and dismissed the others . . . And he, residing many days with the monks and carefully surveying the burnt walls in their upper and lower parts, within and without, did yet for some time conceal what he found necessary to be done, lest the truth should kill them in their present state of pusillanimity. But he went on preparing all things that were needful for the work, either of himself or by the agency of others. And when he found that the monks began to be somewhat comforted, he ventured to confess that the pillars rent with the fire and all they supported must be destroyed if the monks wished to have a safe and excellent building. At length they agreed, being convinced by reason and wishing to have the work as good as he promised, and above all things to live in security; thus they consented patiently, if not willingly, to the destruction of the choir.[6]

As the structure was rebuilt, so it was reglazed. Most of the surviving glass was originally sited in the clerestory; there is some still in place. Eighty-four figures made up the genealogy of Christ. The subjects, taken mainly from Luke, with a further eight from Matthew[7], trace the descent of Christ from Adam – a way of emphasizing His human origins that greatly appealed to the medieval mind. These impressive forbears were grouped two in each window, forming a frieze high up all round the cathedral, which was interrupted only by five windows in the apse depicting the Life and Passion of our Lord. Except for Adam, straining to break the stony ground with his mattock, they are all enthroned – dramatic figures, vigorous in composition, rhythmically rather than rigidly disposed. Some of them, Methuselah for instance, have a grandeur that has never been paralleled.

They are by no means all in their original positions. Some have been moved to the south window of the south-west transept, some to the west window of the nave, one to St Andrew's Chapel. The ancient glass was removed for safe keeping during the Second World War; about twenty years after it had been replaced, it was found to be in a very critical state. Subsequently the windows were given extensive cleaning and restoration. Their true colours revealed, they are now back in place.

One can make certain observations about the design of twelfth-century glass. Because the material was so precious, every scrap of it was used. It was much too expensive to throw away – nor did they know how to make larger pieces. Looking at a panel of this early glass, one can see how such practical considerations influenced style. There is usually a border – this would have used up the tiniest chips of glass – and the design of the figures is boldly conceived and heavily leaded. It is almost a glass mosaic, and little brushwork was used. The art as Theophilus saw it was a combination of pattern and iconography.

I have approached the temple of holy wisdom, and beheld the sanctuary filled with a variety of all kinds of divers colours with the usefulness and nature of each one set forth. Entering forthwith unobserved, I have filled the storehouse of my heart with a sufficiency of all those things . . . and have clearly set them forth for your study, having examined them all individually with careful trial and proved them all with hand and eye. But since [glass-painting] cannot be translucent, I have, like a diligent seeker, taken particular pains to discover by what ingenious techniques a building may be embellished with a variety of colours, without excluding the light of day and the rays of the sun. Having applied myself to this task, I understand the nature of glass, and I consider that this object can be obtained simply by the correct use of glass and its variety.[8]

FROM THE BEGINNINGS

NOTES

1 Both monasteries were destroyed in Scandinavian raids, *c.* 867. For the report by Dr Rosemary Cramp on the discovery of the Saxon glass, see the *Antiquaries Journal*, 1970, Vol. 1, part II.

2 'Apologia' to William, Abbot of St Thierry.

3 The Book of Suger, XXXIII.

4 Book of Suger, XXXIV.

5 F. Sidney Eden dated them towards the end of the century, however, in his article in the *Journal of the British Society of Master Glass Painters*, Oct. 1925.

6 Gervase of Canterbury, a Benedictine monk. His Chronicle is a roughly contemporary account.

7 Luke 3: 23–38, and Matthew 1.

8 *On Divers Arts*, Prologue to Book II.

CHAPTER FOUR

The Thirteenth Century

The first Franciscans or Grey Friars, only nine in number, came to England in 1224 from the monastery of Fécamp in Normandy. Three years earlier, Dominican monks had been welcomed by the Bishop of Winchester who introduced them to Archbishop Stephen Langton. They established themselves chiefly in Oxford, and within forty years had founded as many convents. Being more scholarly than the Franciscan order, however, their influence was less widespread. The Grey Friars, following the precepts of St Francis of Assisi (1181/2–1226), who led a life of extreme poverty and simplicity, travelled without means, depending on the charity of the people among whom they preached and made converts. Their first friaries were set up in Canterbury, Oxford and London, from which centres the movement spread throughout the country. The buildings, usually situated on the outskirts of towns, were not lavish, but functional. They were not all clerics or even learned men, but they went among the people and preached in words their audience could readily understand. This was something quite new in the religious life of the Middle Ages. The monks had set themselves apart; the ordinary man might admire their holy way of life, but he would hardly think of emulating it. The parish priest was in closer touch, but he did not have to be a preacher. In the early days of their mission people respected the Grey Friars and identified with their poverty. Their rhetoric was compelling and their influence gained considerably. In consequence, the established church found itself having to alter its ways and substituted shorter, more intense services for the seemingly unending chanting that had been practised previously. Perhaps it now had to make some effort to explain religion rather than simply present it for the faithful to accept. Therefore, while the friars themselves were not great commissioners of windows, they had a profound influence on the development of a narrative element in thirteenth-century stained glass.

It is perhaps significant that the rise of the narrative element in stained glass in England also coincides with the beginnings of drama; it seems likely that there was a relationship between them. The earliest form of drama in England was the trope[1], performed at the chief festivals of the church, originally as part of the religious celebration with the parts taken by priests. There survives the Easter trope of the Maries at the Sepulchre. The text is extremely simple and short and runs thus:

Angel   *Quem quaeritis in sepulchro, o Christicolae?*
          (Whom do you seek in the sepulchre, O Christian women?)

Maries *Iesum Nazarenum crucifixum, o coelicolae.*
          (Jesus of Nazareth who was crucified, O heavenly ones.)

Angel   *Non est hic; surrexit sicut praedixerat.*
          Ite, nuntiate, quia surrexit de sepulchro.
          (He is not here; He is arisen even as he foretold.
          Go, tell that He has arisen from the sepulchre.)

The aim of this briefest of playlets was to illustrate the Resurrection by expressing it in visible terms; it was first performed at the altar of the church, then later a theatrical tomb (sarcophagus) was put up in the north aisle. These sarcophagi are occasionally portrayed in stained glass. To begin with there was no setting at all, just figures and action. Similarly the narrative stained glass of the thirteenth century shows figures and action, with the minimum of 'props', and with no landscape background unless it is necessary to the theme. Thus in the Parable of the Sower panel at Canterbury there had to be ploughed fields in order to indicate that he was a sower at all. Similarly the Magi in the same window must wear their crowns even when they are asleep, otherwise they would not be recognizable as kings.

Parable of the Sower, early thirteenth century. Canterbury Cathedral

We have come to refer to this narrative element in medieval stained glass as the Poor Man's Bible, for such it is, although this phrase derives from, and should be more correctly applied to, its source material. The windows had to be *read* (left to right, starting at the top – if the arrangement at Canterbury is anything to go by) and must have been supplemented by the spoken word. The iconography for much glass of the period comes from the *Biblia Pauperum*[2] and the *Speculum Humanae Salvationis* (Mirror of Man's Salvation) and both of these works were based on the concept of typology – that is to say, the belief that events in the New Testament parallel those in the Old. This area of theology, which finds its roots in the early Church, became a vital part of the medieval understanding of God's purpose. It was not, in fact, a new concept; as early as the seventh century, Benedict Biscop had brought back sets of pictures from Rome, and arranged them in pairs around the walls of St Paul's Church, Jarrow, New Testament above, and Old Testament parallels below.[3] The typology of some medieval glass may be difficult to grasp at first, but when one knows some of the 'rules' it can provide an endless source of fascination. One example is the sacrifice of Isaac paired with the Crucifixion. The father, whether heavenly or earthly, is willing to sacrifice the life of the son. Both sons carry the wood of their sacrifice.

In thirteenth-century stained glass, besides themes from the Old Testament (among which, if we are to judge from the surviving glass at Lincoln, Moses seems to be especially prominent), New Testament subjects include the following: the Birth of the Virgin; her Presentation in the Temple (this subject was more popular towards the end of the Middle Ages); the Annunciation; the Nativity, together with the coming of the shepherds and the Magi; the Massacre of the Innocents; Christ's Presentation in the Temple; the Transfiguration (again, a subject more favoured in later centuries); the Entry into Jerusalem; the Crucifixion; the Resurrection; Pentecost; the Death and Assumption of the Virgin. Of Our Lord's miracles, only the Raising of Lazarus and the Marriage at Cana were popular subjects. (In the windows at Canterbury, the waterpots develop interestingly into the theme of the Six Ages of Man (colour plate 9).) Again at Canterbury, and also at Twycross in Leicestershire, are shown the spies bearing the grapes from Canaan, their load slung on a pole; the grapes signify the body of Christ and the wine from them signifies His blood.[4] Jonah emerging from the whale prefigures the Resurrection (colour plate 7). In the east window of the corona at Canterbury, he appears unscathed from the jaws of a sea-monster beside a rudimentary and rather Roman-looking ship. Noah's Ark, also to be seen

The Spies and the Grapes of Canaan, early thirteenth century. Canterbury Cathedral

in thirteenth-century glass at Canterbury, signifies the redemption of mankind; and it is shown with three decks because St Gregory had declared that it had one deck for animals, one for birds, and one for men (colour plate 10).

The idea of a Poor Man's Bible presupposes both illiteracy and lack of books. Books, all of which had still to be written out by hand, were scarce in the extreme. But while most men were illiterate it would be a mistake to imagine that the craftsmen who made the windows were. Probably they had these basic skills, having received some schooling before their apprenticeship; they knew at least enough to put their accounts into writing.

Equally it would be a mistake to suppose that the ordinary man, who was to be instructed by the Poor Man's Bible, understood nothing of the content of these windows. Probably he understood a great deal more than his equivalent today. Whether he could *see* them or not is a different matter; as Osbert Lancaster remarks,[5] 'the poor man of the Middle Ages must have enjoyed quite exceptional eyesight'. But the stories of the Bible and the lives of the saints, especially those saints connected with his local church, would have been familiar to him. Attending services on Sunday was obligatory; his vision was generally limited to what he learnt of religious teaching and what he picked up of folklore – travel was unusual and distractions were few. Certainly in an age when it was not possible to look things up in books, the memory had infinitely more exercise. The Poor Man's Bible can be regarded as a visual *aide-mémoire*.

The lives and miracles of the saints became a favourite theme in stained glass. The chief source-book for these was, or was to be, the *Golden Legend*, thought to have been compiled by a Dominican monk called Jacobus a Voragine (Jacopo de' Varazze, 1230–98; he became Archbishop of Genoa). It was originally written in Latin, then in the fourteenth century translated into French by Jean de Vigny, and a printed version was brought out by Caxton in 1483 – the most popular book he produced. Other sources for the lives of the saints were *Dialogue of Miracles* by Caesarius of Heisterbach (d. 1240) and the *Mirror of History* by Vincent de Beauvais (d. 1264).

Saints were identifiable not only by the inscriptions attached to them but by their attributes: St Andrew a cross saltire, St Nicholas three balls, St Edward the Confessor a ring. In thirteenth-century glass we find, for instance, St Edmund offering up the arrows of his martyrdom to heaven (Saxlingham Nethergate, Norfolk), St Catherine of Alexandria with her wheel (West Horsley, Surrey), and St Stephen, almost always shown at the time of his stoning, for example at Grately, Hampshire, and in the Jerusalem Chamber of Westminster Abbey.

Equally important were the local saints, such as William of York, William of Norwich, Hugh of Lincoln, Neot of Cornwall and Thomas à Becket at Canterbury (and in other places). The cult of St Thomas was in fact much celebrated in stained glass. At Canterbury there are historical panels showing the saint and Henry II and also scenes depicting miracle cures. The saint's blood was held to have special healing properties: William the Priest of London was relieved of the palsy by drinking it (window III). Audrey of Canterbury was similarly rid of her quartan fever and Petronilla of Polesworth, an epileptic nun, was cured by bathing her feet in water containing the saint's blood (both in window IV). Juliana of Rochester was cured of her blindness by the touch of this holy water on her eyes (window VI). The liquid is effectively portrayed with ruby glass.

After a miracle it was important to bring thanks-offerings to the saint's tomb. Among the piles of treasure are to be seen coils of silver wire. The custom was that when a person was ill they measured him, or that part of him which was afflicted, candles were burnt to the same length, and the silver measuring wire offered up with prayers to the saint.

One story which is told in some detail is that of the plague in the house of Sir Jordan Fitzeisulf, a friend of Becket's, from Pontefract (colour plate 8). In the first scene the nurse Britonis has died, the inscription warns that 'the funeral of the nurse threatens the survivors with each his own scourge'. The plague strikes next at Fitzeisulf's ten-year-old son, William; he is revived by the water of St Thomas administered by his father. Sir Jordan later neglects his vow to bring coins to the saint's tomb as a thanks-offering for the boy's life. St Thomas appears in a vision to a leper called Gimp, and directs him to warn Sir Jordan of dire consequences if he does not keep his promise. The leper's warning is ignored, a second son dies, and the whole household is stricken with plague. Finally Sir Jordan repents, comes to Canterbury, and heaps gold and silver coins at the tomb of his patron saint. This is only one of several related stories of healing, broken vows, and retribution, in which the significance of making a substantial offering of coins or silver wire to the saint was obviously not lost on later pilgrims, to judge by the wealth amassed by the cathedral.

Dominant though the narrative theme was, it would be wrong to suppose that thirteenth-century glass was invariably pictorial. There is the great exception of the Five Sisters window at York Minster. Dating from the third quarter of the thirteenth century, there are five lancets of uniform height; they contain about 1,250 square feet of glass set in thirteen panels – all of which, with one exception (Daniel in the Lion's Den), one might term abstract in design. That is to say, they are geometric patterns set against a background of greyish foliage. The foliage, however, is that of the plant *geum*; in the Middle Ages the geum was held to have powers of healing and was thus associated with Christ. The geometric patterns are squares, circles, quatrefoils. The general effect is mellow and subtle, soft gradations of greeny-yellow to grey, punctuated here and there with a small piece of red, blue or yellow. While it is classed as grisaille, it is not by any means all grey, nor is it probably as lacking in iconography as one might think.

The complex themes of thirteenth-century glass, however, cannot always have been appreciated by the congregation any more than by the modern viewer, unless he brings binoculars – simply because they were sometimes too high to be seen. This is the case with the great rose window in Lincoln Cathedral known as the Dean's Eye. Its contents, hardly discernible from the ground, would have been known only to a few: perhaps only to the men who commissioned it and the craftsmen who made it.

The 'Dean's Eye': the thirteenth-century rose window at Lincoln Cathedral

The Dean's Eye is a unique survival: a thirteenth-century rose window with its original glass *in situ*. It stands in the north transept, opposite the Bishop's Eye[6], measures 23 feet in diameter, and dates from about 1210. It contains about sixty scenes, principally on the theme of the Passion and Last Judgement, and the Kingdom of Heaven. With its combination of symbols and representation, it gives so much insight into the medieval mind that it is worth analysing in some detail.[7]

First Christ is shown as a triumphant figure and the Passion depicted symbolically rather than representationally, whereas the Resurrection is seen literally. Then there is a good deal of emphasis on the Virgin Mary, implying the reverence in which she was held. Adam and Eve are shown at work in a very fine panel which it is interesting to compare with the great twelfth-century Adam at Canterbury. Finally, the carrying of the body of St Hugh (canonized at about the time that the window was made) is most memorably portrayed (colour plate 11).

It seems fairly certain – although one cannot be dogmatic because few medieval windows have kept their ancient places – that there was a strong link between the sequence of iconography and the architecture. As M.D. Anderson

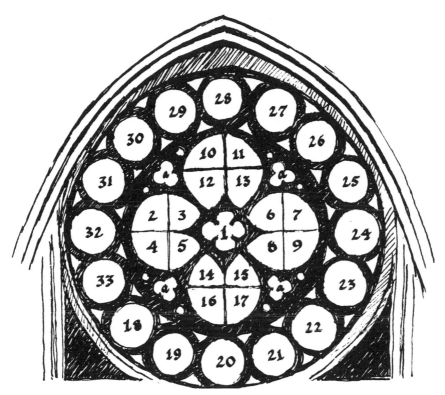

Diagram of the Dean's Eye, Lincoln

1 Christ in Majesty.
2 Entombment scene.
3,4 The Blessed in adoration.
5 St Joseph is chosen as a husband for the Virgin Mary.
6 Men carrying a coffin.
7,8,9 The Blessed in adoration.
10 Four men standing.
11 Mutilated scene, possibly the Foolish Virgins.
12 Three saints seated.
13 Jesus among the doctors in the Temple.
14,15,17 The Blessed in adoration.
16 Scene showing the body of St Hugh (Bishop of Lincoln) carried into Lincoln, apparently by three bishops (probably the archbishops of Canterbury, Dublin and Ragusa in Sicily) and three kings (John of England, William of Scotland and the Welsh Roland of Galloway).

18,19,20,21,22 Figures of bishops, blessing or seated in quatrefoils.
23 Adam delving and Eve spinning. There is also a third figure, who is probably Cain.
24 Two angels blowing trumpets.
25 Damaged panel, seven apostles.
26 The Crowns of Thorns.
27 The Spear, held by two angels.
28 Christ as Judge.
29 The Cross, on green glass with the inscription IHS NAZARENUS.
30 The Three Nails, carried by an angel.
31 The Virgin and Apostles (six figures, including St Peter and St Paul).
32 Two angels blowing trumpets.
33 The Resurrection of the Dead. They rise from their tombs carrying blue slabs on their shoulders.

has pointed out,[8] an ancient scheme exists for the decoration of Greek churches, which was brought to light in 1839 by the French archaeologist, Didron. He found that on Mount Athos monks were still painting their church in accordance with the system outlined in a book that they owned, the *Manual for Painters*. Anderson suggests, and it seems extremely likely, that a similar scheme of work came into use in English churches and applied not only to wall painting but also to glass. The only church in the whole country which still has its original glazing intact and *in situ* is at Fairford (see also Chapter Six). This dates from about 1500. Whether the same arrangement was used two or three centuries earlier we cannot be certain. We do not even know if Fairford is typical of its time. It seems likely, however, that the relative importance of images determined their siting within the church. The Passion and the most significant scenes from the Bible would surely be placed at the east end, the Crucifixion above the cross on the main altar. Didactic theological themes were usually confined to the north aisle of the choir. Above subsidiary altars, the subjects would correspond to their dedications to the saints. Accordingly, the windows to St Thomas at Canterbury were put up in the Trinity Chapel where his shrine stood. In this way, the lay observer might know where to refer to events, using the windows as an illustration to the teachings of the Church.

So the form of the windows tended to be bound up with their iconography. Where the patriarchs of the church were to be displayed, a great single figure window was almost inevitable. Similarly where the narrative element began to call for several episodes to be displayed, a new form consisting of separate panels or medallions seems to have been introduced. However, as regards the appearance of the rose window, we have the innovations of the Early English style to thank, rather than iconography. This style expressed itself not only in pointed lancets and rib vaulting but in a general lightening of the structure, making it possible to pierce the west wall (or the end walls of the transept) with the rose window whose very shape cried out for the use of stained glass.

As for the glass itself, it continued a costly commodity. The account for glazing a chapel in the Tower of London in 1286 mentions a figure of 4d. per foot for white glass, and 8d. per foot for coloured. This was for new glass; but there is also an item for old glass, intended for re-use. This was rather cheaper, at 2¹/₂d. per foot. Frequently it was ordered and sold by weight. This seems to have been the traditional way of measuring glass of all kinds. An early term denoting about 5 lb of glass was the *wey*; one *wey* of glass would be sufficient for about two feet of glazing. In the later Middle Ages the word *wisp* is used; this seems to have meant very much the same quantity as the *wey*. Twenty-four *weys* of glass, or thereabouts (120 lb) amounted to a *seam*. Other words which came to be used instead of *seam* were *case*, *chest* or *cradle*, all coming to very much the same thing.

About the glaziers, however, we know next to nothing, except that the office of King's Glazier was first recorded in 1242, held by a certain 'Edward' at Windsor, but it is unclear whether his job was to design or execute the windows, or both. Only from documents of the next century do we begin to gain real insight into the life and work of the glass-painters of England.

NOTES

1 See Allardyce Nicoll, 'The Development of the Theatre'.
2 Copies survive from the 14th century and were first printed in the 1460s. The *Biblia Pauperum* (ed. Laib and Schwarz, Freiburg, 1892) and *Speculum Humanae Salvationis* (ed. Lutz and Perdizet, Mulhouse, 1907) are referred to by John Lowe: 'The Medieval English Glazier', *Journal of the British Society of Master Glass Painters*, Vol. XIII, no. 2, 1960–1, and no. 3, 1961–2.
3 See Bede: Lives of the Abbots of Wearmouth and Jarrow (available in *The Age of Bede*, Penguin Classics).
4 The extreme similarity in composition between these panels, both thirteenth century, but that at Twycross (which came from Ste Chapelle, Paris) not having been imported until the nineteenth century, underlines the theory that the man who designed the Canterbury glass was French.
5 'Pillar to Post'.
6 The Bishop's Eye is made up of fragments of medieval glass gathered up after the vandalism of the sixteenth century (when the servants of the Dean George Fitz-Hugh shot at them with arrows), and the iconoclasm of the seventeenth (the Earl of Manchester's soldiers in 1644 took pleasure in destroying them), and installed there in the south transept in 1788. The tracery (fourteenth century) is marvellously flowing, but of the iconography it is impossible to make much.
7 For a full discussion on Lincoln's thirteenth-century glass, see the article by M. Jean Lafond 'Stained Glass Decoration of Lincoln Cathedral in the Thirteenth Century', *Archaeological Journal*, Vol. CIII, 1947. The diagram on p. 33 is adapted from this.
8 *History and Imagery in British Churches*, Murray, 1971.

CHAPTER FIVE

The Fourteenth Century

Wouldst thou glaze the gable, and grave therein thy name,
Secure should thy soul be for to dwell in heaven.

William Langland, *Piers Plowman*

There are two things remarkable in this couplet from *Piers Plowman*. One is that the commissioning of a window was, it was thought, enough to buy a man's way to heaven; and for the sake of saving his soul he might plunge his hand fairly deeply into his pocket. The other is that he should put his name on the glass; whether in the form of portrait, or simply in lettering, the identity of the donor was important and should be recorded. Implicit in these two lines of Langland's is a whole new way of looking at things.

Towards the end of the thirteenth century the increase in population had meant that the rewards for labour had become smaller and the demand for cultivatable land greater. During the first half of the fourteenth century the growth in population slackened, with consequent advantage to many among the poorer classes, whose labour was beginning to enjoy demand again. After the Black Death (1348–9), when between a third and a half of the population had died, skills of all sorts became in great demand. So much so in fact that foreign craftsmen were encouraged to settle in England to help produce the glass which the plague had made difficult to import, and to replace the glaziers that had died. The Black Death had other effects. Striking down as it did good and bad alike, it may have done something to shake religious belief. There was certainly a diminishing faith in the Church. Its tenets were no longer accepted without argument. Moreover as an institution the Church was divided in itself. We have only to look in the pages of Chaucer's *Canterbury Tales* to discover the Summoner accusing the Friar of abusing his right to enter peoples' homes, and the Friar accusing the regular clergy of ineptitude. The Monk preferred to spend his time hunting and feasting on roasted swan, rather than labouring with his hands or studying in his cloister. And as for the hangers-on of religion, the corrupt and repulsive Summoner, and the smooth-tongued Pardoner, with his bag of false relics (pigs' bones and bits of pillow-case, which he swore were the bones of saints and fragments of Our Lady's veil), both battened unashamedly on the people's gullibility and their fear of hell-fire, for the fear of hell-fire was still a potent force.

It was generally thought that one could buy one's way to heaven, whether by purchasing pardons 'come from Rome all hot', or perhaps by commissioning a window: 'Secure should thy soul be for to dwell in heaven.'

Where fourteenth-century glass is still *in situ* (which is rare), it is especially interesting. A good example is the so-called Becket window in the Chapel of St Lucy at Christ Church, Oxford (colour plate 12). The subjects include not only the martyrdom of St Thomas, but the heads of a king and queen, St Martin dividing his cloak, St Cuthbert holding the head of St Oswald, St Augustine preaching, shields with the arms of England and France, a kneeling canon (donor), censing angels, Christ in Majesty, and various grotesque creatures – man, woman, dragon, lion, centaur, harpy. Altogether, some – to us – quite extraordinary juxtapositions; but in fact no more extraordinary than the marginal decorations of illuminated manuscripts.

Windows would not always be entirely religious in content, however. There was a growing interest in human individuality, and a secular element began to be introduced. This was expressed in different ways. It might be in the subject itself – examples are the 'Monkey's Funeral' and the Bellfounders' window in York Minster; or it might be by making the donors a major theme in the glass, as in the rows of kneeling figures, dating from *c.* 1300, in the side windows of the chapel of Merton College, Oxford. Each is set under a canopy and bears the name of the donor, Henry de Mamesfield.

Henry de Mamesfield, donor of the glass, late thirteenth century. Merton College Chapel, Oxford (*by kind permission of the Warden and Fellows*)

The Bellfounders' window at York (see p. 38) dating from the

The Bellfounders' window, fourteenth century. York Minster (*photo: RCHME/reproduced by permission of the Dean and Chapter, York Minster*)

1330s, is very largely secular. It was given by a city bailiff called Richard Tunnoc who lived in Stonegate in the centre of the city; he may well have been a bellfounder himself. Tunnoc appears in the bottom centre panel presenting a bell to St William of York. Bells are the dominant motif throughout, and in the side panels are depicted the processes of bellfounding. And curiously while there are monkeys playing musical instruments in the borders on either side of the centre light, the saints, Peter, Andrew and Paul, are relegated to the quatrefoils.

The secular element in stained glass also displayed itself in heraldry which, by the fourteenth century, had become quite a common subject. The whole idea of including it in a scheme of stained glass was the same as that of the chantry chapel; it would, it was hoped, prompt people to pray for the soul and family of the person whose arms were depicted. It might appear in conjunction with figures of saints and such, as at Selling,

Early fourteenth-century east window at Selling, Kent

Kent. Here we find figures under canopies with shields below – St John above the arms of Clare, St Mary Magdalen over the arms of Castile and Leon (referring to Eleanor of Castile), the Virgin and Child over the Lions of England, St Margaret over the French coat of arms, and another saint over the chequered arms of Warenne. The saints are swaying figures set between rudimentary chestnut trees. The panels are set in grisaille, and the colours include very fine deep blues; around are coloured borders with clover leaves. The glass dates from not long after 1300.

Heraldry might also be featured on the figures themselves. There are, for instance, the splendid knights high up on the west side of the choir at Tewkesbury Abbey (colour plate 16). All the clerestory windows seem to date from the second quarter of the fourteenth century, and to have been given either by Eleanor de Clare, 1314–37, or after her death, by her son Hugh Despencer. There are eight knights who were the Lords of the Manor of Tewkesbury: Fitzroy, de Clare, Despencer, FitzHamon on the north side, de Clare, Zouch, and two more de Clares on the south. They display their arms on their heraldic surcoats.

There is in Chaucer's *Boke of the Duchesse* (1369) a remarkable description of glass in a secular setting:

> And sooth to seyn, my chambre was
> Ful wel depeynted, and with glas
> Were al the wyndowes wel yglased,
> Ful clere, and nat an hoole ycrased,
> That to beholde hyt was gret joye.
> For holly al the story of Troye
> Was in the glasynge ywroght thus,
> Of Ector and of kyng Priamus,
> Of Achilles and Lamedon,
> And eke of Medea and of Jason,
> Of Paris, Eleyne, and of Lavyne.
> And alle the walles with colours fyne
> Were peynted, bothe text and glose,
> Of al the Romaunce of the Rose.

FOURTEENTH CENTURY

I would hesitate to say that this richly decorated interior was based on anything more than Chaucer's imagination. But the significant thing is that the idea of a bedroom being adorned with a stained glass scheme based on subjects from classical history and mythology was just credible in the fourteenth century. A hundred years earlier, it would have been unthinkable.

The passage goes on to describe how, when the sun was out,

> Upon my bed with bryghte bemes,
> With many glade gilde stremes

golden rays of light shone through the glass into the room. This, together with the intricacy of the subject matter, suggests that Chaucer had in mind glass stained by a new technique. It was discovered that silver nitrate used on clear glass would produce a yellow stain, generally more delicate in tone than the pot-metal yellow that had been used, for example, in the bells of the Bellfounders' window.

The discovery that silver filings could be used as a colouring agent seems to have stemmed from a work called the 'Lapidario', compiled at the command of King Alfonso X of Castile (1252–84).[1] It is a collection of notes, taken mainly from the Arabic, on the properties of rocks and minerals. Of the stone named Ecce it has this to say:

> The substance is very black in colour, speckled with yellow spots. It is shining and light in weight, porous, easy to break, and by nature cold and dry. It has this virtue that to him who bears it upon him it give great strength and overcomes fear, making him very bold in all feats of arms he undertakes. And if they grind it and knead it with honey and smear glass with it and fire it, it stains the glass a very beautiful golden colour. And it strengthens it in such a way that it makes the material stronger than it was before and it cannot be melted so readily and does not break so easily . . .

For the glazier it was the first time that he had prepared glass specially in his own workshop. Pieces of painted glass were placed on trays and covered with wood ash or quicklime, and the stain was fixed by firing them in a muffle kiln. The first known use of yellow stain on English glass is in the Peter de Dene window at York Minster, thought to date from 1306. Extant accounts for the glazing of St Stephen's Chapel at Westminster in 1351–2[2] mention frequent purchases of silver filings:

> Monday 20th June . . . To John Geddyng for lymayl [silver filings] bought for painting glass for the windows of the said Chapel, 8d.

and again in August and September 1351 silver was in constant demand for just this purpose, on one occasion as much as 7s. being spent.

The new technique was taken up with enthusiasm, because the silver stain could be used to define different colour areas on the same piece of glass. It made a different sort of design possible, larger pieces of glass could be used, and less leading was needed. A head with golden hair, a halo or a crown could be made out of a single piece, and the design was drawn with greater delicacy. Colour is more often subdued than brilliant in fourteenth-century glass, and a good deal of white glass was used. Otherwise greens, yellows, browns and occasional reds predominated (colour plate 14). For the first time these colours might be modified by diaper patterning. For instance, the exquisite Virgin and Child at Eaton Bishop in Herefordshire (colour plate 13) might not at first be noticed in the expanse of the east window. The Virgin is dressed soberly in brown and gold; her head, hands, and the flower she holds are very white, and the background diapered in leaf-green. The painting is done with delicacy; and the figure has that easy swing, the gentle S-curve characteristic of the Decorated period. The figure of St Catherine at Deerhurst, Gloucestershire (colour plate 15) which dates from 1300–40, has an even more pronounced rhythm.

The larger windows, together with the new style of design, created a need for larger, thinner pieces. Rather more white was used, because it was cheaper. In 1338 Thomas de Beneston, vicar-choral at York Minster, paid 6d. a foot for white glass, and twice that sum for coloured. In order to make glass more fusible, so that it could be thinner, more ash was put into the mixture. The trouble was that this weakened the finished metal and caused pitting.

Foreign glass, especially from Lorraine or Normandy, was preferred, even though it was more expensive. In 1317 '639 paice of white glass bought at Rouen' for Exeter Cathedral cost £15 14s. 9d., a price paid quite clearly on account of its superior quality. However, English centres for the making of

white glass were established in the Surrey–Sussex Weald, and also in
Shropshire, Staffordshire and Cheshire. Although foreign glass-makers, such as
Laurence Vitrearius in the thirteenth century and John de Alemayne in the fourteenth, had come over from Lorraine and Normandy where coloured glass was
made, they may not have been the most skilled men in their profession and it
seems that coloured glass was not made in this country. But supplies of foreign
glass were liable to interruption on account of wars and pestilence, in which
case for even the most ambitious projects English glass had to be used. In 1349,
for instance, at the time of the Black Death, the King's Glazier, commissioned
to glaze St Stephen's Chapel, Westminster, bought glass from Staffordshire and
Shropshire. In the accounts for the same work we find the following entry for
4 July 1354:

> To John Geddyng, glazier, going with the King's Commission to the parts of
> Kent and Essex to seek glass for the work of the Chapel, for 4 days going,
> staying away and returning, taking for himself and his horse 12d. a day, 4s.

Then on the 12 December we find this:

> To William Holmere for 60 weys of white glass bought at Chiddinfold for
> the Chapel windows, at 6d. the wey, 30s.

> For carriage of the said glass from Chyddinfold to Westminster, 6s.

Then the lead, or 'soudelett' had to be bought:

> To Master Andrew the Smith for 120 soudelett for the glass of the said
> windows, weighing 190 lbs at 1½d. a pound, 23s. 9d.

The entry continues:

> For ale bought for whitening the glaziers' tables, 3d.

The glass was carried either by cart or by boat. Boat was obviously the
gentler way if it could be done – especially if a completed window was to be

transported. Windows for St George's Chapel, Windsor, were made at Westminster in 1351–2, since Westminster had a very well-established workshop. So we find in the accounts entries for nails and wooden boards 'to make cases for carrying the glass panels from Westminster to Wyndesore'. The glass was packed in straw and hay inside the case (the hay and straw cost 14d., which seems expensive), and the cost of transporting it up the Thames was four shillings.

Large towns had their permanent workshops; the main centres were London, York, Oxford, Norwich and Bristol; some smaller places also had independent establishments, but the general practice was for work for outlying churches to be commissioned from the nearest central workshop. When a great church was being built, various lodges, temporary sheds or lean-tos would cluster round its walls. There would be one for the masons, the carpenters and the smiths, and also one for the glaziers. The King's Glazier at Westminster had a lodge sixty feet long and twenty feet broad. This would have been furnished with a kiln for firing the glass when painted or fixing the yellow stain.

At Westminster they were still designing the glass on wooden tables, as had been done in Theophilus's day. But cartoons were also coming into use. In 1390 Robert Lesyngham, a mason, was called upon to produce a design for the east window of Exeter Cathedral, and a skin of parchment was bought for this purpose for the price of 2d.[3]

Cennino Cennini describes the use of paper in the craftsman's handbook *Il Libro dell'Arte*, written at the close of the century. He outlines a practice whereby a painter prepares a design for a window which the glaziers will execute:

It is true that this occupation is not much practised by our profession, and is practised more by those who make a business of it. And ordinarily the masters who do the work possess more skill than draughtsmanship, and they are almost forced to turn, for help on the drawing, to someone who possesses finished craftsmanship, that is, to one of all-round, good ability. And therefore, when they turn to you, you will adopt this method. He will come to you with the measurements of his window, the width and length: you will take as many sheets of paper glued together as you need for your window; and you will draw your figure first with charcoal, then fix it with ink, with your figure completely shaded, exactly as you draw on panel. Then your glass master takes this drawing, and spreads it out on a large flat bench or table; and he proceeds to cut his glasses, a section at a time, according to the way he wants the costumes of the figure painted. And he gives you a colour which he makes from well-ground copper filings; and with this colour, on the point of a miniver brush, you shape up your shadows gradually, matching up the arrangement of the folds and the other details of the figure, on one piece of glass after another; and you may shade any glass, indifferently, with this colour. Then the master, before he fastens one piece to another, according to their practice, fires it moderately in iron cases with his ashes; and then he fastens them together.

You may execute silk stuffs, upon these glasses, sprig and hatch and do lettering, that is, by laying in with this colour, and then scraping through, just as you do on panel. You have one advantage: that you do not need to lay any other ground, because you can get glass in all colours.[4]

The craft of the glazier, like most crafts, seems to have run in families, which facilitated the keeping of trade secrets. Most stained glass, however, was produced by commercially run firms, and these, if there were enough of them, were organized into guilds. London had a guild of glass-painters by 1328.

Although the workshop was expected to undertake all manner of commissions from the artistic to the simply practical, there were different categories within the craft. Nomenclature is often unclear; the old Latin term 'vitriarius' could mean anyone working with or making glass; 'glass-painter' clearly implied artistic skill; 'glazier' was a term very widely and variously used during most of the medieval period, although later it was to signify someone responsible for no more than leading-up.

A boy who was to take up the craft of a glazier was generally apprenticed at the age of thirteen or fourteen for a period of seven years. The system of apprenticeship had grown up gradually, from the time of Edward I onwards. Many glaziers worked by themselves as independent craftsmen, some were employers. They might be paid in food and clothing, as well as cash. Wages varied according to status and function, as the following accounts for the St Stephen's Chapel illustrate:

Monday 20 June (1351)

. . . To Master John de Chestre glazier working there on the designing (protactacione) of various figures (ymaginum) for the glass windows of the King's said chapel, he receiving 7s. a week, 7s.

To . . . five master glaziers working there on similar designs, for the said five days, to each of them 12d. a day, 25s.

To . . . 11 glaziers, painters in the same craft, painting glass for the windows of the upper chapel for the said five days, to each of them 7d. a day, 32s. 1d.

To . . . fifteen glaziers working there on the breaking and fitting of glass . . . for the said five days and for the said feast day (Friday the Nativity of St John the Baptist) namely for 6 days, to each of them 6d. a day, 45s.

Every member of the workshop is named, including two glazier's mates who appear in later accounts, Thomas Dadyngton and Robert Yersdale, who are only paid fourpence or fourpence halfpenny a day for the labour of cutting glass and grinding pigments for painting it. The chief designer was on this occasion paid a little more than his colleagues, but whether he did five days work or more for his improved rate of pay we cannot know.

Few glaziers gained quite the esteem of Thomas Glazier of Oxford. In the late part of the century he received commissions for windows at both New College, Oxford and Winchester College, and in order to execute both pieces of work he had to employ a large company of glass-painters. Although he was not so privileged as the master mason and master carpenter who were invited to dine at the high table, still he dined with the Fellows of New College; the glazier was gaining a new status in society.

NOTES

1 This is pointed out by John Harvey in *Medieval Craftsmen*.
2 A transcript of the accounts made by L.F. Salzman may be found in *Journal of the British Society of Master Glass Painters*, Vol. I, no. 5, Oct. 1926, and vol. II, no. 1, April 1927.
3 Designs on tables had occasionally been used more than once (e.g. at Fladbury and Warndon near Worcester); but the employment of cartoons made such repetitions easier and far more common.
4 Translated by Daniel V. Thompson, published by Dover Publications, New York, 1954.

CHAPTER SIX

The Fifteenth Century

Good people, things cannot go well in England, nor will they, until all goods shall be in common and when there shall be neither villeins nor gentles, but we shall all be one . . .

. . . We be all come from one father and one mother, Adam and Eve; whereby can they say or show that they be greater lords than we, saving that they cause us to win and labour for that they dispend? They are clothed in velvet and camlet furred with grise, and we be vestured with poor cloth . . .

from *Froissart's Chronicles*

The challenge in this speech, attributed to John Ball (1381) had once spurred peasants to action, but by the turn of the century, their fiercest demands for social equality had subsided to grumbling and suspicion, mainly about the Church. While it maintained its authority in all but extreme cases[1] there could be no major reform. The Church, however, could not claim unique responsibility for the spread of literacy and the founding of grammar schools. Sevenoaks School, where Caxton is said to have been educated, was founded by William Sennocke in 1418, on the stipulation that the headmaster should be a layman and that the tuition should be given free. Instruction was in Latin; the general rule of grammar schools was that boys should speak Latin both in and out of class – the use of the vulgar tongue, English, would be punished by beating.

William Caxton (*c.* 1421–91) began work as a calligrapher and probably learned printing in Cologne. Having set up the first press in England, at Westminster, he printed about a hundred books, many of them in his own translations from French. He was deeply concerned with the standardization of dialects in English, and pioneered the use of English in printed texts. After 1480 he also published woodcuts illustrating the texts; thus images came into wider circulation than had ever been previously possible.

But the potential of reaching a wide public appealed for more mercenary reasons to the wealthier men of the merchant classes. England's new prosperity resulted from the development of the cloth trade. English wool, considered to be the best in Europe, had for years been exported to Italy and Flanders for weaving and finishing. Deriving expertise from foreign traders in cloth, English merchants began to supply wool to local weavers, collecting it as finished cloth, which they were then able to market at home and abroad. An ordinance of 1326 decreed that only members of the royal family, the nobility and those whose rent exceeded £30 a year should purchase foreign cloth in favour of domestically produced wool. The centres of internal trade were London, York, Bristol and the East Anglian country towns, among them Colchester, Coggeshall and Worstead (which gave its name to a wool cloth). It was through fortunes made in cloth that families who had risen to import-ance in society were able to finance the building or rebuilding and embellish-ment of parish churches. The splendid new churches of Lavenham and Long Melford were said to have been built on wool. The motive in establishing such a church and in commissioning windows for it combined a desire for public esteem, if not publicity, with an element of commercial rivalry. The benefactor wished not only to save his soul by immortalizing his name but also to outdo the beneficence of the man whose family fortunes were made in the next town.

With these ambitions went the desire for more illumination in the church. It led to great traceried windows involving huge areas of glass, such as the great east window of York Minster. Sometimes these windows consisted almost entirely of white *quarries* surrounding a motif in stained glass. The technical problems encountered in making good quality, white glass had been largely overcome.

None the less it was foreign glass which was still much more highly valued than anything produced in England. For example, a strict specification occurs in the contract for the Beauchamp Chapel at St Mary's, Warwick (1447) (colour plate 25): the donors charge John Prudde, the King's Glazier, to 'glaze the win-dows with glasse beyond the seas . . . with no glasse of England'. Up until this time, little or no coloured glass was made in England but in 1499 John of Utynam, a Fleming, was granted sole rights in its production in England for a period of twenty years. Even so it is not known how much he made; but it included glass for Eton and King's College, Cambridge.

However, the Wars of the Roses did do something to help the home industry. Because of the uncertainties caused by the wars, we find Robert Glasman of Rugeley supplying 180 lb of English glass to York Minster in 1471. Presumably such a quantity would otherwise have been imported.

Thinner flashings were used now in the making of red glass, and blue flashed glass was sometimes made. Annealing or jewelling came more frequently into use. The method was one in which chips of coloured glass were fixed with flux and fired onto the glass sections. The results of this technique can be seen in an example at St Michael's, Spurriergate, York, dating from about 1430, as well as in the fabulously rich Beauchamp Chapel glass mentioned above. Regional colour characteristics can be recognized in fifteenth-century glass, such as the favoured combination of red and gold with white at Norwich, and red and blue with white at York, and the use of an uncommon hue, aquamarine, at Malvern. It is sometimes possible to detect regional styles also in the brushwork delineation of features. Around the Bristol area and Somerset, there is a tendency for faces in fifteenth-century glass to have heavy eyes and slightly drooping mouths, investing them with a curious melancholy (see p. 108).

There was an increased emphasis on painting rather than leading, calling for very precise delineation. The influence of printing may have had this effect on the style. Stipple shading (with little dots of paint) largely replaced the smear shading common earlier; the new technique gave the glass a greater degree of natural translucency. By this time designs were prepared on paper or parchment scrolls, and were plainly much easier to transport, adapt, transfer and ultimately to bequeath, than the traditional bleached table on which early glaziers had worked. One design could be reversed and used several times, as indeed, the design of a window in All Saints, North Street, York, by John Chamber the Younger, was repeated at St Michael-le-Belfry, in the same city, almost a hundred years later.[2]

A list of twelve prominent glass-painters, including the designer of the original example above, has been compiled by J.A. Knowles[3] for St Helen's Church, Stonegate, where they are all buried. Among the names are those of three members of the Chamber family, father and two sons, who lived and worked in Stonegate. The death of Matthew Petty, also one of a family of glaziers, is recorded (1478), and to this information can be added an entry in the Fabric Rolls for 1446–7: 'In payments to Mathew Pety, glazier, for repairing defects in the glass windows . . . 8s. 6d.' Furthermore, we know that he glazed the lantern tower of York Minster, dating from 1471. A more illustrious member of the same family, John Petty, actually became mayor of the city; he was commemorated in a window, now altered, in the Minster, by a portrait and the inscription:[4]

Orate pro anima Johanis Pety glasiarii at Majoris Ebor . . . qui obiit viii [die] *Novembris AD 1508.*

The social history of York is quite rich with references to eminent glass-painters in the fifteenth century, but prior to that the greater number of crafts-men remain unknown to us. We can, however, identify an important outsider, John Thornton of Coventry, by his monogram near the top of the tracery in the Great East window at York, and the date of its completion, 1408. It is an enormous work, measuring 1,680 square feet, for which he must have employed assistants, but he undertook to paint all the histories and main figures in his own hand. He received the sum of £56 for all his labour (colour plate 20).

The Whole Company of Heaven is shown here, with the Nine Orders of Angels, Patriarchs, Prophets, Israelite heroes and saints ranged in the tracery lights. Panels depicting events from the Creation to the Apocalypse – perhaps linked to the idea of Alpha and Omega – lead on to scenes from the Book of Revelations. In the final sequence below are the English kings, saints and arch-bishops of York, among them the donor, Bishop Skirlaw of Durham.[5]

Glass-painters began to introduce allegorical figures and pure symbol into their windows. The allegories which were most popular were those of Creation, Damnation and Redemption. The symbols which they used derived from morali-ty plays which gradually superseded the narrative style of the old miracle plays. They used abstract concepts in dramatic opposition, embodied in characters named God, Everyman, Death, Strength, Knowledge, Discretion, Beauty and so on. The prevailing interest in the allegorical subjects, was paralleled by increas-ing subtlety in the use of symbolic imagery (colour plate 18). Christ is represent-ed against the Cross by a lily in the Lily Crucifix of the Clopton Chantry Chapel, Long Melford, Suffolk.[6] St Michael, who escorts the dead to the next world, is seen at Martham, Norfolk, weighing souls in the balance (colour plate 31).

At Great Malvern, where the scheme of windows derives its subjects from *Speculum Humanae Salvationis,* an element of realism creeps in, turning sym-bols into incidental details; Judas hides the fish he has stolen inside his cloak; God the Father, seldom before given human form, appears to Abraham as a

St Michael weighing souls, fifteenth century. Martham, Norfolk

similarly old man with a flowing beard and long hair (colour plate 28). The lost scenes from the north choir aisle of Malvern Priory, described by Thomas Habington in the seventeenth century, contained: 'The Pater Noster, Ave Maria, the Creede, the Commandments, The Masse, the Sacraments issuing from the wounds of Our Saviour . . . the whole Christian doctrine and the Doctors of the Latin Church': in short, they brought to the view of the congregation representations of the tenets of their faith, with an immediacy that words may often have lacked through repetition.

There is, as one might expect, even more emphasis on the secular element in fifteenth-century stained glass than there had been in previous centuries – much heraldry, the donors very prominent; examples are at East Harling (colour plates 29 and 30), Norfolk, Sir Robert Wingfield the donor of the east window, or the rows of kneeling donors at Long Melford, Suffolk, and occasionally there is reference to contemporary events. An example of this is at Little Malvern, where the east window has figures of Elizabeth Woodville (queen of Edward IV) and her four children with Bishop Alcock – Alcock had been Dean of Westminster when she took sanctuary there after her husband had fled to France.

Windows were also often didactic in purpose. At All Saints, North Street, York, an early fifteenth-century window of the Corporal Acts of Mercy depicts the following good works: feeding the hungry, the thirsty and the stranger, clothing the naked, tending the sick and visiting prisoners in the stocks. The same figure, dressed in ermine appears in each of the scenes. Reginald Bawtre, the donor, appears below, with a man and a woman, the sun and the seven planets (colour plate 26).

In the same church is the 'Prykke of Conscience' window, of c. 1425, which illustrates the happenings destined to occur during the fifteen final days at the end of the world. Many believed that the Apocalypse was due in the year 1500, Dürer's visions, Leonardo's drawings of areas of natural disaster and the fiends of the Faust legend all contribute to an overriding impression of imminent destruction awaiting the world. The 'Prykke of Conscience' is unusual among 'Doom' windows in that it has a literary origin and is based on part of a poem by Richard Rolle, hermit of Hampole (born 1290). The concluding verses link a presage of the end of the world with the Old Testament flood (colour plate 21).

'Corporal Acts of Mercy' window, fifteenth century. All Saints, North Street, York

Thus tells Jerome their tokens fifteen,
As he in the book of Hebrews had seen,
But for all the tokens that men shall see,
That shall no man certain be
What time Christ shall come to the doom,
So suddenly the doom shall come,
For as befel in Noah and Lot's days,
So shall He come, for Luke in the Gospel says
'Et sicut factum est in diebus Noe, ita erit in illis diebus.'[7]

Reading the glass from left to right, bottom to top, these events are predicted thus: the sea rises; the sea falls; the sea resumes its normal level leaving the earth dry; sea-monsters appear; the sea bursts into flames; trees catch fire; earthquakes begin; rocks and stones burn; men hide in holes in the earth; sky and earth alone can be seen; men emerge from holes to pray; human bones in coffins come to life; stars fall from heaven; men die, the dead are mourned; fire completes the destruction of the world. In the tracery, St Peter receives the blessed in heaven, while Satan prods the souls of the damned into hell. It was in the hope of not being included in the latter selection that the donors below were seen kneeling in prayer.

It can hardly be a coincidence that so many 'Doom' windows were made in the fifteenth century. It is always more exciting to portray the devils and the damned than the angels and the blessed; the emphasis is generally one-sided. Therefore it is the red and blue devils of the Fairford Doom window, for example, that catch our eye. The topography of hell was well known. Dooms usually contained a ladder leading from hell to heaven, and a very narrow bridge; the twelfth-century 'Vision of Tundale' described it as 'two miles long and hardly a handsbreadth across'. Often in the centre, by the ladder, St Michael will be seen weighing souls; sometimes a devil will try to tip the scales on one side, and the Virgin counteracts this by placing her rosary on the other.

At Fairford, where the scheme of glass, from the late fifteenth or early sixteenth century, survives virtually intact, we find that the scenes are disposed according to a deliberate system.[8] Starting in the north aisle with the twelve prophets who foretell the coming of Christ, we then recognize the prefigurations from the Old Testament of the New: Eve tempted (introducing the idea of sin and redemption), Moses, Gideon's Fleece (the incarnation) and the Queen of Sheba bearing gifts (the visit of the Magi). In the Lady Chapel, the Virgin's life and the childhood of Christ are celebrated. The east window depicts Christ's Passion and Crucifixion as was traditional. In the chancel, the sequence of Christ's appearances follow the Entombment and the Transfiguration. In the south aisle are the apostles and Doctors of the Church, faced by oppressors of the Church. In the great west window the cycle is completed as we turn to find the Last Judgement, weird and fearsome (colour plate 33). Satan here is shown with a fish's head, and he has another head with staring eyes and a row of sharp teeth in place of his stomach. Set against this horror is a tiny figure of hope, a soul starting its ascent to heaven.

NOTES

1 One such case was the dispossession of the nunnery of St Radegund in Cambridge where the nuns had freely entertained amorous students. In 1496 Jesus College was founded in its place

2 See M.D. Anderson, ibid. The first use of the design was made by John Chamber the Younger, who died in 1451; the repeat occurs in the St Christopher window of the above mentioned church (1528–36).

3 1414   Robert Wakefield
   1422   Thomas Benefield
   1433   Thomas Rose or Ross
   1437   John Chamber the Elder
   1451   John Witton
   1451   John Chamber the Younger, and son of the above John Chamber
   1451   Richard Chamber
   1458   Thomas Shirley
   1478   Matthew Petty
   1480   William Inglish
   1481   Thomas Shirwyn
   1503   Robert Preston

4 Originally in the third window from the east in south wall of the nave. The translation is: 'Pray for the soul of John Pety, glazier and Mayor of York who died on the 8th November 1508'.

5 A detailed study of this window was undertaken by David O'Connor at the Centre for Medieval Studies, York University.

6 There is a similar panel at St Michael at the North Gate, Oxford.

7 And just as it happened in the days of Noah, so shall it be in those days.

8 There is an interesting theory that some of the faces are royal portraits, including Henry VII and his two sons, Prince Arthur and Henry VIII, his two daughters, Margaret and Mary, and Catherine of Aragon.

CHAPTER SEVEN

The Sixteenth and Seventeenth Centuries

The sixteenth century saw the beginnings of an awkward compromise between Church and State. This is most clearly expressed in the chapel windows of the Vyne in Hampshire, dating from the 1520s (colour plate 37). Each of the three windows has a double theme: secular below and religious above. What catches the eye is the sumptuous figure of the young king, Henry VIII, in the lower light of the central window. Splendidly arrayed in golden armour, crimson tunic, deep blue cloak with an ermine collar, a gold crown and chain, he kneels in prayer on a purple cushion, his sword at his side. Behind him is his patron saint, Henry II of Bavaria.[1] The upper light contains, in rather quieter colours (white, turquoise, mauve, with touches of gold), the Crucifixion.

The window to the left contains, principally, Margaret of Scotland, the king's sister, more sombrely dressed; behind her, her patron saint, St Margaret, and in front of her, her lapdog; in the upper lights, the Resurrection. Similarly, in the window to the right kneels Henry's first queen, Catherine of Aragon, attired almost as richly as her husband, in cloth of gold, a violet mantle and a jewelled cap, against the background of diapered crimson. St Catherine stands in a setting of Renaissance architecture, to the left her lapdog is curled up among the folds of purple cloth at the foot of a *prie-dieu*, and through the archway can be seen a soft green landscape. In the top lights, well above eye-level, is the scene of Christ carrying the Cross.

The windows were made by a team of ten glaziers from the Low Countries. One of their number, David Joris, kept a journal and recorded that they were working on them at the time when the Emperor Charles V was in London, which must have been either in May 1520 or in June 1522.

While the Vyne glass retains a religious content, it is the secular that predominates – on account of the size and above all the remarkably glowing colour of the kneeling figures. Admittedly the window is in a private chapel, but even to

Catherine of Aragon; detail of sixteenth-century glass in the chapel at The Vyne, Hampshire

the Tudor mind there must have seemed something odd in subordinating the Crucifixion to a portrait of the ruling monarch, or even in giving his sister's lap-dog a more important place in the window than the Resurrection.

Although the craftsmen who had come to make these windows came specific-ally to do that job, Henry VII had imported John of Utynam in 1499, a Flemish glazier, to work on glass at Eton and at King's College Chapel. He did not come alone. The official policy towards immigrant craftsmen, including stained glass workers, was one of approbation, and had been for some time. English cloth merchants were trading profitably with Antwerp, and their connections with Flanders brought a noticeable number of immigrants escaping religious persecution and no doubt hoping to find patronage here. In the first quarter of the sixteenth century it might be reasonable to suppose that between one and two thousand craftsmen were arriving here annually. They were not always popular.

Among their number was Holbein. 'He is coming to England', wrote Erasmus to Sir Thomas More, 'to scrape a few angels together.' More replied, 'I am afraid he won't find England as fruitful as he had hoped.' This was true, perhaps, but on Holbein's return to Basel he found Protestantism raging at its most iconoclastic; mobs were breaking into the churches and destroying every sort of image they could find. 'Nothing has survived', wrote Erasmus again. 'The pictures were covered with whitewash, what could burn was thrown on the bonfire, the rest was smashed. Neither monetary nor artistic value was any protection.' Iconoclasm (never as extreme as this) was not to afflict England until later.

The employment of foreign artists probably hastened the spread of the Renaissance style. It was first introduced in other media: Torrigiano designed the tombs in the Henry VII Chapel at Westminster (1512–18), and Giovanni da Maiano was commissioned by Wolsey to make terracotta roundels of Roman emperors for Hampton Court Palace and Whitehall (about 1520). Whether the Renaissance style was appropriate to stained glass is open to question; it attempted to simulate volume, making figures appear rounded rather than flat, introducing perspective, especially in architectural settings, putting in glimpses of landscape – in short, trying to add a third dimension to an art which had always been essentially two-dimensional.

Early sixteenth-century Flemish glass was not always large-scale. There was a specialized type of glass-painting in the form of small roundels, no more than nine inches in diameter and made from single pieces of glass. The early ones are painted in yellow (from silver stain) and black – the only two colours then available that could be used on clear glass. (Later examples, from the seventeenth century, may have enamel colours as well.) The designs were generally of biblical or apocryphal scenes, and were mainly derived from engravings. Since these little panels were essentially portable and relatively cheap at the time of the English cult of the 'Grand Tour', there are probably more of them in English churches than there are on the continent. The village church at Nowton near Bury St Edmunds, for instance, has a fine collection, as has Addington, Buckinghamshire.[2]

By contrast, the glazing scheme at King's College Chapel, Cambridge, was perhaps the most ambitious in the early sixteenth century. Dated 30 April 1526, the contract for part of the work makes it clear to us that glaziers were in general

Detail of Christ before Caiaphas, sixteenth century.
King's College, Cambridge

responsible for producing their own design. This design was referred to, reasonably enough, as a *Vidimus* (Latin: we see), and was the basis for the full-sized cartoon, on which the glass would be made.

Also the said Galyon Hone, Richard Bownde, Thomas Reve and James Nicholson covenaunte and graunte by these presentes that they shalle dylyuer or cause to be delyuered to Fraunces Williamson of the parisshe of Seint Olyff in Suthwerke in the Countie of Surrey glasyer, and to Symond Symondes of the parisshe of Seint Margarete of Westmynster in the Countie of Middelsex glasyer, or to either of them good and true patrons otherwyse called A Vidimus, for to fourme glasse and make by other four wyndowes of the seid Churche . . . The seid Frances and Symond paying to the seid Galyon, Richard, Thomas Reve and James Nycholson for the seid patrons otherwyse called A Vidimus asmoche redy money as shalbe thought reasonable . . .

The windows were commissioned by Richard Foxe and John Fisher as early as 1515 and were begun by Bernard Flower, who was either Netherlandish, or more probably, German. We first hear of him in 1496 being paid £18. 1s. 8d. for glass at the new Hall at Woodstock. He worked for King Henry VII at St Paul's Cathedral, the Tower of London, the Bishop of London's Palace, Westminster Hall, Eltham Palace and Richmond (1500–3), and was made King's Glazier in 1505. In about 1510 he was probably responsible for windows in the Henry VII Chapel at Westminster. He was naturalized in 1514. He did some work for Wolsey at York Place (Whitehall) in 1515 and was paid

£18 2s. 5d. for it; in the same year and again in 1517 he received payments for work at King's College Chapel, Cambridge. He died in 1517 in Southwark, where most of the London glaziers lived. His will is preserved and shows him to have been a man of some substance:

> . . . I bequeth to the ffryers Observants at Grenewiche in the Countie of Kent XXs. to pray for my soule and all christen soules. Also I bequeth to the ffryers Observants at Richemont nere to the king's Place ther XXs. to pray for my soule and all christen soules. The residue of all my moveable goodys . . . I ffrely gyve unto Edy my loving wyff and to my sonnes ffraunces ffloŭre and Lucas floŭre . . .

Flower was succeeded as King's Glazier by another immigrant, Galyon Hone. 'A native of Holland and born subject of the Emperor', Hone was possibly the same as the *Gheleyn van Brugge*, Master in the Guild of St Luke at Antwerp in 1492. We first hear of him in England in 1517, making and repairing glass at Eton, then he was employed at the Castle of Guisnes near Calais, working on commissions in preparation for the Field of the Cloth of Gold. The accounts for 1520 refer to him as the King's Glazier:

To persons in England	
Galyon the glasier	£20
To divers persons on this side the sea [France]	
Galyon the king's glasier	£40
Galyon the king's glasier	£8
Galyon the glasier for setting up the king's glass	£20[3]

He continued to work at Eton, and then in 1526 his name appears in the King's College contract mentioned earlier. Later commissions were at Whitehall 1531, Westminster Palace 1532, Hampton Court, forty-eight lights for the 'mount in the garden' – a kind of summer-house – in 1533, Windsor Castle 1533, heraldic glass for Hunsdon in Hertfordshire 1534, and once again Hampton Court in 1535, where Henry VIII commissioned him to glaze the Great Hall (see p. 230). Accounts indicate:

Payments to Hone for:

Glazing the 11 side windows of the Hall	£20. 4s. 4d.
Two side windows at the nether end of the Hall	£3. 10s.
Also in the side windows:	
30 of the kynges and the quenys armys	4s. apiece
46 badges of the kynges and the quenys	3s. apiece
77 scryptors with the kynges worde	12d. apiece
Serten pecys of harnes	15s.

By 1540 he was doing well enough to employ five servants and own goods assessed at £40, although his fortunes seem to have declined somewhat by the time he died in about 1552. His son, Gerard, carried on his father's profession in the parish of St Saviour, Southwark.

James Nicholson was also Netherlandish or German. We find him in 1518–19 working in Great St Mary's Church at Cambridge; there is an entry, 'Item Jacobo Nycolsoon vitrario pro fenestris in ecclesia beate marie £7'. By 1526 he was living in Southwark, two years later he was employed by Wolsey at Christ Church in Oxford to set up forty-seven sets of arms at 6s. 8d. each. Neither this glass nor the glass in Great St Mary's Cambridge survives. Nicholson was unfortunate in his patron; at Wolsey's downfall he was owed £58 for glass commissioned. He worked for some years on the windows of King's College Chapel (1526–31), no doubt more profitably. But then because of his Lutheran belief he had misgivings about the portrayal of saints and he decided to change his profession to that of a printer.

As we have seen, little love was lost between the Flemings and the indigenous London glaziers, whose work carried on the late medieval tradition while Flemings favoured the Renaissance style. The latter was generally preferred for major commissions, being more fashionable. However the Flemings were subjected to various restrictions. An indenture or work permit was drawn up between the two parties, to allow the Flemings to work, and the Flemish half of it was entrusted to James Nicholson. But after his death in about 1538, his widow married the warden of the London Guild; so the English obtained both halves of the agreement, and had four Flemish glaziers, including Galyon Hone, sent to prison (which perhaps accounts for the decline in Hone's fortunes at this time) – until by royal command they were liberated.[4]

Another of the Flemings who was imprisoned was Francis Williamson (or Willem Zoen). He was living in Southwark by 1526, and also worked on the windows for King's College, as did Symond Symondes, or Simenon, who was, as far as we know, English. He lived in the parish of St Margaret's, Westminster, where in 1521 payment was recorded for 'mendyng of the glass windows and the ymagery works that were broken with the grete wynds before Christmas'.

By 1540 there were few commissions for anything but heraldic glass. The Dissolution of the Monasteries, begun in 1536, was legalized by an Act of Parliament in 1539, and much stained glass was destroyed.[5] From Shaftesbury Abbey, for instance, three cartloads of pieces were taken away; from Becket's shrine at Canterbury twenty-six cartloads of wealth of all kinds, Henry VIII seems to have had a particular grudge against Becket, perhaps because he had been Cardinal Wolsey's favourite saint. Windows depicting him were nearly always smashed. At Nettlestead in Kent, for example, the figure of Becket installed in the fifteenth century by the Lord of the Manor, Reginald de Pympe, seems to have been destroyed at this time. Fragments remain: scenes from Becket's life and a picture of Canterbury Cathedral.

In the reign of Elizabeth I came further iconoclasm: the destruction of what were termed 'superstitious images'. All the glass from the cloister at Durham Cathedral was smashed because its theme was the life of St Cuthbert. And although there was a proclamation in 1561[6] which condemned the defacing of 'monuments of antiquity set up in the churches for memory, not for super-stition', and instructed that those broken already should be restored, it is doubt-ful whether anything was ever done about it.

Patronage for religious stained glass revived somewhat in the reign of Charles I, notably by Archbishop Laud who arranged several commissions in Oxford in the 1630s, and which were executed by Abraham and Bernard van Linge. At Balliol two windows were made by Abraham van Linge (1637) on the unusual subjects of St Philip and the Eunuch, and the sickness and recovery of King Hezekiah; also by him at Queen's are the Last Judgement, the Last Supper and Crucifixion, the Annunciation and Visitation, the Ascension, Resurrection, Adoration of the Shepherds, and Pentecost – all in a good state of preservation and dating from 1635. Other works by him are at University College and at Christ Church, a window of Jonah and the City of Nineveh (colour plate 39).

Jonah and the Whale; seventeenth-century enamelled glass at Lincoln College, Oxford (*by kind permission of the Rector and Fellows of Lincoln College*)

At Lincoln College there is an interesting east window by Bernard van Linge, dating from 1629–30, based on typological parallels. The Nativity is paired with the Creation of Adam (who looks remarkably like Charles I), the Baptism of Christ with the Crossing of the Red Sea, the Last Supper with the Passover, the Crucifixion with the Brazen Serpent, the Resurrection with Jonah newly disgorged by the Whale, the Ascension with Elijah and the Chariot of Fire. Bernard van Linge's work can also be seen at Wroxton Abbey, Oxfordshire[7] and at Lincoln's Inn in London. In the designs of both men large figures are set in landscapes giving the effect of a picture seen through window-panes.

Stained glass of this kind can only be done by the use of enamels. An iron-red enamel that was suitable for flesh-tints was introduced by Jean Cousin of Paris in about 1525, and was named after its inventor. In 1636 the district of Lorraine, which had been the chief source for pot-metal, was overrun by the troops of Louis XIII and all the glass-furnaces were destroyed. So as pot-metal became virtually unobtainable, it was inevitable that glass-makers should turn to enamelling. Initially the technique was used mainly for small panels, which were much in demand, often for domestic settings; but after *c.* 1560 it began to be used for large-scale work.

Of the glass at Lydiard Tregoze, Wiltshire, John Aubrey wrote 'In this it exceeds all churches in this countie.' The east window, Flemish without doubt, dating from about 1633, is a splendidly rich combination of the religious with the heraldic – an olive tree with shields being set in the central light between the two St Johns, St John the Baptist to the left and St John the Divine to the

East window by Abraham van Linge, c. 1630, with St John the Baptist, St John the Divine, and olive tree with heraldic shields. Lydiard Tregoze, Wiltshire

right. The whole design is possibly a rebus on the name of the local lord, Oliver St John. Below the saints and the tree are three armorial bearings; above them four angels carry the signs of the evangelists.

During the period of the Civil War and Commonwealth (1640–8) all sources of patronage for stained glass, whether religious or secular, virtually dried up. The Puritans condemned stained glass as vehemently as they condemned the theatre, and they destroyed much, believing it to be the work of the devil. 'We desire that profane glass windows', declared the Women of Middlesex in 1642, 'whose superstitious paint makes many idolators, may be humbled and dashed in pieces against the ground. For our conscience tells us that they are diabolical and the father of Darkness was the inventor of them, being the chief patron of damnable pride.'[8]

A few windows were taken out and hidden; for example at East Harling the glass was concealed in an attic and at the Vyne it was apparently immersed in the lake. Many windows were destroyed deliberately and systematically, others were attacked in a more random manner. The city of York was besieged by three different Parliamentary armies for eleven weeks before the Battle of Marston Moor. The Minster was fired at, even during divine service, and, according to the report of an eyewitness,[9] the Roundheads 'would not fail to make their hellish disturbance by shooting against and battering the church, in so much that sometimes a cannon bullet has come in at the window and bounced about from pillar to pillar (even like some furious fiend or evil spirit). . . '. After the siege there might have been wholesale destruction of the surviving glass, had it not been for the Parliamentarian general, Thomas Fairfax, who removed it at this time, and so it was preserved.

When the art of stained glass was able to reassert itself once more, it was on a different basis, more commercialized. For the first time glass-painters began to advertise their wares.[10] The earliest trade card was issued by Henry Gyles of York (1645–1709). Under a mezzotint portrait of himself, drawn by Francis Place, is printed:

> Glass painting for windows as Arms,
> Sundyals, History, Landskipt, &c Done
> by Henry Gyles of the City of York.

In the *Athenian Mercury* of 1691 and 1692 appeared advertisements for the glass-painting of Mr Winch and Mr Halsey:

> This art of Painting with the New Invention of Spot Dyals, lately known to many of the Gentry of England, is continued at Mr. Winches, a Glass Painter in Bread-Street near Cheapside, where any Gentleman may be accommodated to his satisfaction in any anneal'd Draughts or Effigies whatever.

Mr Halsey protested he had been left out:

> In a late Question about annealing and painting Glass &c., Mr. Winch in Bread-Street was only taken Notice of, whenas Mr. Halsey's Name (who lives in Holborn over against Fetter-Lane) was by some mistake left out, although his Partner and Fellow Artist in those Admirable Curiosities.

Late seventeenth-century west window, showing monarchs of the Anglican persuasion. St Andrew Undershaft in the City of London

SIXTEENTH AND SEVENTEENTH CENTURIES

A great deal of stained glass in London that had escaped Puritan iconoclasm survived only to be destroyed in the Great Fire of 1666. Most of the Wren churches were designed to have plain glass, for which there was a great demand. St Andrew Undershaft's west window is late in the century and has an uncontroversial[11] historical theme – five lights containing figures of Edward VI, Elizabeth I, James I, Charles I and William III. St George's Hanover Square, an early eighteenth-century church, has seventeenth-century glass from Antwerp, which was not installed until the nineteenth century. It was adapted by Willement with, one must admit, rather confused effect.

The best stained glass of the second half of the seventeenth century was usually armorial. Northill in Bedfordshire has windows by John Oliver of 1664, commissioned by the Grocers' Company, showing heraldry adorned with magnificently swash scrollwork.

During these two centuries stained glass underwent considerable changes in style. The Late Gothic still practised by English craftsmen (in the early sixteenth century) was pronounced old-fashioned and the demand was all for the 'Renaissance' style introduced by the Flemings. Then came the introduction of landscape and the 'picture seen through the window' effect. Some splendid armorial glass was designed, truly baroque in spirit. Then the whole art was denounced as Royalist if heraldic, which was bad enough, and as Popish if religious, which was worse; so that when it dared to re-emerge at the end of the seventeenth century it had degenerated into a minor craft, one that had to advertise for small commissions in the public press.

NOTES

1 973–1024. An apt choice of patron saint. The Emperor Henry remained a layman, essentially an administrator rather than an ascetic, he founded the see of Bamberg, and consolidated the power of the monarchy.
2 There are also some excellent examples in the Victoria and Albert Museum, and in the collection of Dr William Cole.
3 Letters and Papers of Henry VIII.
4 See J.A. Knowles, *Antiquaries Journal*, 1925, Vol. 5, p. 148.
5 Malvern was an exception. The discerning townspeople there happily bought the glass of the priory – which otherwise would have been destroyed – for the sum of £20, and so preserved it.
6 State Papers 12/13/32.

7 See article by H.T. Kirby, *Journal of the British Society of Master Glass Painters*, Vol. XIV, no. 2, 1965.

8 Quoted by Herbert Read, *English Stained Glass*.

9 Thomas Mace, a musician. See F. Harrison, *Painted Glass of York*.

10 See article by John A. Knowles 'Glass-painters' Advertisements' in the *Journal of the British Society of Master Glass Painters*, Vol. II, no. 1, April 1927.

11 Uncontroversial, that is to say, in that all these monarchs supported the Church of England. Those who did not are omitted.

CHAPTER EIGHT

The Eighteenth Century

Nature and Nature's law lay hid in night:
God said, *Let Newton be!* and all was light.

(Alexander Pope, epitaph intended for Isaac Newton)

The lines quoted above imply a belief that science (in the person of Newton) could and would explain the universe. However, they also show a belief in the God who created Newton to do this. Pope, if pressed, might have been more willing to abandon the second belief than the first. Among the educated classes reason was coming to be considered as more important than faith and atheism was gaining ground. These attitudes are brilliantly expressed in the Peckitt-Cipriani window in the library of Trinity College, Cambridge. The window shows the Spirit of Cambridge introducing Newton to George III (colour plate 40).

The Church of England was in a particularly turgid state. As the Established Church it retained a monopoly over the learned professions and the universities – where dissenters had to practise 'occasional conformity' by taking communion once a year (or they were debarred) – but gave no strong spiritual lead. The more powerful clergy vied for promotion, often for political rather than religious motives. At the other end of the scale, many curates were paid less than £20 a year, and such miserly stipends were unlikely to attract men of calibre. Parishes were often combined in order to provide something like a living wage; and the poor parson, unable to afford a horse, had to walk from one to another. His richer colleagues might further enrich themselves with a more profitable plurality, which in its turn led to absenteeism. While lip-service might be paid by the layman to orthodox religion, attendances at church dropped. The country squire might expect his wife, children and servants to go, but he himself would spend his Sunday mornings in other pursuits.

The dissenting churches inspired keener loyalty and some excitement. Methodism began with John Wesley (1703–91) although it did not become a separate sect until after his death. Wesley said that his aim was to 'reform the nation, more particularly the Church, and spread scriptural holiness throughout the land'. He organized open-air meetings, which attracted great crowds. The emphasis was always on the spoken word and when chapels came to be built, they were extremely plain, with nothing to distract the eye – certainly no stained glass.

But in the second half of the century there was also a growing belief in pantheism, which found its most telling expression in the poetry of Wordsworth. God, it was believed, was to be found not in churches but in the forces of nature – here was the 'Wisdom and Spirit of the Universe'.[1]

> One impulse from the vernal wood
> May teach you more of man,
> Of moral evil and good,
> Than all the sages can.[2]

This being the tenor of eighteenth-century belief, it is a wonder that any stained glass was produced at all, and not surprising that it was a time when the art was at its lowest ebb. It became closely linked and, inevitably, subordinated to the art of painting. This trend had already begun in the seventeenth century; by the eighteenth it was widely accepted.

The windows of St Michael's Church at Great Witley, Hereford and Worcester, dating from 1719–21 are characteristic of early eighteenth-century work. Although Italian in design, they were painted in enamels by Joshua Price. They are essentially Renaissance compositions seen through a rectilinear grid and are based on designs by Francesco Sleter or Slater. It is entirely unexpected to

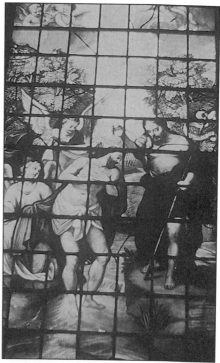

Baptism of Christ; enamelled glass painted by Joshua Price, designed by Francesco Sleter, 1719–21. Great Witley, Hereford & Worcester

70

find anything so richly Italianate in rural Worcestershire. How they found their way there is interesting.

The Duke of Chandos (Handel's patron) had built himself a mansion at Canons near Edgware, described by Defoe as 'the most magnificent in England'. It included a chapel remarkable for 'its building, and the beauty of its workmanship' and, because the duke kept a full choir there, 'the best music, after the manner of the Chapel Royal'.[3] The house was demolished in 1747, and the decorative fittings of the chapel were bought by the second Lord Foley of Stourbridge. He transported them to Great Witley and used them to transform the church adjoining his own great house – now in its turn ruined.

Joshua Price was one of a family of York glass-painters. His brother, William Price the Elder, executed a Nativity at Christ Church, Oxford from designs by Sir James Thornhill (1696), and an east window for Merton College (1702). Joshua apparently did well for himself; Francis Place wrote to Henry Gyles, the glass-painter of York:

I made Inquiry at *Mr. Price's* about *glass painters*, he tells me there is 4 in Towne but not worke enough to Imply one if he did nothing Else . . . He [told] me [their] prises here is 12 or 14 [shillings] p foote for greate work and for small peeces according [as] they can agree. I perceave his cheife traid is glasing by wc I belejve he gets a greate deele of Mony for he is belejved Rich.[4]

The brothers joined in partnership sometime in the first five years of the eighteenth century and both seem to have died in 1722. Joshua's son, William, designed the rose window of the north transept of Westminster Abbey.

There were still plentiful commissions for plain glass, and this must have formed by far the greatest part of a glazier's output in the early years of the eighteenth century. But when a window was coloured the tradition persisted that it should be based on a painting. Clearly this was still the accepted practice when Thomas Jervais published a handbill for his fifth exhibition of stained glass in 1785. Only one of the panels listed is based on nature, all the rest on Dutch, French, or English paintings, or on antique cameos.

It was Thomas Jervais who was responsible for the execution on glass of the Reynolds designs for the great west window of the chapel of New College,

A

CATALOGUE

OF

Mr. JERVAIS's

FIFTH EXHIBITION

OF

STAINED GLASS.

☞ All the undermentioned PICTURES are Painted by *Mr. JERVAIS*, No. 69, *Margaret-Street, Cavendiſh-Square,* after the following Maſters.

FIRST WINDOW.

CENTRE, an oval Flower-Piece, - - *after Nature*
Upper corner, (left ſide) Head of Alexander *in Cameo Antique*
Ditto (right ſide) ditto Hercules - - *ditto*
Bottom corner, (left ſide) ditto Livia, - - *ditto*
Ditto (right ſide) ditto Minerva, - - *ditto*
Lower range, (centre) Moonlight, - - *after Vanderneer*
A Sea View on each ſide, - - *after De Vleiger*

SECOND WINDOW.

Centre of upper part, a Sleeping Cupid, - - *after Guido*
with four compartments of Flow- ⎫
ers, and four ditto Vaſes, ⎬ *after the Antique in Griſaile*
Lower range, (left ſide) a Welch Merry-Making, - *after Ferg*
Ditto, right ſide) Fortune Teller - - *ditto*

THIRD WINDOW.

Upper part, a Landſcape, - - *after Gaſper Pouſſin*
Lower range, (centre) a Smith's Forge, *after Wright of Derby*
Left ſide, a Ship on Fire, - - - *after Vandervelde*
Right ſide, a Candle-Light, - - - *after Schalken*

FOURTH WINDOW.

Upper part, Cows, &c. - - - *after P. Potter*
Lower part, Horſes, &c. - - - *after Cuyp*

FIFTH WINDOW.

Inſide of a Gothic Flemiſh Church, with the Con- ⎫
gregation attending to a Sermon, - ⎬ *after P. Neefs*

Printed by H. REYNELL, No. 21, near Air-Street, Piccadilly.

Catalogue of Thomas Jervais's Fifth Exhibition

Detail from great west window of the Virtues, New College, Oxford, 1778–85. Designed by Sir Joshua Reynolds, executed by Thomas Jervais (*by kind permission of the Warden and Fellows of New College*)

Oxford; they date from 1778 to 1785. Seven vaporous ladies represent the virtues of Temperance, Fortitude, Faith, Charity, Hope, Justice and Prudence. Above is a Nativity, based on a painting by Correggio. While one may admire the technical skill of Jervais in transmuting these subjects into glass, it is an exercise in misplaced ingenuity and an entirely wrongheaded use of the medium. Where there should be firm-edged definition, there is *chiaroscuro*; where there should be two dimensions, there is an unhappy attempt to introduce a third.

The most notable of the eighteenth-century glass-painters was William Peckitt of York. He lived in Micklegate, and in 1752, when he was twenty-one, published the following advertisement:

William Peckitt, son of William Peckitt, the noted glovemaker next door to the Sandhill in Colliergate, York, thinks proper to advertise all gentlemen clergymen and others that by many experiments he has found out the art of painting or staining of glass in all kinds of colours and all sorts of figures as scripture pieces for church windows, arms in heraldry etc., in the neatest and liveliest manner, specimens of which may be seen at the house aforesaid. He likewise repairs old broken painted windows in churches or in gentlemen's houses and will wait upon any person in town or country that desires it.

York Courant, 14 July 1752

In fact Peckitt's technique of enamelling was still a little chancy at this early date, and the windows that he made for York Guildhall in 1754 had to be replaced thirteen years later (these were destroyed in the last war). Other work of his may be seen in York, in the four windows in the south wall of the Minster, depicting Abraham, Moses, Solomon and St Peter, at Oxford in New College Chapel and Oriel College (Presentation of Christ in the Temple), at Audley End, Essex (Last Supper); but his *magnum opus* is the window which Cipriani designed for Trinity College Library, Cambridge, mentioned earlier, and finished in 1775.

William Peckitt's work depended above all on the use of enamelling; he brought this technique to near-perfection. There was still little or no coloured glass being imported. It seems likely that a certain amount was made in

England. William and Joshua Price, as early as 1705, claimed to have rediscovered the secret:

Glass Painting Reviv'd

Whereas the ancient Art of Painting and Staining Glass has been much discouraged by reason of an Opinion generally received, That the *Red Colour* (not *made in Europe* for many years) is totally lost; these are to give Notice, that the said *Red* and all other Colours are made to as great a degree of Curiosity and Fineness as in former Ages by *William* and *Joshua Price*, Glasiers and Glass Painters, near *Hatton Garden* in Holborn, *London* where Gentlemen may have Church History, Coats of Arms &c Painted upon Glass, in what colours they please, to as great Perfection as ever; and draws Sundyals on Glass, Wood or Stone, &c and cut Crown Glass, with all sorts of ordinary Glass, and performs all kinds of Glazing work.

London Gazette, 14 June 1705[5]

In 1733 John Rowell, who was a plumber in Reading, claimed:

the antient art of staining glass, with all the colours, revived and performed by John Rowell at Wycomb in Buckinghamshire.

Craftsman, 3 February 1733

Horace Walpole commented in his 'Anecdotes' that Rowell's colours were generally impermanent, but that he developed 'a very durable and beautiful red'.

The town of Stourbridge in the West Midlands was renowned for glassmaking. 'At Stourbridge', remarked Defoe[6], 'they have a very great manufacture for glass of all sorts.' Dr Pococke in his *Travels through England* is a little more specific about Stourbridge glass. He records that on 8 June 1751 he 'came to Stourbridge famous for its glass manufacture which is here coloured in the liquid in all the capital colours in their several shades, and if I mistake not, is a secret which they have here'.[7]

Stained glass was not rated highly among the arts in the eighteenth century, those who worked in it often had to resort to making sundials in order to obtain adequate commissions. Horace Walpole was an enthusiastic collector of stained glass – one of the first, one imagines. The idea of stained glass being something one might *collect* was new, and perhaps only likely in an age when the actual making of it was in a state of decline. His partiality subjected him to some teasing and abuse, 'His mind as well as his house was piled up with Dresden china and illuminated through painted glass'[8] – especially since he preferred his 'Flemish histories and rich mosaicks' to the smoother, more fashionable products of the century in which he lived.

He displayed his collection in the windows of his house at Strawberry Hill,[9] and employed William Peckitt to set them up. Eight of his windows were damaged when five powder mills exploded at Hounslow in 1772. Walpole bemoaned the state of his 'poor shattered castle', but what is significant is the ruthless vandalism even he would employ in order to replace what had been destroyed, 'I dare not tell how many churches I propose to rob to repair my losses.'

At the end of the eighteenth century and the beginning of the nineteenth century, a fair number of early French stained glass panels came on to the market. It is hard to say whether this was a laudable rescue job as they might have been destroyed in the French Revolution or a piece of commercial opportunism. The best-known dealer in importing this glass was a certain Christopher Hampp who ran a business in Norwich. Thus it is that some fine examples of twelfth-century and thirteenth-century French glass (originating from Paris, St Denis, Rouen, Le Mans, Compiègne) found their way into English churches, such as Twycross in Leicestershire, Wilton in Wiltshire, Rivenhall in Essex (which seems to have been a private transaction), and the chapel of Raby Castle in Co. Durham. It seems that much of the glass was mutilated in the process, and there was little attempt to keep the panels in any logical order. So we find that bits from the St Benedict Chapel at St Denis turn up at both Twycross and Raby Castle. They were not accounted of much value, for it was fashionable to despise the Gothic.

It is not generally realized that during the eighteenth century there was a destruction of glass almost comparable with the iconoclasm that had taken place under Henry VIII and Cromwell. It was not so much for religious motives as that the medieval was disregarded, disliked and thoroughly out of fashion.

Salisbury Cathedral, for instance, lost almost all its stained glass between 1786 and 1790:

Whole cartloads of glass, lead and other rubbish were removed from the nave and transepts and shot into the town ditch.

One small panel that was rescued, presumably from the town ditch, survives in the little church of Grateley near the Wiltshire border of Hampshire.

Other pieces were salvaged, rather unwillingly, by a local plumber; he sent them to a Mr Lloyd of Conduit Street, London with the following note:

This day I have sent you a Box full of old stained and painted glass, as you desired me to doe . . . I expect to Beate to Peceais a great deal very sune, as it his of now use to me, and we do it for the lead. If you want more of the same you may have what thear is, if it will pay you for the taking out, as it is a Deal of Truble to what Beating it to Pecais his.[10]

At Durham Cathedral the fifteen windows of the Nine Altars were destroyed:

The richly painted glass and mullions were swept away, and the present plain windows inserted in their place. The glass lay for a long time afterwards in baskets on the floor and when the greater part of it had been purloined the remainder was locked up in the Galilee.[11]

All this was done in the name of good taste, a poor excuse for vandalism.

NOTES

1 Influence of Natural Objects, & The Prelude, Bk. I, 1. 401.
2 The Tables Turned.
3 Daniel Defoe, *Tour through the Whole Island of Great Britain*, Letter 6.
4 *Francis Place, Engraver and Draughtsman*, by H.M. Hake, Walpole Soc., Vol. X, 1922, p. 65.
5 The advertisement is quoted in an article by John A. Knowles ('Glass-painters' Advertisements') in the *Journal of the British Society of Master Glass Painters*, Vol. II, no. 1, April 1927. Knowles suggests that the Price brothers employed a refugee from Lorraine to make the glass.

6 bid.

7 See article by John Lowe, *Journal of the British Society of Master Glass Painters*, Vol. XIII, no. 2, 1960–1.

8 *Edinburgh Review*, 1818.

9 See 'Horace Walpole and his Collection of Stained Glass at Strawberry Hill', *Journal of the British Society of Master Glass Painters*, Vol. VII, no. 1, October 1937.

10 1788. From *Winston's Memoirs*, quoted in an article on 'Early Nineteenth Century Ideals' by J.A. Knowles, in *Journal of the British Society of Master Glass Painters*, Vol. XIV, no. 1, 1964.

11 This was in 1795. See Raine – Durham Cathedral.

CHAPTER NINE

The Nineteenth Century

The power of glass . . . to convey colour is quite unique; no kind of painting can at all come up to it. It is true, we cannot have the infinite gradations of our great oil colourists; we cannot round one tint imperceptibly
into another, as it is given to them to do; so much we grant; but for power
and brilliancy, or even harmony and sweetness, glass well-made and skil-
fully used has a scale of beauty which no graded pigments laid on to an
opaque surface can hope to equal. Glass . . . is a luminous material, full of
points which catch the light like the facets of a diamond; and it is this
which accounts for the gem-like lustre of old windows. Always light,
because suspended against the day, they yet respond with indescribable
sympathy to every change in the heavens, answering one by one, sweet
vassals of the sunbeams, to the inspiration of the light.[1]

This was written in 1855 by Francis Wilson Oliphant, a glass-painter among
other things, a few years before there was much sign of revival in the art.
Oliphant's turn of phrase is flowery at times, but undoubtedly he understood the
potential as well as the limitations of the medium of glass-painting. What he
does not suggest here is how that potential should be realized in the work of his
contemporaries. We note that he speaks of *old* windows. This is characteristic of
his day. An admiration for the Gothic now bedevilled art, especially ecclesiastical art. If churches were not medieval, they should be made to look as medieval
as possible. And indeed if they were medieval then all too frequently they were
restored to conform to the nineteenth-century idea of what medieval ought to be.

It took a brave man to swim against the tide and expostulate as Charles
Winston did over the reglazing of Glasgow Cathedral:

How completely one sees in all this that the Gothic is not the architectural
style for the nineteenth century! . . . Some day, I suppose, people will
come to their senses, and then we shall see art flourish.[2]

Winston was a profound medievalist, but rightly rejected the medieval pastiche in favour of modern contemporary work. Despite all the dreadful nineteenth-century glass that one sees, there really *was* the revival he predicted, and it was largely due to himself and William Morris.

The problem, as Morris knew very well, was to reconcile art with an industrial age. For commercially the country was prospering. 'It is well known', said Sir Robert Peel when the foundation of a National Gallery was first discussed, 'that our manufacturers were, in all matters connected with machinery, superior to all their foreign competitors; but in the pictorial designs which were so important in recommending the productions of industry to the taste of the consumer, they were, unfortunately, not equally successful.'

At the National Gallery (founded in 1829) and later in the century at the Victoria and Albert Museum, designers found stimulation and perhaps inspiration. But there was a danger of copying past styles indiscriminately, and of applying inappropriate ornament to the products of commerce, as if culture were something you could take by the yard and cut up into trimmings. Art was only an embellishment and not part of the main fabric of society, and if there was one thing that preoccupied Morris it was that art should be integrated into the lives of men, as he believed it had been in the Middle Ages. Quarrelling with the superficiality of so much Victorian decoration, he wrote:[3]

The Aim of Art is to increase the happiness of men, by giving them beauty and interest of incident to amuse their leisure, and prevent them wearying even of rest, and by giving them hope and bodily pleasure in their work; or, shortly, to make man's work happy and his rest fruitful. Consequently, genuine art is an unmixed blessing of the race of man.

Forty years ago there was much less talk about art, much less practice of it, than there is now; and this is especially true of the architectural arts . . . People have consciously striven to raise the dead in art since that time, and with some superficial success. Nevertheless, in spite of this conscious effort, I must tell you that England, to a person who can feel and understand beauty, was a less grievous place to live in then than it is now . . .

The medieval craftsman was free in his work, therefore he made it as amusing to himself as he could; and it was his pleasure and not his pain that made all things beautiful that were made, and lavished treasures of human hope and thought on everything that man made, from a cathedral to a porridge-pot.

It was not that Morris wished to re-create the forms of the art of the Middle Ages – in fact in its earlier days he would not allow Morris & Co. to supply stained glass to any medieval church – but he wished that something of what he felt to be the spirit of those times could be revived in the nineteenth century. His dissatisfaction with things as they were is part of the measure of the man. In the early years of the century, complacency had led artists not only to overvalue their own productions, but to undervalue and perhaps destroy the work of their predecessors.

'Impossible as it may seem', wrote M. Drake in his *History of English Glass-Painting*[4], 'to those acquainted with the works of the eighteenth century, things actually got worse and worse during the first quarter of the nineteenth.'

A stained glass window, it was thought, should be a picture as unencumbered with bar-lines and lead-lines as possible; medieval glass was pieced together with leads only because the craftsman had not the wit to make it without. They wrote with pride of their developed enamelling technique:

In this reign, a new style of staining glass has originated, which is the boast and peculiar invention of our own artists. The deviation from the hard line of the early Florentine or Flemish schools to the correct contour of Michelagnolo [*sic*], or the gorgeous colours of Rubens, is not more decidedly marked, than the design and execution of the Van Lings and Prices, and the masterly performances of Jervais. A striking deficiency in the compostion of the early artists, was the necessity of surrounding the different colours with lead, and destroying, by that means, the harmony of the outline. Harshness was the unavoidable effect, which they knew not either to correct or obviate.[5]

This is James Dalloway, *Observations on English Architecture*, 1806. It was absurdly cranky of Horace Walpole, Dalloway thought, to persist in his admiration for medieval glass, 'so enamoured of Flemish histories and rich mosaics that he was blind to the perfection of the new school of glass-staining'.

Perfection is a strong word. Having, so they thought, achieved it, they felt at liberty to remove and destroy whatever seemed to them less than perfect. Thus during the years 1821 to 1828 the firm of Betton & Evans took out the medieval glass made by Thomas Glazier of Oxford from the chapel at Winchester College, and, instead of restoring it, replaced it with their own copies. Three lights were salvaged, and put first into St Mary's, Shrewsbury, and then in the 1850s bought for the V & A at the price of £8. 6s. 8d. each. The Betton & Evans copies, incidentally, cost about three times as much. They met with great approval. An anonymous writer in the *Literary Gazette* of September 1826 wrote:

Of the modern execution we cannot speak too highly, perhaps there is not an example to compete with it throughout the Kingdom; the colours are exceedingly vivid yet admirably harmonised . . . '

So everyone was happy and the firm of Betton & Evans flourished. They were based at Shrewsbury, and made many windows in that district from 1820 onwards. The partners were Sir John Betton, who died in 1849, and David Evans, also his son Charles Evans. Besides the Winchester glass, their work may be seen in Wadham College, Oxford, and there is armorial glass, done in 1833, at Kenilworth, Warwickshire.

Another well-known firm was that of William Russell Egington (1778–1834), who was appointed glass-painter to Princess Charlotte. Many of Egington's commissions were for secular glass; for instance the library window at Stourhead, which he saw fit to fill with an adaptation of part of Raphael's 'School of Athens' fresco in the Vatican Stanze.

There was also Joseph Backler, who produced a window for Arundel Castle depicting King John's assent to Magna Carta, and an east window for St Thomas's Church, Dudley, based on Raphael's 'Transfiguration'.

William Wailes from Newcastle-on-Tyne, despite the fact that all his children were born deaf and dumb, was said to be 'a very genial man with one of the happiest faces imaginable'. He made a window for Chichester Cathedral in 1841, and his work is widespread; it is a pity that his glass is rather less likeable than his disposition.

There was also the firm of John P. and George Hedgeland, father and son, who worked in Lisson Grove, London. Hedgeland designed the west window of Norwich Cathedral, which at least has the courage of its convictions, and

The east window of East Harling Church, Norfolk, was
donated by Sir Robert Wingfield *(left)* in about 1480.
The detail above depicts the Ascension

Some fifteenth-century devils at work.
Once the scales have been successfully
weighted (as is being attempted at
Brightwell Baldwin, Oxfordshire, *top
right*, and Martham, Norfolk, *above*),
then wicked souls cannot escape the
devil's jaws (as in the detail from the
west window at Fairford,
Gloucestershire, *right*)

St Nicholas is seen saving three unjustly condemned men from death in this detail from an early sixteenth-century window of his life at Hillesden, Buckinghamshire

The Fall and the Expulsion from Paradise (top), and the Nativity and Adoration (beneath), as glazed *c.* 1525 in the east window of the chapel at Hengrave Hall, Suffolk

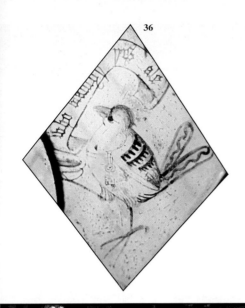

36

Left
A bird from a series depicting the funeral of Reynard the Fox, *c.* 1500, from Yarnton, Oxfordshire

Below Left
Henry VIII, *c.* 1521, from one of the chapel windows in the Vyne, Hampshire

Below right
Flemish sixteenth-century glass showing the Baptism of Christ, from Compton, Surrey

38

Jonah before the city of Nineveh, *c.* 1630, enamelled glass by Abraham van Linge, from Christ Church Cathedral, Oxford

The Age of Reason is typified in this window, designed by Giovanni Cipriani and painted by William Peckitt of
York for Trinity College Library, Cambridge, in 1774 – 5. It shows the spirit of Cambridge introducing Sir
Isaac Newton to George III (reproduced by permission of the Master and Fellows, Trinity College, Cambridge)

The first commission for stained glass from the newly formed firm of Morris, Marshall, Faulkner & Co. came in 1861 from the Church of All Saints in Selsley, Gloucestershire. William Morris, Dante Gabriel Rossetti, Ford Madox Brown and Edward Burne-Jones were all involved in designing windows for the church. That shown above, of the Resurrection, was designed by Burne-Jones and Philip Webb

The Finding of Moses, from a window made by the firm of Clayton & Bell at St Mary Redcliffe Church, Bristol, in 1863

Eve and the Virgin Mary, designed by William Morris in 1865 as part of the east window of All Saints' Church, Middleton Cheney, Northamptonshire

Two Pre-Raphaelite
windows.

Left
The Flight into Egypt, by
William Morris, 1862,
from the Church of St
Michael and All Angels,
Brighton, Sussex

Below
The Fiery Furnace, by
Edward Burne-Jones, 1870,
from Middleton Cheney,
Northamptonshire

Examples of work by two leading Irish artists in stained
glass in the early twentieth century.

Above
South window depicting the life of St Nicholas, 1948–9,
by Evie Hone, from Ettington, Warwickshire

Left
A kneeling angel, a detail from the Roma Spencer Smith
memorial window, 1921, by Harry Clarke, from
Sturminster Newton, Dorset

The 'Salvation' window in
Canterbury Cathedral was
designed in 1960 by the
Hungarian artist, Ervin Bossanyi,
to replace glass destroyed during
the Second World War. It shows
an imprisoned man being lifted by
an angel from darkness into light,
where his wife and daughter
await him

The Baptistery window commissioned for the new Coventry Cathedral was designed by John Piper and made between 1959 and 1962 by Patrick Reyntiens. It offers an abstract representation of the Holy Spirit

The French artist Marc Chagall designed this window, his first in this country, for Tudeley Church, Kent, in 1967. It is a memorial to Sarah d'Avigdor-Goldsmid, who drowned in a sailing accident. The glass was made by Charles Marq at Reims

John Piper is generally recognized as having been the leading artist in the field of stained glass in the latter half of the twentieth century. These two examples, both interpreted in glass by Patrick Reyntiens, typify the colourful and figurative character of Piper's designs of the 1970s and '80s.

Right
Fishes, a detail from the east window at Nettlebed, Oxfordshire, 1970, depicting symbols of the Resurrection

Below
The similarly symbolic and celebratory memorial window to Sir John Betjeman at Farnborough, Berkshire, 1986

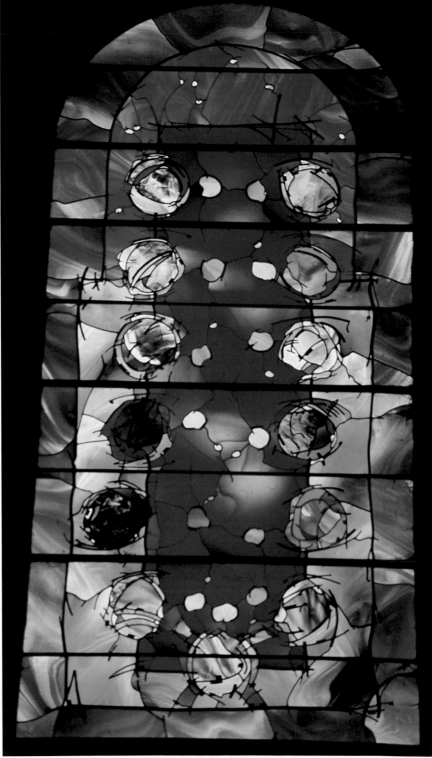

The 'Daily Bread' window by Mark Angus, a bold and imaginative interpretation of the Last Supper, which was installed in Durham Cathedral in 1984

restored the glass of King's College Chapel, Cambridge with rather more con-science than Betton & Evans had shown at Winchester. George Hedgeland's window at the Great Exhibition of 1851 was described by Charles Winston as 'decidedly the best piece of English glass there'.

Apart from the Hedgelands, perhaps the most interesting of this rather dismal bunch was Thomas Willement (1786–1871). He is remembered chiefly for his armorial windows, and also because, unlike most others of his time, he regarded stained glass as a mosaic of coloured pieces. He became heraldic artist to George IV, and 'Artist in Stained Glass to Queen Victoria'. In 1840 he pro-duced a printed catalogue of his work. Perhaps his most notable achievement is the rather splendid glass for the Great Hall and Watching Chamber at Hampton Court. The original Galyon Hone glass was in consequence displaced, and some of it may now be seen in the church of Earsdon, Tyne and Wear.

Charles Winston[6] had no high opinion of the glass-painters who were his contemporaries. 'The great mass can only be looked upon as mere tradesmen at best. They cannot even copy correctly, but have set up a style of their own, which resembles the old work only in its defects.'[7]

Winston was by profession a barrister, but devoted so much of his life to the question of stained glass that one wonders how much was left for the law. In 1847 he published 'An Enquiry into the difference of Style observable in ancient glass-paintings, especially in England, with hints on glass-painting, by an amateur.' Winston was remarkable, first for his stylistic judgements which revealed a very thorough understanding of the medium, second for his technical innovations. He realized very well what had gone wrong with the art in the pre-vious hundred years or so: 'Glass-paintings did not cease to be glass-paintings until the "new manner" in oils was so imbibed by the glass painters that they strove to over-finish and to *imitate the effect of oil*; in which they necessarily failed.' Visually, he said, this was trying to convert the window openings into frescos not allowing for the special characteristics of the medium. Naturalism was not suited to it; if landscape were included, for instance, it should be there as a symbol, not as a representation. Architectural setting he considered vitally important; the glass should enhance it, and never be at variance with it. Dark interiors required more richly coloured glass than light interiors. Similarly the degree of ornamentation should vary according to the nature of the glass, whether it is delicate or strong and dramatic in itself.

Winston was much concerned with the problem of designing glass for medieval churches, and pondered how it could be done. 'At present', he concluded, 'there is no nineteenth century style adapted to a Gothic building of the twelfth or thirteenth.' The tendency was too much towards what he called 'jemmification'[8] of the patternwork and faking antiquity by touching up the glass with oil-paint.

'In designing windows for medieval churches', he wrote, 'there are but two courses – either to adopt modern art (which is the best course where figures are introduced) or to adopt medieval art. There is no middle course, as I once supposed and advocated, of getting a modification of medieval art by good artists; you have entirely convinced me of my error.'

Winston should be remembered most of all for his technical achievements in rediscovering the medieval constituents of glass.[9] He was much aware of the poor quality of the pot-metal available to his contemporaries – in fact enamelling was still widely used instead. From 1850 onwards he made analyses of twelfth- and thirteenth-century glass, especially blue, to try to discover how it was composed. Dr Medlock of the Royal College of Chemistry assisted him. Winston found that the blue glass was obtained not from lapis-lazuli, as had been supposed, but from cobalt. With scientists to help him, he set about reproducing at Powell's glassworks the colours of ancient glass, including 'a soft, bright, intense blue, or rather a sort of neutralised purple', and a 'good olive . . . out of sulphate of iron.' There was no perceptible difference, he claimed, between this and ancient glass – 'we have got the glass perfect as a material' – and proudly he had two windows made of it and installed in the Temple Church.[10] Ruskin, too, was aware of the qualities of the glass itself. There survives a letter he wrote to Edmund Oldfield[11] who had designed an east window for the church of St Giles, Camberwell, where there was also medieval glass (late thirteenth century, possibly German). Oldfield's design had been carried out by Ward and Nixon of Frith Street. Ruskin expressed himself frankly to the designer of the new glass, and condemned its over-brilliance:

> First the modern glass admits much more light, producing a glaring and painful impression on the eye, so that I could not look at it long – the old glass soothed, attracted, and comforted the eye, not dazzling it, but admitting of long contemplation without the least pain . On closer examination,

I found that the *whites* of the modern glass were very bright, looking like the ground glass of a lamp, and were all inclined to *pink* in their hue; while the whites of the old glass were dead, and wanting in transparency . . . all inclined to *green* in hue. Note this please, especially.

He goes on to discuss the differences in the other colours:

Lastly, I find the iron bars twice as thick in the old glass as in the modern, and running through every bit of the window. If ever Ward gives you a bit of whole glass, four inches over, make him smash it and stick it together again.

Ruskin would not have thought much of one of the exhibits in the 1851 Exhbition – a sheet of glass painted by Frank Howard for the St Helens Glass Company, depicting St Michael casting out the Red Dragon, and measuring a record nine feet by five feet.

Twenty-four firms showed stained glass at the Great Exhibition, including Hedgeland, Gibbs and O'Connor, all of London, and Wailes of Newcastle. Most of their work was still in enamels. In the International Exhibition of 1862 there were twenty-eight firms represented, and 'antique' glass was produced – apparently independently of Winston's researches – by William Edward Chance of Oldbury, Birmingham.[12] Winston's glass had been developed by James Powell & Sons, and by the well-known firm of Clayton & Bell.[13] Clayton & Bell's windows vary tremendously in quality; the best of their glass, for instance, in St Michael's Cornhill in the City of London, is both rich and lively; there is a fine Last Judgement window of 1860 in Hanley Castle near Malvern, and a dramatic window of Moses in St Mary Redcliffe Church, Bristol (colour plate 41).

John Hardman & Co. of Paradise Street, Birmingham, also used Chance's glass. His work was associated with Pugin's architecture from 1845 (before which Pugin employed Wailes); an example of it is the Transfiguration window in Bury St Edmunds Cathedral. The Pugin/Hardman collaboration could produce some stunning results. The south transept window of Milton Abbey in Dorset (1847) is a thing of such magnificence, with its hieratic tiers of figures and brilliant colour, predominantly red, that it forces one to revise one's views on mid-nineteenth-century glass.

Detail of the south transept window, Milton Abbey, Dorset, designed by Augustus Pugin, made by Hardman, 1847

At the same time, Michael O'Connor from Ireland established himself in 1845 as a stained glass artist in London (he was joined later by his son Arthur); his windows have a deep, rich tonality – a quality often to be found in Irish artists' work.

Henry Holiday (1839–1927) – perhaps remembered best for his painting 'The First Meeting of Dante and Beatrice' – took over from Burne-Jones as designer for Powell & Sons. His work may be seen at Worcester College, Oxford. He also designed the Moses window at Durham Cathedral. Avoiding archaism and, on the whole, sentimentality, his work has strong, dramatic design with a superb use of colour. Charles Eamer Kempe (1837–1907) worked more in the medieval tradition and particularly favoured tones of olive green. At his best, his windows can be compelling; there is a fine Jesse window at Burford, Oxfordshire (1869), and there are other examples at St John's College, Oxford, Byfield in Northamptonshire, St Mary's, Slough, Horton in Buckinghamshire and many other places. Nathaniel Hubert John Westlake (1833–1921) was not only a stained glass painter (his work may be seen at Worcester Cathedral, St John the Baptist, Brighton, and St John the Divine, Richmond) but also a writer on the subject. His *History of Design in Painted Glass,* Volume 3, was published in 1894.

Better coloured glass was being made than at any time since the Middle Ages. There was a growing interest in the subject and discerning aesthetic judgements were being made. But it would be difficult to speak convincingly of any sort of Victorian renaissance in stained glass were it not for the work of William Morris and his circle.

Edward Burne-Jones, who met Morris at Oxford in 1853, became so closely associated with Morris glass that one tends to overlook the part played by others in its design. He did his first work for Powell & Sons. The St Frideswide window in Christ Church, Oxford, was executed in 1859, when he was only twenty-six. He also designed for Powell's the glass for the east end of Waltham Abbey in Essex. Above the three lights of a Jesse tree – which, though a little over-complex in composition, has great richness of colour (predominantly petrol-blue) – there is a rose window, perhaps the most revolutionary piece of design produced in nineteenth-century stained glass. It dates from 1860–1. Around the central panel of Christ in Majesty are seven roundels representing the seven days of Creation. But they do not so much represent as symbolize; it is near abstract glass astonishingly modern in appearance.[14]

STAINED GLASS IN ENGLAND

The workshop of Morris and Company began in 1861. When his Red House was built by Philip Webb at Bexleyheath, Morris found it impossible to buy any furnishings to suit it; he recalled afterwards how they had to rummage about and in the end 'had to fall back on turkey-red cotton and dark blue serge'. Partly as a result he founded the company, comprising at that time Burne-Jones, Dante Gabriel Rossetti, Ford Madox Brown, Philip Webb, C.J. Faulkner, P.P. Marshall and Morris himself. They set themselves up at Red Lion Square, Holborn, with an original capital of only £7 (£1 from each of them); to this was added £100 from Morris's mother, and a further £19 from each partner. The firm was called Morris, Marshall, Faulkner & Co., Fine Art Workmen in Painting, Carving and the Metals. But they were always concerned with stained glass and their first project was for All Saints, Selsley, Gloucestershire – by various designers including Burne-Jones (colour plate 42). The firm prospered and in 1865 moved to 26 Queen's Square, with George Warrington Taylor as business manager, George Campfield in charge of the stained glass studio, and Charles Holloway as glazier and glass-painter; apprentices were boys from the Boys' Home in Euston Road. The firm of Morris, Marshall, Faulkner & Co. was dissolved in 1875 and became simply Morris & Co., with Burne-Jones as sole designer.

Burne-Jones generally designed in monochrome, and omitted the lead-lines; the glazier would decide on these later. The colour of the glass was chosen by Morris; he supervised, even if he did not execute, the painting, and had the final say about the whole window. The foliage backgrounds, which are a common feature in Morris windows, he designed himself. He bought the glass from Powell's whose glass was based on the researches of Charles Winston. Morris and Winston shared very much the same aims. Morris stressed the need for blackness of outline and transparency of colour; this is how he considered glass-painting should differ from painting of any other sort. Designs had to be simple, bold, with the minimum of shading and the glass should enliven them with colour. Ford Madox Brown emphasized the dramatic nature of the medium – indeed it is this quality which is so apparent in his designs:

With its heavy lead-lines surrounding every part (and no stained glass can be rational or good without strong lead-lines), stained glass does not admit of refined drawing, or else it is thrown away upon it. What it does admit of, and above all things imperatively require, is fine colour; and what it *can* admit of, and does very much require also, is invention, expression, and good dramatic action.

There are so many fine Morris windows that it is difficult to single out examples. Important early ones include St Michael's at Brighton (1892) (colour plate 44) with its golden archangels, St Michael and All Angels, Lyndhurst, Hampshire, designed by Burne-Jones (1862–3), and All Saints, Middleton Cheney, Northamptonshire – the earliest Morris glass there is 1864–5 (colour plates 43 and 45 and p. 117). The windows at Jesus College, Cambridge date from 1873, the glass at Harrow Weald with its beautiful golden-olive tonality, from 1883. The dramatic east window of the Ascension at Birmingham Cathedral was made in 1885. The glass for the two London churches of

Guinevere and Isolde, by William Morris, designed for Harden Grange, Bingley, and now at the Cartwright Hall Art Gallery, Bradford, Yorkshire

St Peter, Vere Street, Marylebone (which Burne-Jones referred to irreverently as Saints Marshall and Snelgrove), and Holy Trinity, Sloane Street, Chelsea with its enormous east window of forty-eight figures, both date from the mid-1880s.

In the early years of the company, Morris designed a good deal of the glass himself, though none after about 1873. Besides Burne-Jones, designs were also made by Rossetti, Ford Madox Brown, Philip Webb, the architect, and occasionally by artists outside the group – Arthur Hughes, Val Prinsep, Albert Moore, Simeon Solomon. Later work was almost always by Burne-Jones, but one must not forget the guiding hand of Philip Webb until 1874 when he broke off his connection with the firm. This was to its detriment. Webb had always made sure of a right relationship between window and architecture, and had been a restraining influence on Burne-Jones whose designs could otherwise become over-pictorial.

Morris died in 1896, Burne-Jones in 1898. The firm continued well into the twentieth century, but tended to reproduce earlier designs (Burne-Jones's in particular), modifying them to different settings.

One wonders if Morris would have approved – probably not. He was very concerned with the relationship of the work to the setting, just as he was of the artist to the craftsman. He opposed the so-called restoration of medieval churches in the nineteenth century – which was not so much restoration as reconstruction – and founded the Society for the Preservation of Ancient Buildings.

'I can only say that, in these times of plenteous knowledge and meagre performance,' he declared,[15] 'if we do not study the ancient work directly and learn to understand it, we shall find ourselves influenced by the feeble work all round us, and shall be copying the better work through the copyists and *without* understanding it, which will by no means bring about intelligent art.'

NOTES

1 'A Plea for Painted Glass', pamphlet.
2 Letter to his friend Wilson, dated 17 September 1857; published in Winston's *Memoirs of the Art of Glass-Painting*, John Murray, 1865, p. 42.
3 William Morris, *The Aims of Art*. First published 1887.
4 London, 1912 (p. 103).
5 Quoted in an article on 'Early Nineteenth Century Ideals', by J.A. Knowles, *Journal of the British Society of Master Glass Painters*, Vol. XIV, no. 1, 1964.

6 1814–64.

7 Letter to C.H. Wilson, 21 March 1856.

8 From the term 'jemmy-Gothic'.

9 In the making of flashed ruby glass, Bontemps was there before him and produced it from 1826.

10 Unfortunately no longer in existence.

11 From Rouen, 18 May 1884. See *Journal of the British Society of Master Glass Painters*, Vol. XV, no. 3, 1974–5.

12 Chance also met up with Clayton and tried to persuade him to develop his glass; Clayton said Chance could make in a week all the antique glass his firm would need in twenty-five years. So Chance set up his own firm.

13 John Richard Clayton, 1827–1913, and Alfred Bell, 1832–95.

14 Study for the Jesse window is in Birmingham City Art Gallery, cartoons for the rose window in the Victoria and Albert Museum.

15 From a speech to the Trades Guild of Learning (4 December 1877). Printed as an essay 'The Lesser Arts' in the *Collected Works of William Morris*, Longmans, Green & Co., 1914.

CHAPTER TEN

The Twentieth Century

The *Art Journal*'s obituary of Morris contained the following assessment:

> His influence has been already productive of conspicuous results; and, although he is no longer among us to direct and encourage the movement, the endurance of what he has established is ensured. He has taught people that real and sincere aestheticism has its place in the scheme of modern existence, and the lesson has been so generally learned that there is little chance of its being ever forgotten again.

In the same year that Morris died Henry Holiday, himself a considerable artist in the medium, had his book *Stained Glass as an Art* published.[1] He remarked on the vague belief general among his contemporaries 'that stained glass should be *rather* medieval. How medieval it should be, or why it should be medieval at all, or which of the totally dissimilar medieval styles it should resemble, is not clear.'

But, holding to precepts worthy of Morris himself, he points out that all the finest stained glass was in its day modern.

> In stained glass we have a noble and enduring material; a material with a strong individuality of its own and possessing beauties all its own; a material fit for elevated art and high purpose, unsuitable indeed for light and ephemeral work. The strange infatuation so generally prevalent that it should be medieval has kept too many of the best artists from having anything to do with it (happily not all . . .); and some who were not misled by this error have fallen into the equally fatal blunder of imitating oil-paintings. Between these two pernicious errors . . . stained glass has been passing through a perilous experience.

The Morris & Co. workshop continued, but with an inevitable slackening of Morris's own principles. John Henry Dearle became principal designer after the death of Burne-Jones, following very much in the style of his predecessor, but with a good deal less conviction. The Paradise window of Rugby School Chapel (Warwickshire), with its seven tall lights of Christ in Majesty and St Michael encircled by angels, was designed by him in 1902; if it lacks assurance, it has at least an ethereal quality appropriate to its subject (see p. 234). The glass of St Stephen's, Tonbridge (1910–11) is also by Dearle; he has had to grapple with the problem of running a design across two or three clearly separated lights, and has made use of horizontal pieces of glass to counteract the vertical rhythm of the architecture. These earlier windows of Dearle's have a certain quality which his later work, static and mock medieval, entirely lacks. When Dearle died in 1932 his place was taken by W.H. Knight. Standards deteriorated, and too often the glass was based on adaptations of paintings. The firm finally closed down in 1940.

Maurice Drake smugly wrote in his *History of English Glass-Painting*[2] (not so much a history as a collector's handbook), 'It is comforting to reflect that though much modern French and German work is good, English work indubitably is better, so that we have the honour now, as in the sixteenth century, to stand at the head of our handicraft throughout the world.' His views were not shared by L.F. Day, who wrote in 1909[3] against the pictorialism practised for instance by the Morris firm in its later years. He emphasized that a picture painted in enamels on one sheet of glass can never have the richness, luminosity and the strength of pot-metal jointed with lead.

The deterioration noted in Morris's firm was not entirely general. At the end of the nineteenth century there had arisen, in opposition to the general trend towards mass-production, the Arts and Crafts movement. Its leader was Christopher Whall (1850–1924), whose work, fluid in design and often streaky in colour,

Window by Mary Lowndes, 1901. Sturminster Newton, Dorset

may be seen at Ashbourne, Derbyshire, the Lady Chapel of Gloucester Cathedral, and Burford, Oxfordshire, among many other places. One of the first notable women glaziers, Mary Lowndes,[4] was an associate of his, and together with Alfred Drury, they set up the Glass House in Fulham; this was to become a very influential centre for stained glass artists working in this style. Others who followed in the Arts and Crafts movement included Henry and Edward Payne (see p. 207), R. Anning Bell, Margaret Aldrich Rope[5], and Douglas Strachan. Strachan's work may be seen at Winchelsea, Sussex (1929), and Hotham, Humberside: full of swirling shapes and bold colour. Pevsner calls it sentimental, but it is striking nevertheless.

There was also Sir Ninian Comper. It is difficult to be enthusiastic about Comper windows; they tend to be stiff and anaemic, as is the Coronation window in the Martyrdom at Canterbury Cathedral (1954). His best work is probably his heraldic glass, such as in the porch of Westminster Hall (1952). The dates of Comper's windows are often rather later than one would guess from their style.

A pupil of Comper's was Martin Travers.[6] He was chief instructor in stained glass at the Royal College of Art from 1925 until his death in 1949; his designs have delicacy and charm and are well integrated with their architectural setting. He designed windows for St Samson's, Cricklade (1928) for example, and also for Tyneham Church in Dorset.

The most astonishing, in fact revolutionary, glass of the early twentieth century is the west window of St Mary's in Slough (Berkshire). It is the very reverse of pictorialism. The designer was Alfred A. Wolmark, better known as a painter. When the four lancets were commissioned by Ellerman (of 'Ellerman's Embrocation'), he insisted that they should be wholly abstract. And so they are, a rich mosaic of colour, darkish in hue, especially the panels at the base. The glass is cut in irregular shapes. The whole effect is staggering, especially considering its date, 1915, when one would not expect much glass to have been commissioned, let alone anything as exceptional as this. To meet its like again, we have to wait until after the Second World War, for the Piper-Reyntiens windows of Coventry Cathedral.

Most commissions in these early years of the century were for memorial windows, and are much dimmer in every respect. Soldiers in khaki seldom made good subjects for stained glass. There is a particularly dreadful example in

Winchester Cathedral, where a soldier in puttees and pith helmet kneels before an angelic mock medieval figure of Patience, who ever obligingly holds his rifle for him.

After the First World War the art was revitalized by developments in Ireland. A school of stained glass was set up in Dublin, called The Tower of Glass. From it came two important glaziers, Wilhelmina Geddes (1888–1955) and Harry Clarke (1889–1931). Their windows were in their day quite revolutionary, designed in an expressive style with powerful use of colour, and an element of Celtic mysticism. Geddes's windows are to be found in Faversham (Kent), Lewisham (St Mildred's, Lee), Laleham (Surrey), Wallsend (Tyne & Wear), and North Chapel (Sussex).

The work of Harry Clarke is more often to be seen in Ireland than in England. It is unique in its brilliant, jewel-like quality, with tiny pieces of glass, heavily leaded. His panel 'Judas' was exhibited in 1913 and won him a gold medal from the South Kensington Museum. A hand holds a rope around the neck of Judas, and scattered across his saffron robe are the thirty pieces of silver.

A Roman Catholic, he seldom designed glass for Anglican churches, but made an exception in the case of a memorial window at Sturminster Newton, Dorset. It commemorates a young Irishwoman called Roma, who died in the influenza epidemic just after the First World War. It is a remarkable window; the style is art deco, but with the subtle sense of pattern one associates with Liberty's, and the flamboyance of the Russian Ballet. In it are portraits; Roma appears as St Elisabeth of Hungary, the artist's wife as St Barbara, and Roma's infant son, daringly, as the Christ Child (colour plate 47 and p. 131).

There was also Evie Hone, outstanding in her day (colour plate 46). She was a pupil of Wilhelmina Geddes. One of her greatest works was the east window in Eton College Chapel, to replace that destroyed by bombing (see p. 112). It is a complex window which includes the Last Supper below and the Crucifixion above, an amazing achievement, but so rich in iconography that it tends to lack unity as a window. Evie Hone's last work (1955) was the west window of the south aisle in All Hallows, Wellingborough, Northamptonshire. The glass is a pattern of Christian symbols with the Lamb of God, the Chalice, the Star of David and the Loaves and Fishes in the centre light, flanked by symbols of the Old Testament on the left and the New Testament on the right. Less complex than the Eton window, it combines drama with clarity.

STAINED GLASS IN ENGLAND

Old Testament window by Evie Hone, 1955.
Wellingborough, Northamptonshire

The end of the Second World War had brought new opportunities to stained glass artists – not just for memorial windows, but for replacing and renewing what the bombing had destroyed. Much of the country's most valuable ancient glass had, wisely and fortunately, been removed for safe keeping. How great the loss would have been at, say, Canterbury had this not been done. Windows considered of lesser importance were left *in situ*, and smashed in the blitz, making way for new commissions. Many of the city churches that had survived as buildings now required new glass. Designers employed to supply this included Laurence Lee (author of the excellent Oxford handbook on stained glass), John Hayward, Brian Thomas, Christopher Webb and Carl Edwards. Edwards was responsible for the new east windows at the Temple Church, Holborn (1957–8). These windows have an overall effect of brilliant mosaic, predominantly blue; they include panels showing London burning during the Blitz, and the Temple Church itself. The central window was presented by the Glaziers' Company and contains their coat of arms.

Canterbury Cathedral's less important glass suffered some casualties and this led to an excessive brightness in the South East transept. To counteract this Ervin Bossanyi was commissioned to design the great Peace and Salvation windows. Bossanyi was a Hungarian, born in 1891. He studied first at the Budapest Academy of Arts and Crafts, then in Paris, London and Rome. Between the wars he worked in Germany; when Hitler rose to power he fled to England and arrived here, quite unknown, in 1934. His first commissions here were minor ones for heraldic glass. Then he was asked to make a window for the Tate Gallery; this led to a major commission in South Africa (the Michaelhouse

Chapel), which in turn led to the Canterbury windows. Of his work there Arthur Lane[7] wrote to the archdeacon, 'It may well be that Bossanyi is closer in spirit to the original designers of the cathedral than any of us are today.' In any event, he approached his task, aware of its magnitude, with humility and passionate faith.

The two great windows each measure 18 by 8½ feet. The Salvation window shows an imprisoned man lifted by an angel from darkness into light, where his wife and daughter await him; above the Prophet holds up a cross of gold (colour plate 48). The other window, 'Peace', shows a majestic grey-haired Christ with huge hands upraised granting peace to the nations of the world, who are represented by children. The windows are conceived with a brilliance of colour characteristic of Central European peasant art, and the eyes are emphasized in a Byzantine way that might seem to the casual observer sentimental; yet of Bossanyi's sincerity of purpose there can be no doubt.

Bossanyi made a point of being responsible for the craftsmanship involved in the actual construction of the window as well as the design of it. To test the effect of the glass which he had assembled in the uniform northern light of his studio, he set up a mirror in the garden which would reflect the rays of the sun, and enable him to see his creation in all shifting conditions of light.

But some of the finest windows made in this century have been the result of a collaboration between designer, who has not necessarily any direct experience of working with glass, and craftsman who has made that experience his profession. The windows of Chagall (like the one in Chichester Cathedral) are, of course, designed by Chagall, but made or constructed by Charles Marq of Reims. His memorial window to Sarah d'Avigdor-Goldsmid (colour plate 50) in the remote country church of Tudeley in Kent is particularly moving. Predominantly blue, its watery nature is further emphasized by the number of lozenge-shapes among the pieces of glass that compose it. The window is now happily complemented by a Chagall-designed glazing scheme for the whole of the rest of the church.

The collaboration of John Piper and Patrick Reyntiens has been particularly rewarding (colour plates 51 and 52). Obviously Piper's designs depend on being translated by Reyntiens's craftsmanship; but when Reyntiens is responsible for the design as well as the execution, as at Marden in Kent, the window somehow lacks quite the power and cohesion of the finest works done by both in collaboration (see p. 165). Some of the best of these are to be seen in Oundle

The Raising of Lazarus, from Miracle and Parable windows designed by John Piper, made by Patrick Reyntiens, 1959–64. Eton College Chapel, Berkshire

College Chapel,[8] in All Hallows, Wellingborough (a church especially rich in modern glass), and the wonderful windows in the chapel of Eton College. There are eight Piper–Reyntiens windows there, the four on the north side representing Miracles and the four on the south, Parables. The Parables are the Wheat and the Tares, the Lost Sheep, the House built on Rock, and the Light under a Bushel; the Miracles are the Miraculous Draught of Fishes, the Feeding of the Five Thousand, the Stilling of the Waters, and perhaps most expressive of all, the Raising of Lazarus. Set against a ground of blood-red below, a hand points upwards to where the bluish, bandaged figure of Lazarus rises from the tomb.

The building of a new cathedral, such as St Michael's at Coventry, or the Roman Catholic cathedral of Christ the King at Liverpool, gives an un-rivalled opportunity for stained glass – both have superb abstract Piper–Reyntiens glass which is integral to the building (colour plate 49). Even the making of a new town may give some scope; the Roman Catholic church of Our Lady of Fatima in Harlow has great curtain-walls constructed of *dalle-de-verre* (made by the monks of Buckfast Abbey). Modern glass can be very much part of the structure; indeed the whole architectural design may be constructed round it. Such opportunities, however, seldom occur.

One would expect the building of the new Church of Christ the Cornerstone in Milton Keynes (completed in 1992) to provide scope for some spectacular stained glass. But this is an ecumenical church, and perhaps in an attempt not to offend anybody, the glass (in my opinion) fails to make a positive statement.

Throughout the ages, stained glass has always been an expensive medium. It is, therefore, remarkable that a number of new windows have been installed in recent years. There was a major commission for the Trinity Chapel of Salisbury Cathedral. It was completed in 1980, five dramatic bluish lights by Gabriel Loire of Chartres, on the theme of the Prisoners of Conscience. It is not easy to make a complete list of modern artists who have done interesting work (one might mention Laurence Lee, Moira Forsyth, Carl Edwards, John Hayward, Anthony Holloway, Alan Younger, Francis Skeat, Jane Gray, Ray Bradley, Brian Clarke, and a few years back, Harry Stammers and Rosemary Rutherford), and I hope that those I have omitted to include will not be too offended.

If I were asked to choose one outstanding artist working now, since the death of John Piper, I think it would be Mark Angus of Bath. His 'Daily Bread' window in Durham Cathedral (1984) makes in symbolic terms a bold statement, colours are strong, clear-cut; and yet it is amazingly in tune with the architecture of this ancient building (colour plate 53).

It is perhaps surprising that this window seems to have met with general approval from the people of Durham. Broadly speaking, there appears to be a resurgence of popular interest in the art. This may not be primarily for aesthetic reasons; there is another element. The fact that when Terry Waite, envoy to the Archbishop of Canterbury, was held prisoner in Beirut, it was a postcard of a stained glass window which did much to cheer him, somehow captured the public's imagination. Stained glass is no longer associated in people's minds – as perhaps it sometimes has been – with fustiness or archaism, but with its ability to inspire.

As to how the stained glass artist should approach this matter of designing windows, there seem to be two diametrically opposed points of view – with, no doubt, many shades and nuances in between. Brian Clarke headed his foreword to the catalogue of the 1978 Glass/Light Exhibition, 'Rescuing Art from Artists'. British stained glass, he said, is bound up with the cult of the past and does not 'articulate the spirit of the modern age'. His meaning is a little unclear but he appears to advocate that the stained glass designer should work in closer collaboration with the architect rather than associate himself in any degree with craftsmanship.

'Precious art', he maintains, 'has no future; art is not sacred, it is functional.

We must come to terms with the electronic age and not hide away from it in nineteenth-century romanticism. For the first time in five hundred years artists are in a position to work with architects on a heroic scale towards the destruction of precious art and the establishment of architecturalism.'

While there are several things here with which one might disagree, it is the desire to work 'towards the destruction of precious art' that is most alarming. This attitude has its antecedents in the iconoclasm of the late eighteenth century, all done in the name of good taste. Moreover, simply to be representative of this or any age cannot be enough. As Bossanyi put it:[9]

> Only works of art done by passionate, burning love bear the mark of validity in buildings of dignity. If the artist would make what he really loves and the craftsman what he really can make well, and the patron would possess and use a really sound judgement, it might happen that quality slowly takes the place of quantity and the flood of unworthy things ebbs away from buildings that should serve as exemplary human achievement.

It is difficult to escape from the fact that this art has always been at its most telling, most lively and most transcendental when it has had a religious theme to express.

NOTES

1 Macmillian, 1896.
2 Published T. Werner Laurie, 1912. The book mostly consists of bargains such as 'A fragment bought in Edinburgh for five shillings in June, 1906, sold for nine guineas three years later.'
3 *Windows*, published by Batsford.
4 The work of Mary Lowndes is notably to be seen at Sturminster Newton, Dorset, where she made memorial windows to both her parents.
5 Henry Payne's glass may be seen for instance in Leicester, in the cathedral, and in the church of St Andrew; there is also much in Gloucestershire, e.g. Chipping Campden, Box, Cherington; his son Edward's may also be seen at Box, and at Birdlip, Chalford, Cheltenham (St Paul's), Minchinhampton and Stonehouse. The work of Anning Bell (1863–1933) is at Cattistock, Dorset, and Bradford City Art Gallery as well as in his native Scotland. Margaret Aldrich Rope's work is to be seen at Chesterfield (St Mary), Leeds (St Chad), and Brent (St Francis, Gladstone Park).
6 For an account of The Travers School of Glass, see *Journal of the British Society of Master Glass Painters*, Vol. XIV, no. 2, 1965.

7 At that time Keeper of the Ceramics Department at the Victoria and Albert Museum.
8 The three very powerful east windows at Oundle School Chapel (Northamptonshire) represent the earliest major works produced by them jointly, a wholly new interpretation of the art of stained glass. They date from 1955–6.
9 Letter to Dean Sayre of Washington, 25 October 1954.

CHAPTER ELEVEN

Conservation

Granted that stained glass is both durable and resilient, and stands up remarkably well to the conditions to which it is generally exposed, it is nevertheless in some ways vulnerable.

It may be difficult at a distance to detect deterioration in a panel of stained glass. Until it can be inspected at close quarters, its problems can seldom be diagnosed. For instance, in an exhibition on cathedral restoration at Canterbury, the untreated twelfth-century figure of 'Cosam' was shown. Blackish accretion was very noticeable around the edges of the leading and wherever the glass was cracked. The whites had in many cases turned to grey-green, the surface was dull and uneven, and some pieces had become entirely opaque. The ancient glass had decayed, we are told, to less than a quarter of its original thickness.

The degree to which glass erodes varies surprisingly. It is not always the most ancient glass that presents the greatest problems. Of two pieces of glass of similar date in the same panel, one may be completely clear and healthy, and the other hopelessly decayed. It depends on their chemical constituents when first made. Nineteenth-century glass may have decayed too. In Dennis King's workshop at Norwich there was recently a panel, perhaps a hundred years old, of the Lost Piece of Silver (destined for the Ely Museum of Stained Glass), where there was viridian green glass in a bad state of decomposition. Opinions vary about what is the main cause of the corrosion of glass; one expert will declare that it is principally water which does the damage, another that it is the spread of lichen, a third that it is the sulphur dioxide in the atmosphere.

Then there is the problem of breakages, whether accidental or the result of vandalism. The Burne-Jones windows for the church of St Michael and All Angels in Brighton, for instance, have apparently been used by boys with airguns for target practice. Then there are the mistakes of past restorers to be rectified. A piece of glass may have been misplaced, or put in the wrong way round, with its painted side exposed to the outer atmosphere. Red flashings on ruby glass are generally on the inside, but in the Norwich workshops, there was a panel from West Rudham, Norfolk, where the flashing was on the back of the glass and was consequently wearing off. Therefore it would be necessary to reverse the ruby glass if possible.

The most common problem that the restorer has to deal with is the deterioration of the leading. Lead is in any case a considerably less durable material than glass and after a century or so it usually (though not invariably) decays, and the solder cracks at the joints. Then the panel will buckle which puts a strain on the glass, causing it ultimately to break, and the panel ceases to be weatherproof.

The cleaning of glass may be done in various ways, one workshop favouring one method and another another. In Canterbury, for instance, fibre-glass brushes are used to clean the inner surface of the glass (once the painted design is fixed) – a new brush being needed for every two square inches of glass. Then it is polished with rotating brushes of nylon. The outside may be cleaned by shooting jets of tiny beads at its surface (the air-abrasive method). At Chartres the glass is cleaned with a certain chemical solution invented by Dr Jean Marie Bettembourg. In Austria the method widely favoured is again the use of glass-fibre brushes; elsewhere, in York for example, the ultra-sonic method is used.

The work of restoration to be described here is largely based on the practice of York: that is to say, the York Glaziers' Trust Workshops, under the direction of Mr Peter Gibson (see p. 104).

First the glass is moved from its normal position – usually it will come out in the form of panels of not too unwieldy size – and taken to the workshop. Before any treatment is begun it is photographed, and a rubbing is made, rather like making a brass rubbing; the purpose is to reveal and record the exact position of the leads. Detail paper is placed over the panel and is worked over with a stick of black wax. Great care is taken not to press on the panel, however, as the glass may be in a very vulnerable state. This done, the panel is dismantled by cutting the leads and carefully removing the glass. The pieces are then placed in position on the rubbing, so that there is no danger of their being jumbled. Quite a small panel may contain hundreds of pieces of glass, so this is a very necessary precaution. Section by section, the pieces of glass are placed in a tank containing a diluted solution of ammonia, to which a small generator is attached, and the glass is cleaned ultra-sonically. This process takes approximately three minutes.

Then the pieces of glass are returned to their positions on the rubbing. They are looked at critically, and any that have been misplaced in previous

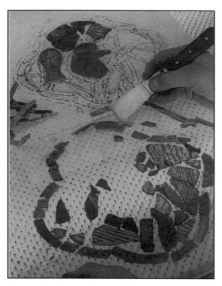

Dismantling glass and re-assembling it against rubbing previously made

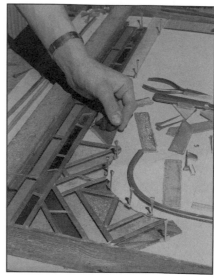

Re-glazing the panel

CONSERVATION TECHNIQUES
Photographs taken at the York Glaziers' Trust Workshops

Soldering the joints

Puttying

restoration are removed and replaced in a 'bank' of glass. The workshops at York have a considerable bank of this kind, containing glass of many different periods. From it, something more fitting may be found to substitute for misplaced pieces. Ideally replacements should be contemporary but sometimes a piece of Victorian glass may be placed in a medieval panel and look reasonably appropriate. Otherwise a piece of modern pot-metal may be used. On occasion, when the Trust are restoring York Minster glass, if a head or the detail of a heraldic coat of arms is missing then these are newly painted, in the style of the period, at the workshop of Dennis King of Norwich.[1] This is not done with any intention of faking, but in order that the window will make sense again, and each newly painted piece has marked on it the year of its insertion.

Cracked pieces from the original windows have to be mended. The edges are glued together with silicone adhesive and then the joined piece is sandwiched between two layers of plain glass. At York, the panels are reglazed on illuminated perspex benches, using new lead calms. The depth and width of the flanges vary according to the nature of the panel. (At Canterbury the calms arc not bought new, but are made by melting down the lead.) The new leads are soldered at the joints, using tallow as a flux. The minimum of heat is used for fear of cracking the glass.

The re-assembled panels are made weatherproof by brushing under the calms a rather liquid form of cement.[2] Then the whole panel is covered in whitening, left to dry for twenty-four hours, brushed off, and left to dry again. Any corroded glass is waterproofed with a butyl mastic compound. Photographs arc taken and careful records are kept of the whole restoration process, so that future generations will know exactly what has been done and when. New copper ties are soldered on; and where new saddle-bars are needed these are made from lengths of manganese bronze. These have the virtue of not rusting, so they will neither damage the glass nor the surrounding stonework.

When the panel is replaced in its original position, it is rendered in with lime-mortar cement. The window should then last in good repair for another century or so.[3]

Various techniques have been evolved for protecting the glass after it has been restored. In some workshops the whole panel is given a resin coating (Viacryl). In Canterbury a plaster cast is made of the outer surface of the glass, and then molten glass is poured into the cast, thus making an outer layer of

STAINED GLASS IN ENGLAND

plain glass which will fit the stained glass exactly. However, this method is expensive. Since the main object is to protect the ancient glass from the outer atmosphere, the practice at York (in almost forty windows) is to fix an extra layer of leaded sheet glass on the outside. Thus, with limited time and resources, more glass can be treated and preserved.

But, as Dennis King points out, it is impossible to make rules about conservation, each panel is a new problem.

NOTES

1 At Dennis King's own workshop in Norwich, however, the practice preferred is to use toned glass to replace missing pieces – suggesting rather than attempting to reproduce the original.
2 The cement used at Canterbury is made of whiting, red lead, gold size and linseed oil.
3 A new technique of using lasers for cleaning stonework has been developed in France, specifically for the restoration of Amiens Cathedral. It is thought that the same system could be adapted to the cleaning of stained glass windows; it will be interesting to see if this proves feasible. See article by Stella Hughes in the *New Scientist*, 27 June 1992.

Gazetteer

Avon

Banwell, St Andrew

Medieval glass in E windows of aisle, Flemish glass in vestry. Elsewhere much mid-19th-century glass, including work by Warrington.

Bath, Bath Abbey

Early 17th-century heraldic glass in a N aisle window and in clerestory. E window of 1873 by Clayton & Bell.

Bath, Mountview, Southdown

Window by M.C. Farrar-Bell.

Bath, St Bartholomew

Near-abstract E window by Mark Angus, 1980. W windows also by him (1980, 1982), based on the elements of fire and water.

Bath, St Stephen

E window of Lady Chapel designed by Mark Angus (1983), a mosaic of colour evoking, rather than depicting, the martyrdom of St Stephen.

Bristol, Cathedral

Lady Chapel: parts of a Jesse tree of 1360 survive in the E window, the rest is restoration of 1847. In S window, St George and armed knights.

N chancel aisle: E window of late 16th century, reputedly given by Nell Gwynn.

S chancel aisle: E window has some German glass of the early 16th century.

N transept: 14th- and 15th-century fragments in the E window.

Cloister: 14th- and 15th-century pieces in the windows.

The cathedral also has a modern 'Holy Spirit' window by Keith New, 1965.

Bristol, All Saints, Corn Street

Colston Window of 1907–8 by Henry Holiday.

Modern windows by Patrick Reyntiens and Gillespie.

Bristol, St Mark, College Green

A good deal of glass dating from 15th to 18th centuries was brought in to the church in 1823; it came largely from the sale of Beckford's Fonthill, and includes some good French glass of the early 16th century.

Bristol, St Mary, Redcliffe

The Chapel of St John in the NW corner of the church has impressive 15th-century figures in the W window, in particular St Michael with sword upraised, also Virgin and Child, and St John the Baptist. N window of the chapel has interesting fragments including some good heads.

Fine 19th-century glass by Clayton & Bell in the Moses window (W window of S aisle), rich colour (colour plate 41). S window of S transept is early 20th century, by Comper; Cabot and his ship in the upper lights.

The Lady Chapel windows of the

Fifteenth-century figure of St Michael at St Mary Redcliffe, Bristol

1960s and broadly on the theme of the Virgin Mary, are all by Harry Stammers; the designs became bolder and the colours more stunning as he progressed.

Bristol, St Peter, Henleaze
E window of 1967 by Alan Younger.

Brockley, St Nicholas
Stained glass by Egington, *c.* 1825, in chancel and in the Pigott Pew.

Churchill, St John
Sixteenth century medieval glass in a N window.

Claverton, St Mary
Interesting 14th-century German glass.

Clevedon, Christ Church, Chapel Hill
13th- and 14th-century glass in E window, French; it includes a 13th-century king from a Jesse tree.

Clifton, Bristol, Clifton Cathedral (RC)
Dalle-de-verre glass by Henry Haig.

Clifton, Bristol, All Saints
Fibreglass windows designed by John Piper: tall and sinuous River of Life and Tree of Life in Baptistery, 1967.

Dyrham and Hinton, St Peter
15th-century glass in four tracery lights of E window – Virgin, St John the Baptist, St John the Evangelist and a female saint. W window of 1846 by Willement.

Farleigh Hungerford, St Leonard
In a N window, late 14th-century head of a knight.

Great Badminton, St Michael
Aisle windows by Thomas Willement, 1846–7.

Hawkesbury, St Mary
Medieval glass (St Giles) in a N window.

Iron Acton, St James
15th-century glass in N window of chancel, including a king, a pope and a bishop.

Kelston, St Nicholas
Chancel S window has 14th-century saint, French, and the chancel N window a 15th-century saint.

Keynsham, St Dunstan
W window by Mark Angus, a white cross on a purple ground, with fiery red on either side, 1979.

St Catherine, St Catherine
Late 15th-century glass, though restored in the 19th century, in four lights; it includes the Virgin, Crucifixion, St John and St Peter, with donor figure of Prior Cantlow who commissioned the glass in 1490.

Tickenham, St Quiricus and St Julietta
In S chapel, small early 14th-century figures of Crucifixion and Christ in Majesty. Also 14th-century fragments in two N aisle windows.

Tortworth, St Leonard
15th-century glass in tracery of E windows of S aisle: angels with the emblems of the Passion on either side of a portrait of Edward IV. E window and W window of S aisle by Powell's.

Walton-in-Gordano, St Paul
Fragments of imported 13th-century glass in E window.

Weston-super-Mare, St John the Baptist
In S aisle, a 15th-century figure of a saint.

Wick, St Lawrence
E window by M. Lassen, 1987.

Wickwar, Holy Trinity
W window by Christopher Whall, 1911. Two windows by John Hayward in N aisle (1978 and 1987).

Winscombe, St James
Very find 15th-century glass in E and N windows of N chapel, including in E window a Crucifixion with the Virgin, St John and St Anthony; kneeling donors below and angels above. St Anthony leads his pig, and the angels bear the symbols

St Anthony's pig; detail of fifteenth-century glass at Winscombe, Avon

109

of the Passion. 15th-century glass in the S windows include St James of Compostella flanked by bishops. N window of chancel has early 16th-century silver stain figures of the three St Peters, rather brassy in colour. The W window also appears to be 16th century. Splendid E window of three lancets is dated 1863: kings, prophets and sibyls of brilliant colour, interspersed by panels of richly glowing apples. Is it by William Morris or, as has been suggested, Fred Weeks for Saunders & Co.?

Bedfordshire

Bedford, Bunyan Meeting Free Church
A set of windows commemorating the tercentenary of the publication of *The Pilgrim's Progress*; they include that of Bunyan in Bedford Jail (of which a postcard was sent to Terry Waite when he was imprisoned as a hostage).

Bunyan in prison; one of the *Pilgrim's Progress* windows in Bedford Free Church

Bolnhurst, St Dunstan
N window of nave has 15th-century figure of the Virgin.

Cockayne Hatley, St John the Baptist
Early 14th-century glass in N aisle E window: four saints under canopies, also 15th-century figures. E window of 1829 by Willement. Armorial glass also by Willement in S and N windows of 1839.

Dean, All Saints
Early 14th-century fragments in E window and W window of S aisle.

Dunstable, Priory
Modern glazing scheme by John Hayward (1974, 1989).

Edworth, church
14th-century figure of St Edmund with the arrows of his martyrdom, also another saint, set against 13th-century grisaille, in S chancel. 15th-century figure of St James in S clerestory.

Houghton Conquest, All Saints
Fragments of medieval glass in many windows.

Luton, St Mary
15th-century glass in E window. In S transept, 1979 Magnificat window by Alan Younger.

Marston Moretaine, St Mary
Three large figures designed by Burne-Jones for Morris & Co. in S window of chancel; *c*. 1893.

Melchbourne, St Mary Magdalene
Glass of *c*. 1902 by Mayer of Munich in E window.

Northill, St Mary
17th-century windows by John Oliver, commissioned by the Grocers' Company – heraldic with splendidly baroque scrollwork, 1664.

Tilsworth, All Saints
Fragments of medieval glass in a N window include a 15th-century head.

Totternhoe, St Giles
E window by John Piper, made by Patrick Reyntiens, depicting Tree of Life (1970–1).

Berkshire

Aldermaston, St Mary
Two 13th-century roundels in N window of chancel (Annunciation and Coronation of the Virgin).

Binfield, All Saints
15th-century glass in SE window, including complete figures.

Bracknell, St Michael and St Mary Magdalene
Much glass by Morris & Co. including E window of Last Judgement – designed by Burne-Jones, 1876.

Bradfield, Bradfield College
Two Burne-Jones windows in dining hall, made by James Powell & Sons, 1857.

Brightwalton, All Saints
Remarkable Wrouhgton Window of c. 1860.

Bucklebury, St Mary
Glass designed by Sir Frank Brangwyn in E, N, and S windows of chancel. Also stained glass sundial of 1649.

Cranbourne, St Peter
W window by Morris & Co., 1862, designed by Morris (Cana), Ford Madox Brown (Christ and a child), and Webb (ornament). Also by Morris the S chapel window of 1861.

Dedworth, St Peter
Good Morris & Co. glass of 1863–87. E window has Nativity, designed by Burne-Jones, Resurrection designed by Morris, and Crucifixion designed by Rossetti. Central window of S aisle, 1873, was designed by Morris and Ford Madox Brown. More Morris glass in the S and N aisles, including Annunciation, designed by Burne-Jones.

Easthampstead, St Michael and St Mary Magdalene
Morris & Co. glass. Chancel E window of Last Judgement 1876, St Mary Magdalene window of 1877, and St Maurice window of 1884.

Eton College Chapel
Very remarkable for its modern glass. E window is by Evie Hone, 1952. The symbolism is complex, but the main themes are the Last Supper, between (left) Melchisadek and (right) Sacrifice of Isaac; above these, the Crucifixion. The background is predominantly deep ultramarine with greenish tones here and there. The N and S windows of the eastern half of the chapel are designed by John Piper, made by Patrick Reyntiens (1959–64); the four on the N side showing the Miracles, and the four on the S showing Parables, the lower half of each window depicting failure or predicament, the upper half achievement and fulfilment of hope. On the N side, from W to E, the Miraculous

East window, showing Last Supper, by Evie Hone, 1952. Eton College Chapel, Berkshire

Draught of Fishes, the Feeding of the Five Thousand, the Stilling of the Waters, the Raising of Lazarus; on the S side, the Wheat and the Tares, the Lost Sheep, the House built on Rock, the Light under a Bushel. The most dramatic are perhaps the two easternmost windows; the Lazarus window has a pointing hand seen against blood-red, and above rises the bluish grave-wrapped figure of Lazarus; the Light under the Bushel a small flame below and a burst of brilliance above (see p. 98).

The N and S windows in the western half of the chapel are heraldic glass designed by Moira Forsyth (1959). W window is surviving mid-19th-century glass by Willement.

Farnborough, All Saints

W window designed by John Piper and made by Joseph Nuttgens, 1986. It shows a Tree of Life, with fish and butterflies on either side; brilliant in colour and painterly in effect, it is the most cheerful of memorial windows, and commemorates Sir John Betjeman (1906–84) (colour plate 52).

Fawley, St Mary

Chancel E window of two lights, with Mary and Joseph, by William Morris & Co., 1866.

Greenham, St Mary

Parts of a Jesse tree of 1618 set in quarry glass.

Lambourn, St Michael

16th-century glass in N chapel. Glass by Willement, *c.* 1855, in outer S chapel.

Langley Marsh, St Mary

N window of N chapel has fragments of 15th-century glass.

Ockwells Manor House

15th-century heraldic glass (eighteen shields) in Hall.

Sandhurst, Royal Military Academy, Chapel

E windows of apse are by Powell & Sons, but the two W windows are modern glass by Laurence Lee. He also designed four large windows in the nave, and 3-light window in S transept.

Slough, St Laurence

Stained glass by Willement (S window in S aisle), and much by Kempe, 1877–93.

Slough, St Mary

Four lancets in W have really astonishing glass designed by Alfred A. Wolmark in 1915. It was commissioned by Ellerman (of Ellerman's Embrocation), and is entirely abstract – surely unique at this date: a rich mosaic of colour, fairly dark, made of pieces of irregular shape. Unforgettable. Also a good deal of Kempe glass, not bad, but prosaic by comparison.

Warfield, St Michael

14th-century angels in head of E window, 15th-century fragments in S window of S transept. 15th-century figure in W window of N aisle.

Wargrave, St Mary

Modern glass by John Hayward, 1962, in a S window.

Wasing, St Nicholas

16th- and 17th-century imported glass.

West Woodhay, St Laurence

Morris & Co. glass in chancel windows, 1883 and 1890.

Windsor Castle, St George's Chapel

W window of nave has 65 standing figures, most of them early 16th century. 15th-century armorial glass in Bishop King's Chapel. Two abstract windows, John Piper, 1969, in George VI Memorial Chapel.

Buckinghamshire

Addington, St Mary

Many 16th–17th-century Flemish roundels.

Amersham, St Mary

E window is imported 17th-century glass, and repositioned here in 1760.

GAZETTEER

Aston Sandford, St Michael

13th-century seated figure of Christ, very small, in upper E window; mainly in green, yellow robe underneath. The panel is much improved by being cleaned by M. Farrar Bell in 1983. Farrar Bell himself designed the N window in memory of R.H. Good of Aston Sandford Manor, 1969; the theme is 'He that soweth to the spirit shall of the spirit reap life everlasting'.

Aylesbury, St Mary

19th-century glass by Willement, O'Connor, Oliphant, Burlison & Grylls.

Beaconsfield, RC church

St Francis of Assisi window by J.E. Nuttgens (1938), fine bold design.

Bletchley, St Mary

Window of 1868 by Powell & Sons in S aisle, designed by Holiday.

Bledlow Ridge, St Paul

Lovely W window designed by John Piper, symbolizing Heaven, 1968.

Chenies, St Michael

Early 16th-century donor in E window.

Chetwode, St Mary and St Nicholas

Notable medieval glass in three lancets in chancel; the centre one is of *c.* 1260–70, and has three panels set in delicate grisaille: at the bottom, the arms of England (see p. 3), then above this is the figure of a bishop in red and green (probably St Nicholas), and at the top, a swaying figure in yellow, representing St John the Baptist. The other two lancets have 14th-century glass; again, the grisaille looks original. In the left one, a figure under a canopy, above that a green cross, then a star pattern. In the right, a bishop (? St Thomas) in green and red, above that two figures in yellow and white, and at the top a roundel with what appears to be a ship.

E window by William Holland of Warwick, 1842, using similar almond-shaped panels. In NE window, a George and the Dragon, 1939.

Drayton Beauchamp, St Mary

15th-century glass, ten complete figures, in E window. Two figures, rather restored, in W window.

Fawley, St Mary

In E window of N aisle, recent single lancet memorial window designed by John Piper (who lived here), a Tree of Life in glowing colours.

Fenny Stratford, St Martin

18th-century coat of arms, supported by angels, in a N window.

Frieth, St Peter

E window made by John Hardman, 1849, to design by Augustus Pugin.

Fulmer, St James

Glass of 1840s by G. Hoadley of London. 16th-century Flemish roundels with themes from Petrarch's Triumphs.

Gerrards Cross, United Reformed Church

Celebration Window by David Wasley, 1992.

Haddenham, St Mary

13th-century glass in E window of N chapel. Much glass by Michael Farrar Bell.

Hillesden, All Saints
E window of S transept has early 16th-century glass, eight panels showing the Story of St Nicholas, very cheerful and full of incident, some of the faces verging on caricature (colour plate 34). S window of S transept done in the same style by Burlison & Grylls, 1875.
Some 15th-century glass, fragmentary in E window of chancel. In E window of S aisle a 15th-century bishop and two heads of bishops.

Hitcham, St Mary
In main lights of N and S windows of chancel, 14th-century figures of feathered angels; they stand on little wheels, with their upper wings crossed behind their heads – but unfortunately most of the heads are missing. The angel on the best-preserved wheel (to S) has yellow feathers; that on the left side of the N window opposite has white feathers among which there are eyes peeping out. In tracery lights above are seated figures of saints, mainly brownish, that to the NE being the most complete.

Horton, St Michael
Kempe window of 1882–3 in memory of the poet John Milton who lived here.

Ickford, St Nicholas
Much stained glass by Comper.

Little Marlow, St John the Baptist
15th-century glass, fragmentary. E window by Heaton, Butler & Bayne.

Long Crendon, Our Lady of Light (RC)
24 windows by Goddard & Gibbs, slab glass set in resin, very much part of the architecture of this polygonal modern church; near-abstract, but effectively suggesting rays of light on either side of altar (1971).

Ludgershall, St Mary
N aisle window has 14th-century fragments.

Milton Keynes, Church of Christ the Cornerstone
The building of this great new church should have given scope for new stained glass as remarkable as Coventry Cathedral or the RC Cathedral at Liverpool; but Alexander Belechenko's designs, perhaps in an attempt to be inter-denominational, somehow fail to compel. Church opened 1992.

Milton Keynes, Crownhill Cemetery Chapel
Two windows by Graham Pentelow (1982) on the theme of the cycle of life.

Radclive, St John the Evangelist
Fourteenth-century fragments, nave N window.

Stoke Poges, St Giles
In Hastings Chapel, 17th-century armorial glass. In the S aisle a window of c. 1845 by Mayer of Munich.

Turville, St Mary
Semi-circular window symbolizing the Magnificat, John Piper, 1975. A lovely thing.

Wavendon, St Mary
Glass is by O'Connor, c. 1849.

Weston Turville, St Mary
E window contains a 15th-century Virgin.

Weston Underwood, St Laurence
A number of 14th-century fragments in the E window.

Cambridgeshire

Babraham, St Peter
Splendid E window with emblems of St Peter, designed by John Piper, 1966.

Barnack, St John the Baptist
Stained glass by Marsham Argles, who was rector here; one window is dated 1873. 1930s Hugh easton window in S aisle.

Brinkley, St Mary
In the E window, two 14th-century angels. Other fragments of medieval glass in the chancel.

Buckden, St Mary
15th-century figures in heads of W and E windows of S aisle.

Burghley House
In the Hall, 15th-century scenes including Joseph in the Pit, and the Harrowing of Hell. They came from Tattershall, Lincs., placed here in 1757.

Bury, Holy Cross
Medieval glass in N window of chancel, also fragments in N aisle windows.

Cambridge, All Saints, Jesus Lane
Splendid E window by Morris & Co. 1865–6; designed mainly by Burne-Jones, much use of silver stain. Also glass by Kempe, and good windows by Douglas Strachan (1944).

Cambridge, Christ's College Church
In N windows 15th- and early 16th-century glass.

Cambridge, Churchill College Chapel
Abstract glass by John Piper, 1970.

Cambridge, Corpus Christi Chapel
16th-century German glass in N and S windows. E window by Heaton, Butler and Bayne.

Cambridge, Downing College Chapel
Apse windows of 1962–3 by L.C. Evetts.

Cambridge, Jesus College Chapel
Remarkably rich in Morris & Co. glass; dates from 1873–7.
S window of chancel has Nativity and Jesus in the Temple; effective in the Nativity are the streaky blue of the sky and the textured green of the grass.
S window of S transept has Saints and Angels of the Hierarchy – decisive use of colour especially reds and blues. Side window of S transept has Saints Matthew, Mark, Luke and John with attendant sibyls; the Erythraean sibyl to the left of St John and the St Matthew between the Persian and Cumaean sibyls much influenced by Michelangelo's Sistine Chapel. In the N aisle, the virtues overcoming the vices, Temperance over Wrath etc. In the N transept, Faith, Hope and Charity, also Patience, Obedience and Docility.
Mostly this was designed by Burne-Jones; two drawings for the glass by him are preserved in the chapel, also one design by Morris. (The other designs are in the Tate Gallery, the V & A Museum, Birmingham City Art Gallery, and the William Morris Museum.) Ford Madox Brown designed the S window of S transept, SE window of S transept, and lower scenes in the W window of S side of nave.
Hall has armorial glass by Morris & Co.

Nativity; Morris glass of the 1870s. Jesus College, Cambridge

Cambridge, King's College Chapel
World famous for its early 16th-century glass: the most complete set of stained glass windows from the time of Henry VIII. For full notes on the subject matter, see Pevsner's 'Cambridgeshire' in the *Buildings of England* series.

Designers employed on the windows included Bernard Flower, from 1515 to 1517, then Galyon Hone, then in 1526 Galyon Hone again, Richard Bond, Thomas Reve and James Nicholson, assisted by Francis Williamson and Symond Symondes. It has been suggested that the Betrayal Window of *c.* 1515 is possibly by Dirick Vellert.

Generally speaking, the glass is pictorial, the 'picture seen through a window' grid technique, but there is some graphic and telling draughtsmanship.

Cambridge, Magdalene College Chapel
E window by Pugin.

Cambridge, Peterhouse
Chapel: The E window of the Crucifixion is Flemish glass of 1639.

Hall: Secular glass by Morris & Co., designed by Burne-Jones and Madox Brown. The bay window has an arrangement of 21 lights derived from the Jesse tree idea: Burne-Jones series on the theme of Chaucer's 'Dream of Good Women'.

Cambridge, Robinson College

Fine chancel window by John Piper, resembling a cascade of leaves and flowers (1978–80). Also glass by Piper in the antechapel (1982), an Adoration of the Magi with green pagan beasts below, and under that, a Last Supper with Adam and Eve (based on a Romanesque tympanum).

Cambridge, St Edward, St Edward's Passage

Armorial glass designed by James Hogan for Powell & Sons, 1946.

Cambridge, St John's College

Chapel: has 19th-century glass by Clayton & Bell, Hardman and Wailes.
Hall: has 18th-century figure of St John and 19th-century heraldic glass by Clayton & Bell.
Combination Room: has roundel of 1630 with portrait of Queen Henrietta Maria.

Cambridge, Trinity College

Chapel: Stained glass by Holiday, 1871.
Library: N window of 1704–7 is by Henry Gyles of York (shows arms of Queen Anne). S window is by Peckitt of York (Fame introducing Newton and Bacon to George III), 1774–5, from a design by Cipriani (colour plate 40).

Cambridge, Trinity Hall

In the antechapel, two windows by John Hayward commemorating Runcie's elevation to the archbishopric of Canterbury.

Cambridge, Westminster College

Thirteen windows by Douglas Strachan.

Diddington, St Lawrence

15th-century glass including two female saints, parts of a Resurrection, and a female donor.

Doddington, St Mary

Very early Morris & Co. glass in E window of N aisle (*c.* 1865), a Crucifixion with St Peter and St Paul. Crucifixion was designed by Rossetti, St Peter by Morris and St Paul by Ford Madox Brown. The glass came from Langton Green in Kent.

Dry Drayton, St Peter and St Paul

E window by Thomas Willement, 1853.

Eaton Socon, St Mary

Four Flemish roundels in E window of S chapel.

Elton, All Saints

Morris & Co. glass in three windows (dates 1891–1901).

Ely, Cathedral

The Stained Glass Museum opened in 1979 with the purpose of displaying interesting glass from redundant churches and other buildings. The collection includes, among other things, small 14th-century yellow stain figures which came from the cathedral's Lady Chapel, a mid-14th-century Annunciation from Hadzor (Herefs. & Worcs.), and 14th-century figures from Woodwalton (Cambs.).
The glass in the cathedral itself is almost all 19th century, largely by Wailes, also Clayton & Bell. Choristers' window in N aisle with music-making angels is by Oliphant, designed by William Dyce.

Godmanchester, St Mary
S aisle window by Morris & Co., *c.* 1896; also much glass by Kempe.

Grantchester, St Andrew and St Mary
In chancel and N window of nave, fragments of 14th- and 15th-century glass.

Haslingfield, All Saints
Two 14th-century figures in a vestry window.

Hemingford Abbots, St Margaret
18th-century heraldic glass in N aisle E window.

Hilton, St Mary Magdalene
E window by Wailes (1861), W window by Constable of Cambridge (both bad, Pevsner says).

Horseheath, All Saints
In E window, two medieval flying angels.

Kimbolton, St Andrew
15th-century figure in S chapel, fragments in E window of N chapel.

Kirtling, Our Lady Immaculate and St Philip
16th-century Swiss glass, from a Crucifixion scene originally in Wroxton Abbey.

Landbeach, All Saints
Assorted medieval fragments in E window; they may have come from Cambridge.

Landwade, St Nicholas
15th-century fragments, including complete figures.

Leverington, St Leonard
Splendid 15th-century Jesse tree in E window of N aisle. 13 of its 61 figures are entirely medieval, 17 are medieval but restored, the rest renewed. The figures are linked together with vine branches.
In E window of S chapel a 15th-century Pietà and kneeling donors.

Madingley, St Mary Magdalene
In S windows of chancel, 15th-century figure of Virgin, 16th-century Crucifixion, also fragments.

Orton Longueville, Orton Hall
Armorial glass on staircase by Willement, 1831.

Peterborough, Cathedral
N chancel aisle: window by Wailes, 1856.
S transept: Morris, Marshall & Faulkner window, 1862.
N transept: windows by Clayton & Bell, 1860, Cox & Son, 1849, O'Connor, 1865, and Heaton, Butler & Bayne, 1852 and 1865.
Abbot's House Chapel: lancet by Patrick Reyntiens, 1958.

Ramsey, St Thomas of Canterbury
Morris & Co. glass, mainly late – about 1920.

St Neots, St Mary
19th-century glass by Clayton & Bell and Hardman – including Hardman's 'Woman of Samaria', shown at 1878 Paris Exhibition.

Swaffham Prior, St Mary
Glass by Ward & Hughes, 1910–20, designed by T.F. Curtis. An odd mixture

of little scenes (e.g. Statue of Liberty, Wicken Fen, and a First World War trench) placed inappropriately under Gothic canopies.

Thorney, Abbey Church of St Mary and St Botolph
Late 15th-century German glass, six scenes from the Passion and Resurrection, installed here in 1638.

Trumpington, St Mary and St Michael
In a N chancel window, 13th-century figures of St Peter and St Paul. Fragments of medieval glass in E window.

Waresley, St James
N window possibly an early work by Burne-Jones.

Westley Waterless, St Mary
Early 14th-century fragments in N and S aisle windows.

Wimpole, St Andrew
14th-century heraldic glass in N chapel. 18th-century heraldic glass in W gallery.

Wisbech, St Peter and St Paul
15th-century figures in clerestory windows.

Wisbech St Mary, St Mary
Many panels of continental glass, and a small amount of English 14th- and 15th-century work. Two panels in chancel dated 1535.

Wistow, St John the Baptist
15th-century W window of S aisle, complete – figures of the Virgin of the Annunciation, Resurrection and angels. It was originally in the E window of the chancel.

Cheshire

Acton (near Nantwich), St Mary
Much stained glass by Kempe, late 19th century.

Alderley Edge, St Philip
Centre window of S aisle has Morris & Co. glass (1874).

Astbury, St Mary
Stained glass of c. 1500 in W window of N aisle (three figures). W window of S aisle and S window of S aisle have medieval fragments in tracery.

Birtles, St Catherine
16th- and 17th-century Flemish glass in several windows.

Chester, Cathedral
Mainly 19th-century glass, by Wailes, Heaton, Butler & Bayne, Clayton & Bell, Kempe, Hardman, but an interesting modern E window by W.T. Carter Shapland, 1961.

Chester, St Mary-on-the-Hill
Early 16th-century glass in tracery of E window of S chapel.

Daresbury, All Saints
Alice in Wonderland window by Geoffrey Webb, 1932.

Disley, St Mary
E window has 16th-century glass, scenes from the Passion, and life of St Elisabeth of Hungary. 16th-century glass also over the chancel arch. In S wall, small 15th-century window of the Risen Christ with St Mary Magdalene.

Gawsworth, St James
15th-century fragments in several windows.

Grappenhall, St Wilfred
Some 14th-century glass in the chapel. Three windows in the S aisle by Mayer of Munich.

Knutsford, St Cross, Mobberley Road
W window and a S aisle window by Morris & Co. (of 1890s).

Malpas, St Oswald
Panels of early 16th-century glass in N chapel, probably Flemish.

Nantwich, St Mary
14th-century fragments in tracery of a chancel window. Good glass by Harry Clarke (1919) in S aisle. Also 19th-century glass by Clayton & Bell, Hardman and Kempe.

Over Peover, St Laurence
In S chapel fragments of 15th-century glass.

Shotwick, St Michael
14th-century Annunciation in tracery of E window of N aisle.

Tabley, Chapel of St Peter
A window of 1895 by Morris & Co., also some early Netherlandish glass.

Tattenhall, St Alban
In the chancel, 14th-century figures of St Alban and St Stephen (restored).

Wilmslow, St Bartholomew
Late Morris & Co. glass (1920), designed by Dearle.

Cleveland

Kirklevington, St Martin
Glass designed by H. Holiday for Powell & Sons in S aisle, 1884.

Skelton, Christ the Consoler
Good 19th-century glass by Saunders & Co., designed by F. Weeks (*cf.* Studley Royal, Yorks.), 1870s.

Yarm, St Mary Magdalene
S window of Moses by William Peckitt of York, 1768.

Cornwall

Antony, St James
19th-century stained glass by Clayton & Bell and Kempe.

Breage, St Breaca
Fragments of 15th-century glass in N aisle.

Chacewater, St Paul
E window has glass originally from St Mary, Truro.

Cotehele House
Early 16th-century glass in the chapel; in the E window, Crucifixion with Annunciation above; in the S window St Anne teaching the Virgin to read, and a St Catherine.

Falmouth, Church of King Charles the Martyr
In Lady Chapel, old glass imported from Italy.

Feock, St Feoca
E window by Beer of Exeter.

Golant, St Samson
Some 15th-century glass: figures of St Samson and St Antony.

Ladock, St Ladoca
E window of chancel with St Mary Magdalene, 1863, designed by Burne-Jones. E window of S aisle (1869–70) and W windows (1896 and 1897) are also Morris & Co. glass.

Lanteglos-by-Camelford, St Julitta
In tracery of S aisle windows, fragments of 15th-century glass.

Lanteglos-by-Fowey, St Willow
S aisle E window has some late 15th-century glass.

Lostwithiel, St Bartholomew
19th-century glass by Willement: Faith, Hope and Charity.

Luxulyan, St Ciricius and St Julietta
W tower window has fragments of 15th-century glass.

Par, St Mary
19th-century stained glass by Wailes.

Penzance, St Mary
New E window to replace that and the John Piper reredos lost in the fire of 1985.

St Enoder, St Enoder
In tracery of SE window, a 15th-century head.

St Eval
RAF memorial window by Crear McCartney.

St Germans, St Germanus

A good E window, Morris & Co. glass, designed by Burne-Jones, 1896.

St Kew, St James
Important 15th-century glass in NE window (1469), depicting the Passion, with donors and a small Nativity scene; coats of arms in the tracery, including Henry VI's. Parts of a Jesse tree, also 15th century, in SE window, and in the E window fragments include St Michael and St Laurence.

St Michael Penkevil, St Michael
Chancel E window of Crucifixion, 1866, is William Morris glass.

St Michael's Mount, church and Chevy Chase Room
A varied collection of roundels and panels, mainly Netherlandish, dating from 15th–17th centuries, and executed largely in yellow stain and enamels.

St Neot, St Anietus
Important 15th- and early 16th-century glass in fifteen windows, some of it rather heavily restored by John Hedgeland in *c.* 1830; still a remarkably complete series. It consists largely of saints, including local as well as international ones (the whole story of St Anietus is there), also Old Testament stories, and donors.

St Winnow, St Winnow
In E window of S aisle 15th-century and early 16th-century glass: saints, donors and heraldry.

Sheviock, St Peter and St Paul
E window by Wailes, designed by G.E. Street, *c.* 1850.

Hell's Mouth; a vivid evocation in paint and yellow stain. Roundel of *c.* 1500. Chevy Chase Room, St Michael's Mount, Cornwall (*photo: Roger Thorp*)

South Petherwin, St Paternus
Some medieval glass, heraldic, in a S window.

Truro, Cathedral
Clayton & Bell glass, and earlier 19th-century glass by Warrington in S aisle (part of the old parish church).

Cumbria

Armathwaite, Chapel of Christ and Mary

E window is late Morris & Co. glass of 1914.

Beetham, St Michael
15th-century fragments in S chapel. Also four 14th-century figures under tower, including crucifixion.

Bootle, St Michael
19th-century glass: E window by Hardman, N window of chancel (1899) by Holiday.

Bowness-on-Windermere, St Martin
Late 15th-century E window of the Crucifixion, with donors below – impressive, said to have come from Cartmel or Furness.

Brampton, St Martin
Very important Morris & Co. glass – the church was designed by Philip Webb, Morris's associate, his only church; executed with the patronage of the Howards, Earls of Carlisle.
E window of chancel, of the Good Shepherd, angels, saints and pelican, designed by Burne-Jones, 1880.
E window of S aisle, 1888, by Morris.
Second window of S aisle, 1888, by Morris.

Brough, St Michael
In a N window, fragments of 15th-century glass.

Brougham, St Wilfred's Chapel
Some 14th-century fragments.

Carlisle, Cathedral
E window is by Hardman, but has some 14th-century glass in the tracery, including a seated Christ. 14th century doom in tracery of great east window. Later glass by Wailes and Whall.

Carlisle, St Cuthbert, St Cuthbert's Lane
14th-century glass in a N window (figure below canopy), also 15th-century fragments. 1930s–40s glass on Life of St Cuthbert by A.K. Nicholson and G.E.R. Smith.

Cartmel Fell, St Anthony
In the E window 14th- and 15th-century glass of the Crucifixion and five scenes, fragmentary, of the Seven Sacraments; also St Anthony with his pig, St Laurence, female donors, and fragments including the Lamb and Flag of St John the Baptist.

Cartmel Priory
Medieval glass includes a king and six prophets from mid-14th-century Jesse tree (E window, S aisle), and 15th-century figures of Virgin and Child, St John the Baptist and an archbishop (fragmentary) in main E window. Good Shrigley & Hunt glass in the nave.

Casterton, Holy Trinity
Stained glass by Henry Holiday (as are the wall-paintings in the chancel), 1894–7.

Cockermouth, All Saints
19th-century glass. E window by Hardman, 1853, and W window by Kempe, c. 1897.

Crosthwaite, St Kentigern
Some 15th-century glass in a N aisle window. Otherwise 19th-century glass by Kempe and Wailes.

Crosthwaite, St Mary
Harry Stammers window of the Virgin with Henry VI and William of Wykeham. Symbolic window by L.C. Evetts. Both c. 1950.

Dufton, St Cuthbert
18th-century glass by Faucet of Appleby.

Edenhall, St Cuthbert
E window has two early 14th-century figures, also Netherlandish roundels.

Greystoke, St Andrew
E window of 15th-century glass (reassembled in 1848): apocryphal story of St Andrew and his adventures in Wronden, the City of Dogs.

Kendal, Holy Trinity
15th-century head of a king in S chapel.

Keswick, St John the Evangelist
E window by Holiday, 1888–9. Also by him, the side windows of the chancel and one S window.

Kirkbampton, St Peter
E window by Morris & Co., 1871 (Christ with eight music-making angels).

Kirkby Ireleth, St Cuthbert
Seated Christ and other 14th-century fragments in chancel windows.

Lamplugh, St Michael
Late 19th-century glass by Kempe.

Lanercost Priory, St Cecilia
Morris glass of 1875–96. St Cecilia window by Evie Hone (1948).

Martindale, St Peter
Eight lancets by Jane Gray, *c.* 1960s.

Muncaster, Muncaster Castle
A number of 16th- and 17th-century Flemish roundels and panels, mainly in yellow stain and black paint, at the foot of the stairs and on the staircase.

Newbiggin, St Edmund
14th- and 15th-century glass in E window, fragmentary.

Penrith, St Andrew
15th-century glass in a N aisle window, and some in a S aisle window.

Ponsonby, parish church
Burne-Jones glass of 1875 in E window.

Staveley, St James
Chancel E window by Morris & Co., 1882, designed by Burne-Jones (Crucifixion, Ascension and angels).

Troutbeck, Church of Jesus
E window by Morris & Co., 1873, includes Crucifixion, Baptism of Christ, Christ blessing the children, the Charge to St Peter, Supper at Emmaus. Designers were Burne-Jones, Morris and Madox Brown.

Ulverston, St Mary
19th-century glass. E window by Grey of London *c.* 1805, also windows by Wailes, Powell, Heaton, Butler & Bayne.

Wetheral, Holy Trinity
Two 15th-century saints, with donors, in W window.

Witherslack, St Paul
17th-century heraldic glass, possibly by Henry Gyles of York.

Wreay, St Mary
Stained glass includes fragments of medieval French glass imported in *c.* 1830.

Derbyshire

Ashbourne, St Oswald
Five 13th-century Nativity scenes in N transept.

Ault Hucknall, St John the Baptist
16th-century Crucifixion window of three lights (E window of S aisle), 1527.

Birchover, parish church
Three S aisle windows by Brian Clarke, 1977.

Caldwell, St Giles
Two roundels of *c.* 1400 in W window.

Chesterfield, St Mary
Glass is largely 19th century (Hardman, Warrington, and Heaton, Butler & Bayne). In St Peter's Chapel, window by Margaret Aldrich Rope in the Arts and Crafts style. Early 20th-century glass by Christopher Webb.

Dalbury, All Saints
Extremely interesting early 12th-century winged figure, probably St Michael, in second window from W on S wall. He stands frontally with hands raised in prayer; surely one of the earliest panels in the country. Restored by the York Glaziers' Trust in 1980 (colour plate 2).

Darley Dale, St Helen
Morris & Co. window in S transept, designed by Burne-Jones as memorial to Raphael Gillum; subject is the Song of Solomon; 1862–3. E window of 1892 also by Burne-Jones.

Derby, Cathedral Church of All Saints
Modern glass. E windows in both aisles designed by Ceri Richards, made by Patrick Reyntiens, mainly blue and yellow, depicting All Souls (N) and All Saints (S); 1967.

Dronfield, St John the Baptist
14th-century fragments in two chancel windows, also in nave, nearest window to east.

Eggington, St Wilfred
13th-century fragments of Crucifixion, Virgin, St John.

Elvaston, St Bartholomew
19th-century N window of chancel by Burlison & Grylls.

Haddon Hall, Chapel
15th-century E window of Crucifixion, St Mary and St John, inscribed '*Orate pro animabus Riccardi Vernon et Benedicite uxoris eius qui fecerunt anno dni 1427*'.
N and S windows of the Apostles are of the same date.

Hathersage, St Michael
Stained glass by Kempe, transferred from Derwent Church in 1949 (Derwent Church was about to be submerged in a reservoir).

Killamarsh, St Giles
15th-century Virgin in S window of chancel.

Melbourne, St Michael and St Mary
E and S windows of chancel are by Hardman (1867 and 1869), N window of 1869 by Clayton & Bell.

Morley, St Matthew
Glass of 1482 which came from Dale Abbey at the time of the Dissolution. The 15th-century glass is mainly in the N chancel chapel, and shows the legend of St Robert of Knaresborough (colour plate 27) and the Discovery of the True Cross.

Restored in 1847 by William Warrington, but much 15th-century glass survives.

Norbury, St Mary
14th- and 15th-century glass. Side windows of chancel have 14th-century glass, mainly heraldic. 15th-century figures in E window, and in SE chapel (saints and donor's family).

Staveley, St John the Baptist
Heraldic glass by Henry Gyles of York, commissioned by Lord Frecheville, Governor of York, 1676.

Swanwick, St Andrew
E window of 1923 by Martin Travers, W window of 1953 by J.E. Nuttgens.

Tideswell, St John the Baptist
Jesse tree in E window, 1875, by Heaton, Butler & Bayne.

West Hallam, St Wilfred
15th-century figure of St James the Less, holding a club, in a S clerestory window; in S chancel quarries with birds painted and silver-nitrate stained.

Wilne, Willoughby Chapel
Dramatic 17th-century glass, probably by the Van Linges; the chapel was built in 1622, and the glass is likely to be of the same date.

Winster, St John the Baptist
S window of chancel by Burne-Jones, made by Morris & Co.

Wirksworth, St Mary
Burne-Jones and Morris window of 1909 in N transept (though both were dead by this time).

Youlgreave, All Saints
E window and chancel S windows designed by Burne-Jones.

Devon

Abbots Bickington, St James
In E window fragments of medieval glass, including a Crucifixion, St Andrew, St Christopher: 14th–15th century.

Ashburton, St Andrew
W window by Kempe, c. 1880.

Aston, St Michael
15th-century glass, mainly armorial, also includes angel from an Annunciation, kneeling knight and saint.

Bere Ferrers, St Andrew
Early 14th-century glass in E window: seated Christ, donors and saints.

Buckfastleigh, Buckfast Abbey
The monks of Buckfast Abbey are renowned for the designing and making of modern stained glass especially *dalle-de-verre* both for their own building and elsewhere (see Harlow New Town, Essex).

Burlescombe, St Mary
Stained glass by Powell & Sons, 1858.

Clovelly, All Saints
E and W windows both by Kempe (1885 and 1898).

Cockington, St George and St Mary
In N window, 14th-century figure of St Paul. 15th-century saints in S window.

Culmstock, All Saints
1896 window by Morris & Co., designed by Burne-Jones.

Doddiscombsleigh, St Michael
Notable for its 15th-century glass – five windows of it. N aisle windows contain figures of saints and Virgin, and below each figure a coat of arms – all set in white quarries. E window has 19th-century Christ (Clayton & Bell), but around this are medieval scenes of the Seven Sacraments – highly interesting.

Dunsford, St Mary
15th-century figures in heads of N windows, St Margaret, St Catherine, St Barbara. Four sets of tracery lights on S side include angels, yellow stained, and elders of the church.

Exeter, Cathedral (St Mary and St Peter)
Early 14th-century grisaille glass in SE and NE chapels.
14th-century glass also on a clerestory window (saints under canopies) and in E window.
W window by Peckitt of York, 1766.

Exeter, Royal Clarence Hotel
Surprisingly, 30 panels of 16th–18th-century glass of continental origin.

Exeter, St Mary Steps
Modern E window by John Hayward.

Haccombe, St Blaise
Early 14th-century glass in a few windows.

Horwood, St Michael
E window of N aisle has 15th-century glass in tracery.

Ifracombe, Holy Trinity
19th-century glass by Hardman, Willement, Lavers & Barraud, O'Connor etc.

Inwardleigh, church
E window of N aisle has 14th-century angels in tracery.

Ipplepen, St Andrew
E window by Kempe, 1906.
In the tracery lights, coats of arms (Henry VII, Bishop Grandison, Bishop Lacy), 15th-century figures of Cardinal Beaufort, St John the Baptist, St Thomas, and a female saint with roses in her hair.

Kelly, St Mary
Large 15th-century E window of the Crucifixion (with St Mary, St John and Edward the Confessor) in the N aisle. Considerably restored.

Little Hempston, St John
15th-century figures of St Stephen and St Christopher, with donors; the glass came from Marldon.

Littleham, St Margaret with St Andrew
In a N window 15th-century figures of Christ, St Michael and St Roch.

Manaton, St Winifrid
In the head of a N aisle window 15th-century figures.

Northleigh, St Giles
In E windows of N chapel, three late 15th-century figures.

Ottery St Mary, St Mary
Glass is 19th century, by Wailes, Warrington, Hardman, O'Connor and

Gibbs – most 1850–60.

Payhembury, St Mary
Interesting 15th-century glass in tracery lights of N aisle, including figure of St Apollonia, holding an enormous tooth, also Saints Blaise, Laurence, Stephen and Vincent.

Plymouth, St Andrew
Six fine windows by Piper/Reyntiens, mainly 1960s: Tower window with Symbols of the Passion; Chancel window of the Four Elements; E window, Lady Chapel, with Symbols of the Virgin; E window, St Catherine's Chapel, St Catherine's Wheel; Dr Harry Moreton window, N transept, with golden harps; S transept window, Hand of God with doves and fishes.

Shobrooke, St Swithin
Shelley memorial window by Burlison & Grylls, 1869.

Tavistock, St Eustace
N aisle E window by Morris & Co., 1876. Other 19th-century glass by Wailes, Ward & Hughes, Powell & Sons, Clayton & Bell, Kempe etc.

Torbryan, Holy Trinity
15th-century figures of female saints in E window; in S chancel the four Doctors of the Church.

Torquay, St John the Evangelist, Montpelier Terrace
Chancel E window designed by Burne-Jones for Morris & Co., 1865, also W window.

Weare Giffard, Holy Trinity
15th-century Jesse tree, although fragmentary, in E window of S aisle.

Whitestone, St Catherine
15th-century Virgin in a N window.

Yarnscombe, St Andrew
In E window of S aisle, 14th-century angel with shield.

Dorset

Abbotsbury, St Nicholas
Late 15th-century half-figure of sorrowing Virgin from a Crucifixion, wringing her hands: a moving piece.

Almer, St Mary
Early 17th-century Swiss Last Judgement (very small).

Bournemouth, St Peter
Burne-Jones, window of 1864 in S chapel, depicting the Miracles of Christ, also good glass by Clayton & Bell (1866 and 1874).

Bournemouth, St Stephen
Rather dark but fine quality glass by Clayton & Bell (1881–98).

Bradford Abbas, St Mary
Some 15th-century glass in vestry and S window of chancel.

Bradford Peverell, St Mary
Annunciation and Coronation of the Virgin, 15th century, in a N window. Also in a N window, arms of William of Wykeham, probably medieval. The E window was presented by New College, Oxford in 1850.

Cattistock, St Peter and St Paul
S aisle window by Morris & Co., 1882 (two lights with six angels against a blue

ground). Early 20th-century glass by Walter Tower and Anning Bell.

Cerne Abbas, St Mary
15th-century heraldic glass in E window.

Charborough, St Mary
Early 19th-century glass, including Christ in W window based on Raphael's Transfiguration.

Cranborne, St Mary and St Bartholomew
15th-century fragments in a S window.

Creech Grange, Creech Grange
17th-century heraldic glass in drawing-room, 19th-century glass by Willement in Hall.

Creech Grange, St John the Evangelist
Willement glass of 1849 in N transept.

Dorchester, St George, Fordington
Late Morris & Co. glass in W window (1903) and S transept (1913).

Hampreston, All Saints
Stained glass by Kempe in W, NW and a S window.

Hazelbury Bryan, St Mary and St James
Several pieces of 15th-century glass especially in N window.

Ibberton, St Eustace
15th-century fragments and 16th-century roundels.

Lyme Regis, St Michael
Several windows by Willement, mid-19th century.

Marnhull, St Gregory
E window is late Morris & Co., 1911. 15th-century fragments in a N window.

Melbury Bubb, St Mary
In two N windows, 15th-century glass, showing Sacrament of Ordination, Annunciation, and Christ Showing His Wounds. Below are arms of Warre and Matravers and the date 1466. Fine quality glass.

Milton Abbas, Milton Abbey
Fragments of 15th-century glass in E window of chancel, of much less account than the S window of S transept, designed by Pugin for Hardman in 1847. This is a splendid affair: tiers of figures, glowing colour, red predominant.

Moreton, St Nicholas
Engraved glass by Lawrence Whistler in the apse windows, very delicate.

Parkstone, St Osmund, Bournemouth Road
Abstract glass designed by Prior for Prior's Glass.

Portland, St Andrew
In S aisle, memorial window to 106 people who lost their lives in the collision of the ships *Avalanche* and *Forest* in 1887; symbolic rather than representational, fine use of colour, designed by Jon Callan, 1981.

Sherborne, All Hallows (Abbey Church)
In St Catherine's Chapel, 15th-century glass, including complete figures. Medieval glass also in Mary-le-Bow Chapel. 19th-century glass designed by

Pugin for Hardman in two windows, and by Clayton & Bell in clerestory.

Sherborne, Almshouse of St John the Baptist and St John the Evangelist
In S window of chapel, 15th-century Virgin with the two St Johns on either side, *c.* 1475.

South Perrott, St Mary
In N window of chancel, two 18th-century roundels.

Sturminster Newton, St Mary
SE aisle window by Harry Clarke of Dublin, 1921, very rich in colour and art deco in style; three standing figures, St Elisabeth of Hungary, Virgin and Child, St Barbara. A rare and exceptional piece (colour plate 47).
S chapel window (1901) and Tower window by Mary Lowndes, pioneer among women glaziers. E window by Hardman, 1865, N aisle window by Webb, 1911.

Symondsbury, St John the Baptist
S window of S transept by Lethaby, *c.* 1880.

Trent, St Andrew
E window has splendid array of 16th- and 17th-century Swiss and German panels, many of them enamelled. Fine S transept window by O'Connor (1871), showing Christ in glory.

West Lulworth, Holy Trinity
Good glass by Kempe, 1898–1901.

Whitchurch Canonicorum, St Candida
Medieval fragments in E window of chancel.

St Elisabeth of Hungary; detail from 1921 window by Harry Clarke. The saint's features are those of young Roma Spencer Smith, whom the window commemorates. Sturminster Newton, Dorset

Wimborne Minster
16th-century Flemish Jesse tree in E window of choir, damaged.
N and S choir aisles have armorial glass by Willement, 1838. N window by Heaton, Butler & Bayne, 1857.

Durham

Darlington, St Cuthbert

Extensive 19th-century glass by Clayton
& Bell, Hardman, Wailes, Burlison &
Grylls, Wallace, Atkinson and others.

Durham, Cathedral

Very little medieval stained glass survives: early 15th-century fragments and
figures in W window of Galilee, including
top half of 14th-century bishop under
canopy, *c.* 1435; scene of the Sacrament
of Matrimony, 15th-century figures of St
Bede and another saint, also heraldic
glass. Central W window has in tracery
lights a fine Crucifixion between the sun
and the moon. In the S transept, a good
15th-century figure of St Leonard; charming bird quarries of this period in the
Chapter House.

In W window of nave, Jesse tree by
Clayton & Bell, 1867. The 'Good
Shepherd' window in the N aisle is by
Wailes.

S window of S transept by Clayton &
Bell.

The striking Moses window in the S
transept (1895–6) is by Henry
Holiday.

There is also modern glass: three windows by Hugh Easton. Bede window in
the Galilee Chapel by Alan Younger
(1973), and in the N aisle, 'Daily Bread'

Sacrament of Matrimony, *c.* 1435. One of the surviving panels of medieval glass in the Galilee Chapel,
Durham Cathedral

window by Mark Angus (1984), a fine symbolic composition on the theme of the Last Supper (colour plate 53).

Durham, Castle
In the chapel, Jesse tree window of 1542. In the Great Hall, four-light window by Kempe (1888), with Saints George and Cuthbert, and Bishops Hatfield and Fox.

Durham, St Oswald
Good Morris & Co. glass in W window, designed by Ford Madox Brown, 1864.

Escomb, Saxon church
There are a few small fragments of c. 7th-century Saxon glass in a case in the porch, excavated from around the church.

Lanchester, All Saints
Three very high quality panels of imported French glass, 13th century. Flight into Egypt, Annunciation to the Shepherds, Adoration of the Magi.

Raby Castle, Chapel
Remarkable 12th- and 13th century glass, which seems to have come from St Denis near Paris, including very early panel of c. 1144 showing the Three Magi, and figure of Isaiah (from Infancy of Christ window); and a kneeling monk (from a St Benedict window). Also Flemish roundels, and a panel of a kneeling king (early 16th century).

Staindrop, St Mary
Glass mainly by Clayton & Bell, c. 1865, though some medieval pieces in E window of S aisle and in vestry.

Ushaw, St Cuthbert's College Chapel
The mid-19th-century W window (it was

originally the E window of Pugin's chapel) is by Oliphant; Pugin referred to it as 'the finest work of modern times'.

Wolsingham, St Mary and St Stephen
Morris & Co. window in the baptistery: Jacob's Ladder. The design was probably by Burne-Jones, and the date c. 1896.

Wycliffe, St Mary
14th-century tracery lights in S chancel: music-making angels, Christ in Majesty, St John the Baptist, and Virgin and Child (twice), of c. 1375.

Essex

Abbess Roding, St Edmund
15th-century glass, including figures of a bishop and a female saint, in S window of chancel.

Audley End, House
18th-century enamelled window of the 'Last Supper', by William Peckitt.

Basildon, St Martin
Recent window by Joseph Nuttgens.

Broomfield (Chelmsford), St Mary
E window of the Resurrection and three memorial windows by Rosemary Rutherford, 1951–66.

Chelmsford, Cathedral (St Mary)
E window by Clayton & Bell, 1858. Other glass mainly by A.K. Nicholson.

Clacton-on-Sea, St Paul
Dalle-de-verre (slab glass and concrete) in almost the whole E wall: Conversion of St Paul. Designed and cut by Rosemary Rutherford, set by Goddard & Gibbs, 1965.

Clavering, St Mary and St Clement
15th-century glass in N aisle windows, fragmentary and rather pieced together – all the inscriptions are in the same light. The colour is attractive: olive green to yellow shades, with deep blue and touches of red.

Coggeshall, St Peter ad Vincula
Modern glass by L.C. Evetts.
In St Catherine's Chapel, a window installed in 1975 showing St Catherine kneeling – over her head is a sword set in a red disc, above that the crown of martyrdom, and on either side of her, broken Catherine wheels.
At N end of N aisle, another L.C. Evetts window of 1975, on the theme of peace, the turning of swords into ploughshares.

Dedham, St Mary the Virgin
Chancel windows by Kempe (first decade of 20th century).

Easthorpe, St Edmund
German or Swiss glass of *c.* 1530 in S window.

Elmstead, St Ann and St Laurence
Fragments of 14th-century glass in S chapel and S window of chancel.

Good Easter, St Andrew
14th- and 15th-century fragments in two windows of S aisle.

Great Bardfield, St Mary the Virgin
Late 14th-century glass in N aisle, mainly in tracery lights, including a Crucifixion.

Great Dunmow, St Mary
15th-century glass in a S aisle window, fragmentary.

Great Leighs, St Mary
In N windows of chancel some 14th-century glass survives.

Greensted, St Andrew
In W window, a head of a man of *c.* 1500.

Harlow, Harlow New Town, Our Lady of Fatima (RC)
An extensive, exciting, colourful glazing scheme, designed by Gerard Goalen and executed by the monks of Buckfast Abbey. The glass, whole walls of it, is set in concrete with plain glass outside for protection. The grid-design predominates, and the general pattern is to have scenes depicted only in the centre of each panel.

Harlow, Harlow Old Town, St Mary the Virgin
Small 14th-century figure of Virgin in N vestry.

Hatfield Peverel, St Andrew
14th- and 15th-century glass, fragmentary, in N windows. In S windows, some 16th–17th-century imported glass.

Heybridge, St Andrew
In N chancel window a late 13th-century female saint.

Hornchurch, Church of the English Martyrs
Small, brilliantly coloured rectangular windows on the theme of the Creation, by Goddard & Gibbs Studios, 1981.

Lambourne, St Mary and All Saints
Five 17th-century panels, German or Swiss.

Layer Marney, St Mary the Virgin

In E window of N chapel, early 16th-century figure of St Peter.

Leigh-on-Sea, St Clement
Modern glass by Francis Stephens, Madonna and Child, 1971.

Leigh-on-Sea, St Margaret
Epiphany window by Francis Stephens in Lady Chapel, 1950.

Lindsell, St Mary the Virgin
In E window, fragments of medieval glass of 13th–16th centuries, including two 13th-century figures of saints, a grisaille medallion in the centre of the window, two 16th-century panels each showing a husband and wife praying – done in yellow stain and dark red glass. Assembled and restored in 1929.

Little Baddow, St Mary the Virgin
Fragments of c. 1400 in E window, including St Michael and the Dragon.

Little Easton, St Mary
Six 17th-century German panels in S windows, installed in 1857.

Margaretting, St Margaret
E window of three lights is a 15th-century Jesse tree, Flemish (for Jesse trees, see Matthew 1). The glass was in the N wall until it was restored in 1870, and probably used to fill above five windows. There are shown 25 characters who lived after Jesse, and five before; the Virgin is at the top of the centre light, and the others are mainly in pairs, e.g. Jacob and Joseph to her left, and Abiad and Zarubabel to her right.
A tricky church to reach: one has to walk across a level-crossing over a very busy railway line.

Messing, All Saints
In E window 17th-century glass of the Works of Mercy, also Faith, Hope and Charity, probably by Abraham van Linge.

Newport, St Mary the Virgin
Early 14th-century glass in the N transept (bought early 20th century). In the central section of the two lights are found (on left) St Katherine, (on right) St Michael; above and below is 14th-century glass, but rather jumbled.
In S transept, 19th-century window by Clayton & Bell, of Elijah and his Chariot of Fire: a dramatic composition across three lights, executed in memory of Robert Morgan Tamplin of Keble College, Oxford, who was burnt to death in the great fire at Exeter on 5 September 1887, aged 23.

Prittlewell, St Mary
Twelve early 16th-century panels, originally from St Ouen's Church, Rouen. Purchased at the time of the French Revolution but not installed until the 1880s, their design is strongly influenced by Albrecht Dürer.

Rivenhall, St Mary and All Saints
In all the country, one of the most important churches for 12th-century glass. The glass is undoubtedly French; it was bought by the Revd B.D. Hawkins (then the incumbent at Rivenhall) from the *curé* of Chénu, near Tours, in 1839. Like the Canterbury glass, it was stored during the war, and it was re-arranged and re-installed in 1948. It has been suggested that the central roundels date from as early as 1145; but see the article by F. Sidney Eden, *Journal of the British Society of Master Glass Painters*, Oct.

GAZETTEER

Twelfth-century French glass from Chénu-sur-Sarthe, near Tours. Rivenhall, Essex

1925, who dates the roundels as late 12th century and the knight in the bottom right hand corner as early 13th century. The knight is entitled 'ROBERT/US LEMAIRE' in Lombardic capitals. Altogether this is extremely impressive stained glass.

Roxwell, St Michael and All Angels
Two small German panels of *c.* 1600.

Saffron Walden, St Mary the Virgin
19th-century glass by Powell & Sons and Lavers & Barraud.

Shalford, St Andrew
Fragments of 14th-century glass, mainly in E window.

Sheering, St Mary the Virgin
E window has late 14th-century Coronation of the Virgin, with two censing angels and eight orders of angels.

South Weald, St Peter
In W window, two panels of late 15th-century Flemish glass; the rest of the window is 19th century, by Powell & Sons. E window and S aisle window by Kempe (1886 and 1888).

Southend (Prittlewell), Annunciation of the BVM (RC)
In E window of S aisle, 16th-century German or Swiss glass.

Southend, St Clement, Leigh-on-Sea

In E window, 18th-century Crucifixion.

Stambourne, St Peter and St Thomas

Two early 16th-century figures of donors in E window (Henry MacWilliam and his first wife – d. 1530).

Stapleford Abbots, St Mary

In N vestry a small early 14th-century figure of St Edward the Confessor.

Stisted, All Saints

16th-century fragments in chancel windows.

Thaxted, St John the Baptist

Fragments and figures in N and S windows, much of it jumbled. Early 16th-century figures of saints in the N windows, unfortunately with their heads missing (but see details of watermill and ship in St Christopher window). In S window of S transept a late 14th-century figure with underneath a (?) 16th-century figure of Abraham. In a S aisle window, Stories from Genesis, in four panels, dating from *c.* 1450 (slightly patched, but note the purple angel and the varied plants and textures of the Paradise garden).

Expulsion from Paradise; fifteenth-century glass at Thaxted, Essex

Thundersley, St Peter
Apse windows are by Ray Bradley, on the theme of St Peter, 1966.

Toppesfield, St Margaret of Antioch
15th-century Coronation of the Virgin and censing angel in E window of S aisle.

Waltham Holy Cross, Waltham Abbey
The glass at the E end was designed by Burne-Jones and made by Powell & Sons in 1861 – it is thus a little earlier than the work he was to do for Morris & Co. The E window consists of three lights (a Jesse tree) and a rose window above (God the Creator and the Seven Days of Creation). It is all most vivid. Note the petrol-blue background to the side lights of the Jesse tree, the predominant scarlet of the central light – also the general sense of focus, the movement towards the central stem of the composition.
The rose window is even more remarkable; God is seated on a rainbow in the centre, and the other roundels are almost abstract in their landscape forms. Note the horizontal but waving lines of various shades of turquoise in the two lower roundels. Quite astonishing work for this date – or indeed for any date.
E window of S aisle and window above the entrance to the crypt by Henry Holiday (1867 and 1861).
(The cartoons for the Burne-Jones rose window are in the V & A Museum, and those for the Jesse window in Birmingham City Art Gallery.)

Wethersfield, St Mary Magdalene and St Mary the Virgin
Many 14th- and 15th-century fragments.

White Notley, St Etheldreda

In the E wall of the N vestry a tiny mid-13th-century window which was found buried in a wall when the vestry was built in the 19th century (colour plate 6). The glass was embedded in a Saxon tombstone; it still is – surely one of the oddest frameworks for a panel of stained glass. The glass is of a figure which may represent St Etheldreda (7th-century foundress of Ely Cathedral and patroness of the University of Cambridge), or it may equally well be a king.

Widdington, St Mary
In a N window, a sundial dated 1664.

Woodham Walter, St Michael
15th-century glass in a S aisle window.

Writtle, All Saints
19th-century and early 20th-century glass by Clayton & Bell, Powell & Sons, C.P. Bacon and H.W. Bryans.

Gloucestershire

Abenhall, St Michael
14th-century glass, fragmentary, in N window of chancel.

Aldsworth, St Bartholomew
In S porch, fragments of 15th-century glass, including blazing star and white rose.

Arlingham, St Mary
Two windows on N side of nave have glass of c. 1340:
1. St Mary and St John, with gently swaying figure of St Catherine in tracery.
2. St Margaret and the dragon, with a crowned female saint.
15th-century glass in SW window of chancel.

Avening, Holy Cross
Glass of 1908 by Christopher Whall in two windows of nave. E window by Clayton & Bell, 1889.

Badgeworth, Holy Trinity
Fragments of medieval glass in N chapel (tracery) and in vestry.

Bagendon, St Margaret
15th-century glass in S windows of chancel, fragmentary, but include figure of the Virgin and St Catherine's wheel. 15th-century glass also in E window of N aisle (St Margaret).
N chancel window by Whall, 1906.

Barnsley, St Mary
W window has medieval fragments including St Laurence's gridiron. Mid 19th-century glass by Willement in E window, N and S windows of chancel and one window in nave.

Barnwood, St Lawrence
Glass mainly 19th century (Hardman and Clayton & Bell), but window in S aisle by Veronica Whall, 1932.

Bibury, Museum
Stained glass version of Holman Hunt's 'Light of the World', mainly enamelled.

Bibury, St Mary
E window by Willement, 1885.
In chancel, small 13th-century grisaille window, and fine Karl Parsons window of 1927.

Bishop's Cleeve, St Michael and All Angels
In W window of S aisle, fragments of 14th- and 15th-century glass.

Bledington, St Leonard
Late 15th-century window to the Virgin, possibly by John Prudde of Westminster (*cf.* Beauchamp Chapel, St Mary's, Warwick). The Virgin is in blue and carries a rosary and a sceptre; also St Christopher. In the clerestory, St George and the Dragon, Pietà, St Mary Magdalene and donors.
In the chantry chapel, Coronation of the Virgin, with six disciples above.

Bourton-on-the-Water, St Lawrence
Most of the glass is by Kempe or Walter Tower. M.C. Farrar-Bell window in nave, 1936.

Bromsberrow, St Mary
Much glass by Kempe. 17th-century and medieval fragments in E window of chapel.

Buckland, St Michael
E window has three panels of late 15th-century glass, *c.* 1475, representing the sacraments of Baptism and Confirmation, Holy Matrimony, Extreme Unction. Restored by William Morris, at his own expense, in 1883. Other fragments of 15th-century glass in S window.

Chaceley, St John the Baptist
14th-century glass in E window (Crucifixion) and E window of S aisle.

Chedworth, St Andrew
In two chancel windows fragmentary medieval glass.

Cheltenham, Cheltenham College
S side of chapel has two fine windows by Louis Davis.

Cheltenham, St Christopher, Warden Hill
Eight painterly windows by Tom Denny, based on the Parables (1987–1990s).

Cheltenham, St Mary
19th-century glass – by Lavers, Barraud & Westlake, also Clayton & Bell, Heaton & Butler, Hardman, Burlison & Grylls, Joseph Bell.

Cheltenham, St Paul, Paul's Road
Window by Edward Payne, 1963.

Chipping Campden, St James
Some medieval glass in tracery of E window. Hardman window over chancel arch, 1878.

Cirencester Agricultural College
Benedicite Window in Chapel, by Paul Quail.

Cirencester, St John the Baptist
In S window of S aisle, and in E and W windows of nave, fragments of *c.* 1525, installed in late 18th century. The rest of the glass from the 42 windows was packed in crates; all but one crate was tipped into a ditch at Oakley Hall in *c.* 1890. The contents of the case that was saved are in a two-light window in S sanctuary wall.
E window: glass of *c.* 1480, originally from Siddington, installed in *c.* 1800. The rest of the glass is 18th century, designed by an antiquary named Lysons.
S window of S aisle: *top:* St Jerome, St Gregory, St Ambrose; *centre:* St Catherine, St Margaret, St Dorothy; *below:* St John of Beverley, St William of York, St Zita, St Bathilda.
Lady Chapel: N windows have figures and canopies of *c.* 1450.

Elsewhere, 19th-century glass, mainly by Hardman; W window of S aisle by Easton.

Coln Rogers, St Andrew
In a N window of nave, 15th-century figure of St Margaret.

Daglingworth, Holy Rood
In tracery of W window, 15th-century glass with the Prince of Wales's feathers.

Daylesford, St Peter
Good 19th-century glass by Clayton & Bell, also by Wailes.

Deerhurst, St Mary
A delightful church. W window of S aisle includes rhythmic figure of St Catherine with her wheel, early 14th century (colour plate 15): also mid-15th-century glass of St Alphege, donors and armorial shields in tracery.

Didbrook, St George
15th-century panel of two angels incorporated in E window, also inscription commemorating the building of the church.

Duntisborne Abbots, Cotswold Farm
In the dining-room, Morris & Co. window of three lights, showing the life of St Cecilia – designed by Burne-Jones (came from Bowden Hall, Upton St Leonards). Morris glass also in small window on back stairs.

Eastington, St Michael
Fragments of 16th-century and earlier glass in a nave window, including figure of St Matthew.
A window depicting the River of Life has been commissioned from Tom Denny and Richard Webb for the N wall of the nave.

Eastleach, St Michael and St Martin

Fragments of medieval glass in E, N and N chancel windows.

Ebrington, St Eadburga

17th-century armorial glass in E window of S chapel. E window by Christopher Webb, 1964.

Edgeworth, St Mary

14th-century bishop in a N window of chancel.

Fairford, St Mary

Extremely important: the only church in the country which still has its medieval glazing scheme *in situ* and virtually intact. There are 28 windows (over 2,000 sq ft) of late 15th- or early 16th-century glass, possibly by Barnard Flower. The church was commissioned by John Tame in 1497.

The whole of the Catholic faith is embodied here. It begins on the N side (opposite the organ) with the Temptation of Eve and the stories of Moses, Gideon and Solomon, leads through into the Lady Chapel with the parentage and life of the Virgin Mary (Annunciation, Nativity, Adoration of the Magi) and the childhood of Jesus. Then in the chancel is the Life of Christ, the Crucifixion occupying a central position. In the Corpus Christi Chapel, the Resurrection (including interestingly, the Risen Christ visiting His Mother) and Pentecost.

In the nave, S side, the windows of the Twelve Apostles, then the Four Fathers of the Church (St Jerome, St Gregory, St Ambrose, St Augustine).

The three windows to the W of the S side were damaged in a storm in 1703.

The W window has Last Judgement in the lower half – St Michael weighing souls, St Peter, and some fierce red and blue devils; in the upper half, Christ in Majesty with St Mary and St John and the circles of the blessed (colour plate 33).

On the N side of the nave, the Evangelists and twelve prophets.

In the S clerestory, twelve martyrs and confessors of the faith; above them are angels. Opposite, in the N clerestory, twelve persecutors of the Church, and above them are devils.

Forthampton, St Mary

E window of the Virtues – is it by Morris & Co.?

Frampton-on-Severn, St Mary

Various medieval fragments, including 15th-century glass of the Seven Sacraments in E window of Clifford Chapel, also heraldic glass.

Gloucester, Cathedral

Great E window of the choir is 14th-century glass, virtually intact. Completed in 1357, releaded by Ward & Hughes in 1862. The subject is the Coronation of the Virgin, with many saints, the twelve apostles and angels – done in blue, red, and yellow-stained glass with a good deal of white. Tiers of figures, and below them is heraldic glass: the arms of Arundel, Berkeley, Warwick, de Bohun, Pembroke, Talbot, Sir Maurice Berkeley, Thomas Bradeston, and in the centre Ruyhale, Edward I, Edward III, the Black Prince, Henry of Lancaster, and the Instruments of the Passion; below them the arms of England, Edmund Duke of York, Edward III, Henry of Lancaster.

E window of Lady Chapel is made up of fragments of 14th- and 15th-century glass. Possibly the work of Barnard Flower. The heads of the smaller lights at the side contain Stories of the Virgin. Central lights at the top have 15th-century glass, including fragments of a Passion, which have been brought in from another window. Lower lights have 14th-century glass, part of a Jesse tree, which probably came from the N transept.

There is much 19th-century glass in the cathedral, Clayton & Bell, Kempe and Hardman. Lady Chapel windows by Christopher Whall and his son and daughter Christopher and Veronica.

Herbert Howells centenary window. Modern glass by Tom Denny and Caroline Swash.

Gloucester, St Paul, Stroud Road.
Modern glass by Hugh Easton.

Gloucester, St Peter (RC)
E window has good 19th-century glass by Clayton & Bell.

Hailes, church (dedication not known)
E window contains 15th-century glass, which came from Hailes Abbey, installed in 1903: panels of nine apostles, and fragments of tracery.

Hardwicke, St Nicholas
E window by Francis Skeat, 1971.

Harnhill, St Michael
In E window, fragments of medieval glass.

Hartbury, St Mary
Three-light E window of the Ascension, by Roy Coomber, 1990.

Hatherop, St Nicholas
19th-century glass by O'Connor, and by Lavers, Barraud & Westlake.

Hempsted, St Swithun
In tracery of N window, under tower, a 15th-century mitred head, said to represent Henry Dane, who after being Prior at Llanthony, Gloucester, became Archbishop of Canterbury.

Highnam, Holy Innocents
Mid-19th-century glass by Clayton & Bell (E window), Wailes, Hardman and O'Connor.

Horsley, St Martin
Medieval armorial glass in tracery in N and S transept windows.

Kempsford, St Mary
Medieval glass in N chancel window – St Anne teaching the Virgin to read.

Lechlade, St Lawrence
Medieval heraldic glass in tracery of S clerestory windows.

Matson, Matson House, Oratory
Window with 18th-century enamelled figures by William Peckitt.

Meysey Hampton, St Mary
14th-century glass, fragmentary, in several windows, including figure of St Michael weighing souls.

North Cerney, All Saints
15th-century E window: Virgin and two bishops, also flaming sun device of the Yorkists.
15th-century glass also in N transept windows – one a memorial to Rector William

Whitchurch (inst. 1464), the other given by John Eycote (figure of the donor is below the Crucifix). Unfortunately releaded inside out in 1732; put back correctly in 1912.

North Nibley, St Martin
Good E window by Clayton & Bell, W window by Powell & Sons.

Northleach with Eastington, St Peter and St Paul
Medieval glass in N clerestory, and in tracery of S windows, including figure of St Lawrence.
E window of 1963 by Christopher Webb.

Notgrove, St Bartholomew
Virgin and Child of c. 1300 in vestry window.

Pauntley, St John
N window of chancel has 14th-century heraldic glass, the Whittington arms. 14th-century glass also in W window of tower.

Poulton, St Michael
Glass by Geoffrey Webb (1946) and Christopher Webb (1959) on S side of nave.

Preston, St John the Baptist
A S aisle window contains medieval Crucifixion with Virgin and St John.

Prinknash, Prinknash Abbey
The modern glazing scheme designed and made there by Brother Gilbert Taylor in the *dalle-de-verre* technique (slabs of glass one inch thick set here in resin), richly coloured, seemingly abstract but actually symbolic forms (see p. 10).

Randwick, St John
Three-light window by Edward Payne, c. 1990.

Rendcomb, St Peter
Glass of c. 1520, rather fragmentary. It has been associated with Fairford, but seems later in date, and Renaissance rather than medieval in style.

Saintbury, St Nicholas
E window has two panels of 16th-century glass.

Sandhurst, St Lawrence
Modern glass in W window of N aisle, by H.J. Stammers.

Selsley, All Saints
Very notable for its William Morris glass – probably the earliest Morris & Co. made. The general scheme of the glazing was devised by Philip Webb. Rossetti designed the Visitation, Ford Madox Brown the Nativity (in the apse), Morris the Annunciation, Webb and Morris the Creation. Burne-Jones and Campfield were also involved in the designing (colour plate 42).

Slimbridge, St John Evangelist
Fine memorial window to Peter Scott, by Tom Denny, 1994.

South Cerney, All Hallows
Fragments of medieval glass in S chancel and N aisle windows.

Stanton, St Michael
In E window, two 15th-century figures under canopies (from Hailes Abbey), 15th-century fragments also in S window. Otherwise, glass by Comper, 1926.

Stone, All Saints
Medieval heraldic fragments in two N windows (Berkeley arms), and one S window (arms of Edward IV).

Sudeley, Castle
Queen Katherine Parr's Room and S staircase have glass partly 16th-century Flemish and partly mid-19th-century by Willement.

Sudeley, St Mary
13th-century glass in two lights of N window in N projection. Two martyrdoms are represented – in one a kneeling figure is being struck with a sword by a man in chain armour, in the other a knight is striking down a figure in pink. In E window of this projection, Tudor female donors and a figure of a bishop.

Swell, St Mary the Virgin, Lower Swell
Clayton & Bell glass, relating the Story of the Passion, 19th century.

Syde, St Mary
15th-century roundel of St James of Compostella.

Temple Guiting, St Mary
Late 15th-century or early 16th-century panels of the Virgin, St Mary Magdalene and St James the Less.

Tewkesbury, Tewkesbury Abbey
Very remarkable 14th-century glass. There are seven windows of it high up in the choir; they date from between 1340 and 1344 and were presented by Eleanor de Clare, wife of Hugh Despencer. In the E window, Christ in Judgement, with the Virgin and an archangel (Michael ?). The side panels have the twelve apostles and

St John the Baptist. The smaller lights below have Last Judgement scenes and the figure of the donor, Eleanor de Clare, in her shift. In the circular window, music-making angels surrounding a Coronation of the Virgin.
In the two windows to the W, splendid knights in armour; their heraldic bearings show them to be:
(N) Robert Consul, Gilbert de Clare, Hugh Despencer, Robert Fitzhamon (colour plate 16).
(S) Three of the de Clare family, and Lord de la Zouche of Mortimer.

Toddington, Toddington Manor
16th-century German glass (Last Judgement) in the staircase window. Armorial glass in the cloisters.

Tredington, St John the Baptist
In N window of chancel, a quatrefoil of 14th-century glass (the crowned head of a king).

Upper Slaughter, St Peter
19th-century glass by Clayton & Bell.

Warden Hill, St Christopher
See Cheltenham.

Wickwar, Holy Trinity
Two windows by John Hayward; one largely heraldic of 1977, the other of 1988 showing St Clement, St Nicholas and St Peter against a map of southern England – St Nicholas stands on the Isle of Wight and holds a small yacht.

Winchcombe, St Peter
15th-century glass, fragmentary, in E window of S chapel, W window of S aisle, and window next to S door.

Woolaston, St Andrew
In chancel, two windows by Francis Skeat, 1963.

Wormington, St Catherine
In N and S aisle, westernmost windows have medieval glass. E window by Morris & Co., 1912.

Wyck Rissington, St Laurence
Fragments of 14th-century glass in the chancel, including Crucifixion with sun, moon and stars.

Yanworth, St Michael
Fragments of medieval glass in E and other windows.

Hampshire

Aldershot, Garrison Church of St Michael and St George
W window of N aisle by Isobel Gloag and Mary Lowndes in the Arts and Crafts style (1909).

Aldershot, Royal Garrison Church of All Saints
E window by O'Connor, 1863.

Basingstoke, All Saints
E window by Burlison & Grylls. Remarkable W windows designed by Cecil Collins, made by Patrick Reyntiens (1988 and 1989).

Basingstoke, St Michael
Early 16th-century glass in S chapel and S aisle.
Christopher Webb windows in chancel (1949) and N chapel (1950).
Early 17th-century heraldic glass in N chapel includes arms of Charles I.

Bramley, St James
14th-century and other fragments in a N window. Early 16th-century Swiss glass in S transept, arranged by Burlison & Grylls in 1889.

Chandlers Ford, St Edward the Confessor
Modern window by David Wasley.

Deane, All Saints
Glazing scheme of 1818, contemporary with the church.

Dibden, All Saints
E window of Christ Triumphant, by Derek Wilson, *c.* 1955.

Droxford, St Mary and All Saints
Glass by Martin Travers.

East Tytherley, St Peter
In side windows of chancel, three small figures of saints, 13th century. The two on the S side seem to be bishops, that on the N with a red halo holds either a book or a stone (? St Stephen). All three set in plain quarry glass. Did these come from Salisbury Cathedral, like the glass at Grateley?

Fareham, Holy Trinity
Copy of Reynolds's Faith, Hope and Charity windows in New College, Oxford, made by Thomas Jervais of Windsor, *c.* 1770–90. Restored in 1835 by J.A. Edwards.

Froyle, St Mary of the Assumption
Heraldic glass of 1300–20 in E window, including arms of Edward the Confessor, and arms of England of 1198–1340. Below this, a Jesse tree by Burlison &

Grylls (1896). Medieval fragments in two nave windows.

Grateley, St Leonard
In the head of the largest window on the S side, a 13th-century panel, square but resting on a point, representing the Stoning of St Stephen. It came from Salisbury Cathedral, according to Pevsner, from somewhere near the E end of it. Colours predominantly blue, the head of St Stephen very red and those of the stoners brownish.
In heads and bases of the three lancets in the chancel, more 13th-century glass, fragmentary and mainly blue.

Hambledon, St Peter and St Paul
Late Victorian and early 20th-century glass, mainly by Ward & Hughes, also by Dixon (E window, S aisle) and R. Anning Bell (N and S windows of chancel).

Harbridge, All Saints
16th- and 17th-century German roundels.

Havant, St Faith
E window by Clayton & Bell, 1873.

Headley, All Saints
13th-century panel showing the beheading of a female saint.

Heckfield, St Michael
Window in S side of nave, to E, by Morris & Co., designed by Burne-Jones, 1884.

Herriard, St Mary
Reset 15th-century St Margaret and other fragments in chancel. Modern glass by Hugh Powell, including window of the Cross (1968).

Highclere, St Michael
Early Kempe window in S aisle, with four seated music-making angels (*c.* 1872).

Hinton Ampner, All Saints
E window of two lancets, 'Pillars of Cloud and Fire' by Patrick Reyntiens (1969).

Hound, St Mary
Virgin and Child by Patrick Reyntiens, 1959, in E window – highly interesting. Four more windows by him in the chancel.

Hursley, All Saints
Stained glass by William Wailes to a design by William Butterfield, including W window of 1858 of the Last Judgement; a complete glazing scheme.

Lyndhurst, Our Lady of the Assumption
War memorial window by A.J. Dix (1919).

Lyndhurst, St Michael and All Angels
E window of chancel by Morris & Co., designed by Burne-Jones, 1862–3: angels playing instruments.
S window of S transept showing Joshua, Elijah, St Stephen stoned and St Peter liberated, also by Morris & Co.
N transept window by Clayton & Bell, N chancel window by O'Connor, W window of nave by Kempe.

Michelmersh, St Mary
S window of chancel has 15th-century fragments: four delightful heads.

Mottisfont, St Andrew
E window of 15th-century glass:

Crucifixion with St Peter on the left and St Andrew on the right. Above are smaller figures of Coronation of the Virgin with saints; in these the original glass is better preserved. Angels in the small tracery lights, also in the side windows of the chancel.

North Stoneham, St Nicholas
Heraldic glass of 1826, fragmentary.

Odiham, All Saints
Two fine bold windows by Patrick Reyntiens, of 1968 (N chancel chapel) and 1969 (E window).

Penton Mewsey, Holy Trinity
15th-century fragments in S window of nave.

Portsmouth, St Cuthbert, Hayling Avenue, Copnor
E window with figure of Christ, by Osmund Caine, 1959.

Portsmouth, St Jude, Southsea
Colourful E window of 1874; who was the artist? Other chancel windows and W window of nave are by Wailes.

Rowner, St Mary
Annunciation window by Hugh Easton, 1950, in E window of S chapel.

Rownhams, St John the Evangelist
The church contains 52 medallions of Flemish glass, but it is not known how they came there.

Selborne, St Mary
Window commemorating Gilbert White, with St Francis and 82 species of birds, by Hinckes, of G. Gascoyne & Son of Nottingham (1920).

Sherborne St John, St Andrew
E window of N aisle has early 16th-century Netherlandish and 17th-century glass (one panel dated 1638 – bottom central panel with St Laurence). Rather a hotchpotch but generally pleasing.

Southampton, Ascension, Cobden Avenue, Bitterne Park
A.K. Nicholson windows in aisle, executed between the wars: designed in collaboration with Eric Milner-White, later Dean of York.

The Vyne, chapel
Very good stained glass probably done in 1521 by ten Netherlandish glaziers in Basingstoke – an account kept by one of them, David Joris, says they were working when the Emperor Charles V was in London, either May 1520 or June 1522. The windows are an interesting combination of the secular with the religious: in centre E window, Henry VIII with his patron saint Henry II of Bavaria, and above, the Crucifixion and the royal coat of arms; to the left of this, Queen Margaret of Scotland with her patron saint St Margaret, and above, the Resurrection; on Henry VIII's right, Queen Catherine of Aragon with her patron saint St Catherine, and above, Christ carrying the Cross.
Reputedly hidden from the Cromwellian soldiers by being put in the lake, it is the finest glass of its date in southern England.

Winchester, Cathedral (St Swithun)
NE chapel has fragments of medieval glass, as has the great W window.
Chancel has 15th- and 16th-century glass in side windows, and early 16th-century

glass in tracery of N chancel aisle, also some in S chancel aisle.

N windows of nave have fragments of 15th-century glass.

W aisle of N transept has Morris & Co. windows of 1909. There is 19th-century glass by David Evans and by Kempe. Early 16th-century panel in library.

Winchester, St Cross
Late 15th-century E window with Virgin, St John, St Catherine, St Swithun. In E window of N transept, 15th-century St Gregory.

Winchester, St Matthew, Stockbridge Road, Weeke
15th-century fragments in E window, also later roundels.

Winchester, Wessex Hotel
Internal screen of foliate heads, designed by John Piper, 1964.

Winchester, Winchester College Chapel
E window is Betton & Evans copy (1822–3) of medieval Jesse tree of 1393 – fragments of the original that have been recovered are in Thurbern's Chantry.
Thurbern's Chantry: Thomas of Oxford's 14th-century glass is in the W window. Also glass of *c.* 1502.
Fromond Chantry Chapel: more glass of *c.* 1502.

Wymering (near Portsmouth), St Peter and St Paul
Good early Clayton & Bell glass of *c.* 1861, including delightful St Christopher window in N aisle (based on a wall-painting formerly in the church).

Yateley, St Peter
W window designed by Holiday for Powell & Sons, 1885.

Hereford and Worcester

Abbey Dore, St Mary (Dore Abbey)
Fragments of medieval, 16th- and 17th-century glass in S chapel and ambulatory. In the three lancets of the E wall, 17th-century glass of the Ascension, eleven apostles, and cherubs.

Abbots Morton, St Peter
15th- and 18th-century glass in N window of N transept. Flemish medallions in E window, 16th century.

Alfrick, St Mary Magdalene
Panels of Netherlandish glass, 16th and 17th century.

Allensmore, St Andrew
14th-century glass, Crucifixion and angels in tracery of E window.

Birtsmorton, St Peter and St Paul
Fragmentary glass of 14th and 15th century, including Baptism of St Christopher (unique subject).

Bredon, St Giles
Two 14th-century figures of female saints in N chancel window: St Mary of Egypt and St Mary Magdalene.

Bricklehampton, St Michael
W window by Kempe, also side windows in chancel.

Bridge Sollers, St Andrew
Good E window by Powell & Sons, 1871.

Brinsop, St George

14th-century glass in E window, including panel of St George. In NW window of N aisle, tiny seated Christ. Two windows commemorating female relatives of William Wordsworth.

Brockhampton-by-Ross, All Saints

E window of saints and angels by Christopher Whall. The W and S transept windows also by him, but later.

Burghill, St Mary

Small window in baptistery by John Petts of Abergavenny in memory of Blake family (1988).

St George; fourteenth-century panel from Brinsop, Hereford & Worcester

Chaddesley Corbett, St Cassian

Good window by A.J. Davis of the Bromsgrove Guild, 1920s.

Credenhill, St Mary

In a S chancel window, figures of St Thomas à Becket and St Thomas of Cantelupe of Hereford, c. 1330.

Dilwyn, St Mary

Early 14th-century glass, two censing angels, in S window of chancel – rather restored.

Eaton Bishop, St Michael

Remarkably lovely 14th-century glass – the date is c. 1330.

In E window: kneeling donors below, and above are three saints (one is St Michael), and delightful swaying Virgin with the Child chucking her under the chin (colour plate 13 and p. 42). In the central panel above, a Crucifixion.

In SE window, more 14th-century glass: angel, Crucifix, Christ in Majesty. Also some in head of NE window.

The colour is predominantly green, yellow and brown, with a sparing but effective use of red.

Evesham, All Saints

14th-century seated Christ in N window.

Fladbury, St John the Baptist

14th-century panel of Virgin and Child at E end of S aisle (Lady Chapel), set in a wooden cross over the altar and lit by electric light (switch by second pew, in S wall). The panel was in the vestry until 1968, then in the Louvre, then in the V & A Museum. The Virgin is crowned, her face very formalized; she is set under a canopy against a ground mainly olive

St Michael weighing souls, 1328. Eaton Bishop, Hereford and Worcester

green (colour plate 14). N window has 15th-century heraldic glass, including the shield of Simon de Montfort – probably brought from Evesham Abbey at the time of the Dissolution of the Monasteries.

Foy, St Mary
Window of 1675 – cf. E window of St Tysilio, Sellack, Hereford and Worcester which it much resembles.

Goodrich, St Giles
15th-century glass in E window of N aisle – angels holding shields.

Great Malvern, Malvern Priory
Extremely important 15th-century glass, dating from c. 1440 to c. 1506:
E window: of c. 1440. Lowest tier shows the donors, Besford, Harewell, Lygon, Lyttelton. Above these are scenes from the Passion, with the Nailing to the Cross and the Crucifixion in the centre. The twelve apostles and an Annunciation and Coronation of the Virgin in the tracery.
S chancel aisle: stories from the Old Testament, from Genesis to the Worship of the Golden Calf (colour plate 28).
N chancel aisle: rather fragmentary, it includes the Four Doctors of the Church, parts of a Seven Sacraments window, and fragments of Baptism of Christ, St Nicholas and the Sailors, Mass of St Giles.
N chancel clerestory: the first two windows from the E illustrate the Story of the Virgin. Then the Founder's window: the Legend of St Werstan – the saint kneels below a vision of the consecration of his chapel (1460–70).
S chancel clerestory: mainly saints and angels.
N window of transept: the Joys of Mary, with saints and angels; below are the donors, Henry VII with Elizabeth of York, Arthur Prince of Wales and Sir Reginald Bray (the window given by Henry VII in 1501 or 1502).
W window of transept: Last Supper, also St Paul, St John the Evangelist and St John the Baptist.
N aisle: one window contains Annunciation, Visitation, Nativity, Presentation, Temptation, Pool of Bethesda, various miracles of healing, Marriage of St Anne, Annunciation to St Anne.
W window: bishops, saints, St Anne and the Virgin.

Great Witley, St Michael and All Angels
The glass was made by Joshua Price in 1719–21, to designs by Francesco Sleter or Slater, a Venetian painter who was working for the Duke of Chandos at Canons. It is painted in enamels and was commissioned by the Foley family of Stourbridge.
Starting from the window to the right of the organ, the glass depicts: the Worship of the Golden Calf, the Visitation, the Adoration of the Magi, Baptism of Christ, St Peter Healing the Sick, the Ascension, the Miraculous Draught of Fishes, the Adoration of the Shepherds, the Annunciation, the Supper at Emmaus.

Hampton (near Evesham), St Andrew
New window by Ray Bradley.

Hampton Lovett, St Mary
Heraldic glass of 1561 in N window of nave.

Hanley Castle, St Mary
Highly dramatic Last Judgement W window by Clayton & Bell, 1860.

Hanley Swan, St Gabriel
Modern window by Tom Denny.

Hentland, St Dubricius
In E window three 15th-century figures.

Hereford, Cathedral
Late 13th-century glass in Lady Chapel, W bay on S side, including Christ in Majesty – of very fine quality.
Early 14th-century glass in SE window of NE transept, in S chancel aisle, and fragments in S aisle of nave.
Also 19th-century glass by Warrington, Heaton, Butler & Bayne, Pugin and Hardman, Burlison & Grylls, Wailes, Kempe, and Clayton & Bell (Hunt memorial window).

Hereford, St Martin
Window of the Good Shepherd in N wall of nave, by Hobbs of Hereford, 1992.

Himbleton, St Mary Magdalene
13th-century female figure (St Mary Magdalene) in E window. 15th-century saint in NE window of aisle. In E window of Shell Chapel, St Mary and St John of c. 1400. Some good donor figures.

Hoarwithy, St Catherine
Good 19th century glass, the artists not known.

Holt, St Martin
15th-century Annunciation, fragmentary, in S chapel.

Huddington, St James
In E window, an early 16th-century Crucifixion with Virgin and St John – rather restored.

Inkberrow, St Peter
Late 15th-century saints and angels in E window of N chapel (St Catherine and St Margaret).

Kempsey, St Mary
In side windows of chancel, eight figures dating from the 14th century. High quality; specially fine are St Catherine, St Margaret with dragon, and a bishop who may be Thomas à Becket.

Kentchurch, Kentchurch Court
In the chapel, Swiss glass dated 1521.

King's Caple, St John the Baptist
Some 15th-century fragments in N chapel.

Kingsland, St Michael
14th-century glass in chancel windows, including Coronation of the Virgin, Christ in Glory, Tobias and the Angel, and saints.

Kington, St James
Two recent windows by John Petts.

Ledbury, St Michael
Some 15th-century glass in E window, which is otherwise by Kempe. Medieval glass also in W window of N chapel, including two 13th-century panels. Heraldic glass of c. 1500 in NE window of this chapel.
In N aisle, copies of the Reynolds windows for New College, Oxford, c. 1820.
Large Benedicite window in N wall of nave, by John K. Clark of Glasgow, 1991.
Three lancets, flame-like in design.

Leominster, Priory of St Peter and St Paul

Some glass by Kempe. In the Lady Chapel, window of 1948 begun by Martin Travers and finished by Laurence Lee.

Little Malvern, St Giles

15th-century glass in E window (kneeling figures) and in one N window of chancel (God the Father).

Llanwarne, St John the Baptist

16th- and 17th-century Flemish roundels in two windows of nave.

Madley, Nativity of the Virgin

Very fine medieval stained glass. 13th-century roundels and early 14th-century Jesse tree figures in the E window, also fragments of medieval glass in the SE and NE windows. 13th-century roundels include an Adoration of the Magi, the Presentation, the Last Supper, the Death of St John.

Mamble, St John the Baptist

Early 14th-century Crucifixion panel in E window: a drooping figure set against a red lattice and blue diamonds.

Moccas, St Michael

Early 14th-century glass with pairs of figures under canopies.

Much Marcle, St Bartholomew

A good deal of Kempe glass, 1870s and 1880s.

Oddingley, St James

Glass of *c.* 1500 in E window (showing St Martin, St Catherine and donors), also in N window of chancel. Fine impressive figures.

The Prophet Hosea, from a fourteenth-century Jesse tree. Madley, Hereford and Worcester

Pembridge, Pembridge Castle

17th-century armorial glass.

Preston

Remarkable early medieval Crucifixion panel in this remote and tiny church.

Queenhill, St Nicholas

Good 14th-century glass in N window of nave, including shield with arms of England, and St Anne teaching the Virgin to read.

Ribbesford, St Leonard

W window by Morris & Co., designed by Burne-Jones, 1875.

15th-century St George in W window of S aisle.

Richard's Castle, St Bartholomew
14th-century glass in E window of transept, also in S chancel and S aisle.

Ross-on-Wye, St Mary
Four 15th-century figures in E window, originally from the bishop's house in Stretton Sugwas.

St Weonards, St Weonard
E window of N aisle has some 15th-century glass – the rest is by Baillie & Mayer, 1875. 16th-century German panel in a S window in nave.

Sarnesfield, St Mary
E window of S transept has four small 14th-century figures, also 15th-century fragments.

Sedgley, All Saints
St Hubert & Madonna window in N aisle by Rosemary Rutherford, 1971.

Sellack, St Tysilio
E window of 1630, but contains 15th- and 16th-century fragments.

Severn Stoke, St Denys
Fragments of *c.* 1300 glass in S transept.

Shobdon, St John the Evangelist
18th-century armorial glass (1753).

Tarrington, St Philip and St James
Fragments of 14th- and 15th-century glass in S window of chancel.

Thruxton, St Bartholomew
Small Crucifixion, early 14th century, in tracery of S window of chancel.

Ullingswick, church
15th-century Virgin and Child in E window.

Upton Warren, St Michael
E window by Taylor & O'Connor, 1880, described by Pevsner as 'uncommonly horrible'.

Warndon, St Nicholas
Early 14th-century Virgin in E window, with St Peter and St Paul below, looking up. Fragments of 15th-century glass in N and S windows, including St Andrew, also 14th-century Annunciation. The glass has been lovingly restored.

Weobley, St Peter and St Paul
15th-century seraphim in tracery of N window.

West Malvern, St James
19th-century glass by Hardman and Wailes.

Weston-under-Penyard, St Lawrence
Window of St Francis of Assisi in N wall of nave, by Hobbs of Hereford, 1984.

Wigmore, St James
Glass by Evans of Shrewsbury, 1849.

Wilden, All Saints
William Morris glass in all the windows, *c.* 1900–14 – after Morris's death, but using earlier cartoons by Burne-Jones. The church was built at the expense of Alfred Baldwin – his sister-in-law was Lady Burne-Jones.

Wolverley, St John the Baptist

Two windows by Morris & Co., 1889, in S wall of chancel.

Worcester, Cathedral
Mainly 19th-century glass, much of it by Hardman. Elgar window in N aisle of nave.
Kneeling figure in tabard of royal arms in S choir aisle is probably Prince Arthur; is this late 15th–early 16th century, or a 19th-century copy of glass from Malvern Priory? Fragments of medieval glass border it.

Worcester, All Saints
Some 15th-century fragments in W window and in W window of N aisle.

Wormbridge, St Peter
Medieval fragments in N and S chancel windows, including small 15th-century figures.

Yazor, St Mary
Good glass of 1866 in two lancets in chancel.

Hertfordshire

Abbots Langley, St Lawrence
15th-century half-figures of St Lawrence in N window of chancel.

Aldbury, St John the Baptist
Early 16th-century German glass in N window of nave, possibly from Ashridge (Crucifixion and Pietà) – canopies are English 15th century.

Aldenham, St John the Baptist
The stained glass is largely by Kempe; 1891–1900. Also Heaton, Butler & Bayne (N window of chancel).

Aldenham, School Chapel
William Morris glass in heads of windows, 1895–1903 (moved from the older chapel).

Anstey, St George
15th-century angel in tracery of N window in nave.

Ashwell, St Mary
Clerestory has 14th-century fragments.

Barkway, St Mary Magdalene
In E end of S aisle, four kings from a mid-14th-century Jesse tree – in the centre light. In the side lights, 15th–16th-century fragments, including St John and St Petronilla. 15th-century music-making angels in the tracery.

Barley, St Margaret
Some 14th-century glass in E and W windows of N aisle, and 15th-century fragments in a S aisle window.

Berkhamsted, St Peter
Late medieval glass in N windows of chancel. W windows by Heaton, Butler and Bayne, 1867–70.

Bourne End, St John
Early glass by Alfred Bell in apse (1854).

Bovingdon, St Laurence
Modern window of 1984, showing symbol of St Laurence and Cross of St Alban, by Alfred Fisher. E window of 1856 by Lavers.

Caldecote, St Mary Magdalene
15th-century glass in E window (roundel) and S window of nave (figure of Rector William Makesey).

Clothall, St Mary
Some 14th-century stained glass, and 15th-century quarries decorated with birds and flowers.

Cuffley, St Andrew
Modern glass of 1965 and 1975 designed by Alfred Fisher for the Whitefriars Studio, and made by the fused technique of overlapping layers of pot-metal; the theme of the fifteen aisle windows is 'The Earth is the Lord's and all that therein is', and the S window is a Tree of Life.

Furneux Pelham, St Mary
15th-century fragments in E window of N aisle, and very good Morris & Co. glass in the S chapel, designed by Morris and Burne-Jones (1867 and 1874).

Gorhambury House
Many fragments of glass in the entrance hall, mainly 17th century; some are designs from prints of *Continents and Elements* by Marcus Gheeraerdts the Elder (1580).

Hatfield, St Etheldreda
S transept window, rich in colour, is Morris & Co., designed by Burne-Jones, 1894. More 19th-century glass by Clayton & Bell and Burlison & Grylls.

Hatfield House, chapel
Twelve panels over the altar with typological themes; eleven of them are early 17th century, by Lewis Dolphin & Richard Butler of Southwark, the other is by Warrington of 1835.

Hemel Hempstead, St Mary
SW window of chancel by Clayton & Bell, 1859.

Hexton, St Faith
Modern E window, 1964, by Stammers.

High Cross, St John the Evangelist
Interesting W window by Selwyn Image, 1893.

Hunsdon, St Dunstan
15th-century glass, but fragmentary, in N and S windows of nave.

Kelshall, St Faith
E window of Faith, Hope and Charity by (?) Heaton, Butler & Bayne, 1868.

Kings Walden, St Mary
S aisle window *c.* 1869 by Morris; archangels Raphael, Michael and Gabriel.

Little Hadham, St Cecilia
Late 14th-century glass in N window of chancel and S window of nave.

Much Hadham, St Andrew
15th-century Virgin and saints high up in tracery of E window.

Northchurch, St Mary
Glass by Kempe, including E window of 1883.

Pirton, St Mary
Fragments of 14th-century glass in N window of nave.

Preston, St Mary
E window a Jesse tree by Christopher Whall, 1900.

Rickmansworth, St Mary
Morris & Co. E window, designed by Burne-Jones, 1896.

Royston, St John the Baptist
In a N window, 14th-century angels.

St Albans, Cathedral
Fragments of medieval glass in N transept (14th century) and N aisle of nave (early 15th century).
Modern rose window by Alan Younger.

St Albans, St Peter
Fragments of medieval glass, 14th century onwards, in the N windows.

St Paul's Walden, All Saints
Early 14th-century Virgin and Child in W window of tower (Virgin in green and brown, Child in red). E window by Hugh Easton, 1946.

South Mimms, St Giles (RC)
Kneeling figures of donors, not very high, set in plain quarry glass – possibly the local Frowyk family who were city merchants; 1526.

Tewin, St Peter
19th-century E window by Powell & Sons, 1874.

Ware, St Mary
Glass by Christopher Whall in the N aisle (1905) and in N transept (1910). In the S aisle, New Testament scenes by Shrigley & Hunt (1885); E and W windows by Wailes.

Waterford, St Michael
Very remarkable for its William Morris glass. E window a Nativity by Burne-Jones with angels by Morris. In S window of chancel, David and Miriam designed by Burne-Jones, Annunciation by Morris; N window of chancel also by Morris (St Michael) – all these date from 1872.

In S windows of nave, more glass designed by Burne-Jones (St Peter, 1876, Christ and angels *c.* 1896, Virgin with Christ, 1917). Figures in W window designed by Ford Madox Brown (St Philip) and Philip Webb (St John the Baptist). Also work by S. Image and Karl Parsons.

Wyddial, St Giles
Flemish 16th-century panels in two N windows.

Humberside

Barmston, All Saints
In tracery of a S window, medieval figures of a crowned Virgin and a headless man with a sword. E window by L.C. Evetts, 1965.

Barnoldby-le-Beck, St Helen
14th-century glass in E window of S aisle, Crucifixion, Virgin and St John.

Barton-upon-Humber, St Peter
In E window, two panels of early 14th-century glass, St James and St George.

Beverley, Minster
Fragments of medieval glass, 13th, 14th, and 15th century, in E window, largely relating to the life of St Martin. Most of the Minster's medieval glass was blown out in a gale in 1608; this is all that survives. The rest of the glass is mainly 19th century, by Hardman.

Boynton, St Andrew
18th-century glass by William Peckitt of York.

Bridlington, Priory
Stained glass mainly by Wailes (19th century).

GAZETTEER

Bubwith, All Saints
15th-century fragments, mainly in E window and two N windows.

Burton Agnes, St Martin
18th-century donors (Roger de Somerville and his wife) with heraldry.

Cottingham, St Mary
Much glass by Capronnier (19th century).

Croxton, St John
In a S window, 14th-century panel of the Crucifixion.

Harpham, St John of Beverley
18th-century glass by Peckitt in the St Quintin Chapel and S side of the nave.

Hayton, St Martin
16th-century Flemish glass in E window.

Hotham, St Oswald
Much glass by Douglas Strachan.

Hull, Holy Trinity
Two interesting windows designed by Walter Crane, 1897 and c. 1907.
17th century continental glass in vestry.

Leconfield, St Catherine
Some fragments of 14th- and 15th-century glass in chancel and N aisle, Virgin, angel and arms of Neville and Percy.

Lockington, St Mary
Panel of 14th-century fragments in E window.

North Cave, All Saints
Modern E window is by Strachan.

Owston Ferry, St Martin
Ward & Nixon window of 1836, with fig-ures of Christ, St Peter and St Paul under canopies. E window of S aisle is also by them, but later.

Redbourne, church
This used to house an enamelled window, late 18th century, based on John Martin's 'Opening of the Sixth Seal'; necessary to check if it has been put back again.

Roos, All Saints
In clerestory on S side of nave, fragments of medieval glass including angel from an Annunciation. Also 17th- or 18th-century heraldic glass.

Seaton Ross, St Edmund
E window by Stammers, 1953.

South Cave, All Saints
18th-century E window. The glass is probably continental.

South Dalton, St Mary
Good E window by Clayton Bell, Last Judgement (1861), W and S transept W windows also by them.

Welton, St Helen's
Six windows of William Morris glass: S transept and chancel windows of 1877. Nave W window designed by Burne-Jones, 1879. W window of S aisle also by Morris and Co. 1882, W window of N aisle 1896, SE of chancel 1898.

Isle of Wight

Bonchurch, St Lawrence
William Morris glass of 1873 in W wall, designed largely by Morris, but figure of Peter is by Burne-Jones, and those of Saints Luke and John are by Ford Madox Brown.

Gatcombe, St Olave
Chancel E window of the Passion, 1865–6, by William Morris & Co.

Newport, St Thomas
Fine E window by Henry Holland of Warwick, *c.* 1857.

St Helens, St Helen
Sermon on the Mount window of 1913 by Morris & Co.

Ventnor, Holy Trinity
Good quality Clayton & Bell E window of 1861.

Kent

Aldington, St Martin
Medieval fragments in two N windows.

Badlesmere, St Leonard
Two lights by Frederick Cole (Sower and St Francis), 1989.

Barham, St John the Baptist
Glass by Martin Travers, 1925.

Bekesbourne, St Peter
13th-century grisaille in NE lancet.

Bexley, St John
Window of sundial and globe by Nicola Kantorowicz (1991).

Bickley, St George
Window depicting the phoenix rising from the ashes, by Alisoun Howie (1990).

Bicknor, St James
E window of 1861 by Clayton & Bell.

Bidborough, St Lawrence

Much glass by Morris & Co., but late (1909–25); mainly from designs by Burne-Jones.

Bilsington, St Peter and St Paul
In heads of N nave windows Trinity and Virgin and Child, *c.* 1400.

Birchington, All Saints
Memorial window to D.G. Rossetti in S aisle, 1882.

Bishopsbourne, St Mary
Late 13th-century glass in side windows of chancel. Armorial glass of 1550 in S chapel. Grisaille by Ghysbrecht Eelkens, 1615.

Blean, St Cosmas and St Damian
E window by H. Holliday.

Bobbing, St Bartholomew
Early 14th-century borders in N chapel, vine and buttercup design.

Bonnington, St Rumwold
In N nave window, 14th- and 15th-century fragments.

Borough Green, Church of the Good Shepherd
Window of the Transfiguration by Patrick Reyntiens (1984).

Boughton Aluph, All Saints
Late 14th-century figures in E window, 14th-century fragments in N transept.

Brabourne, St Mary
Notable for the easternmost window of the N wall, which is entirely 12th-century glass in its original setting. The design is near-abstract and incorporates semi-

circles with white-petalled, yellow-centred flowers, and in the spaces between them, formalized flowers with four yellow petals and rose-pink centres. Restored in 1851.

In heads of three main lights in largest N window of nave, fragments of 15th-century glass.

Brasted, St Martin

Notable new glass here: E window by Laurence Lee showing the pilgrimage of mankind towards heaven (1992); S transept window by John Hayward relating to St Martin's time as a soldier (1992); Hayward also designed the E window of the parish room, its theme the church's connections (1992).

Bredgar, St John the Baptist

In E window of N aisle, 14th-century and 15th-century fragments including Man of Sorrows.

Broadstairs, St Peter

Good glass of *c.* 1869 in N aisle and elsewhere by Heaton, Butler and Bayne.

Brookland, St Augustine

Good 14th-century canopies in N aisle.

Canterbury, Cathedral

As Chartres is to France, so Canterbury is to England. No detailed analysis of Canterbury's superb medieval glass can be accommodated here; for a small handy guide, see either *The Stained Glass Windows of Canterbury Cathedral* by Bernard Rackham, published by SPCK, 1957, or *The Stained Glass of Canterbury Cathedral* by Revd D. Ingram Hill, MA, published by the Friends of Canterbury Cathedral – this is slightly more up to

date. The definitive study on the subject is *Early Stained Glass of Canterbury Cathedral* by M.H. Caviness – a volume of the *Corpus Vitrearum Medii Aevi.*

Very briefly, Canterbury Cathedral's glass includes the following:

N aisle of choir: two 'Poor Man's Bible' or typological windows, 13th century (colour plates 9 and 10 and p. 27).

N triforium of choir: windows of St Dunstan and St Alphege.

NS transept clerestory: windows of *c.* 1178 from an unrivalled genealogical series (more of this series is now in the SW transept and in the W window of the nave).

N wall: the great rose window is partly

Methuselah; late twelfth-century figure from a genealogical series in Canterbury Cathedral (SW transept)

original 12th-century glass, partly restored. The centre piece appears to be original glass, dating from 1178.

Clerestory of choir: the genealogical figures are mainly reproductions, although the armatures are original.

Trinity Chapel: in both N and S aisles, much glass of *c.* 1220 showing the miracles of St Thomas (colour plate 8). Eight out of twelve windows retain their 13th-century glass, all have their original armatures.

Corona or Becket's Crown: New Testament scenes from the Passion to Pentecost, with parallels from the Old Testament (colour plate 7 and p. 29). Part of a 12th-century Jesse tree, and a 19th-century reconstruction of this theme.

SE transept: glass by Ervin Bossanyi (1960), notably the 'Salvation' and 'Peace' windows (colour plate 48). The rose window is 19th century, but contains some 12th-century glass.

Water Tower: glass of 13th–16th century.

Chapel of Edward the Confessor: 15th-century glass (colour plate 23).

Crypt: some 13th–15th-century glass.

Library Passage: glass of 16th and 17th centuries.

SE transept clerestory: four genealogical figures (Neri, Rhesa, Judah, Phares).

S choir aisle triforium: windows with three medallions in each, largely 13th century.

S choir aisle: three windows of imported French 13th-century glass, installed in 1958 and 1962.

SW transept: S window has a tremendous collection of late 12th-century genealogical figures. They came from the choir clerestory and were arranged here in 1793. Also 15th-century heraldic and figurative glass and 13th-century fragments.

Nave: great W window contains late 14th-century heraldic glass together with figures of kings – eight survive from a series of probably twenty-one – and 12th-century genealogical figures, including the famous 'Adam Delving' (colour plate 4).

NW transept (Martyrdom): N or Royal window contains much original work of the 15th century, probably by William Neve, including portraits of Edward IV, his Queen, Elizabeth Woodville, their children, also heraldic glass. Insipid N window by Sir Ninian Comper.

Canterbury, St Dunstan
E window by Aikman. In Thomas More Chapel, E window by Laurence Lee, window by John Hayward next to it.

Canterbury, St Mildred
In S chapel, 15th-century figure of St Mildred.

Chartham, St Mary
A good deal of the late 14th-century glass, especially in the N and S windows – grisaille with coloured borders of growing naturalism, including clover, hop and passion-flower leaves.

Cheriton, St Martin
E window of N chapel has crucifixion in a quatrefoil.

Chevening, St Botolph
E window by Moira Forsyth, also glass by her in Chantry Chapel. New window by Keith and Judy Hill showing the youthful King David with harp.

Chilham, St Mary
15th-century glass in heads of N aisle windows – figures of saints and angels in tracery, canopies below.

GAZETTEER

Cobham, St Mary Magdalene
E window by Lavers & Barraud, also modern window by Brian Thomas.

Cowden, St Mary Magdalen
Modern glass; W window by Carl Edwards, W window in N aisle by Laurence Lee.

Cranbrook, St Dunstan
Early 16th-century window in N aisle, probably Flemish: figures of St George (central), knight (left), and saint (right) in rather misty coloured glass against grisaille. Three armorial bearings below, two more in tracery lights, surrounded by mosaic effect of softly coloured fragments.

Crundale, St Mary
Chancel E window includes roundel of Coronation of Virgin, restored, but of *c.* 1300.

Dartford, Holy Trinity
Window of St John the Evangelist designed by Derek Hicks and made by Keith and Judy Hill (1991).

Ditton, St Peter ad Vincula
14th-century glass in N window, including censing angels.

Doddington, The Beheading of St John the Baptist
Small 13th-century roundel in S lancet in E wall of chancel. Very dark and decayed, but just about discernible is a Flight into Egypt with the Virgin full-face in the centre, and St Joseph carrying the Child.
The rest of the glass was made in 1855, using the 13th-century panel as a basis.

Dover, St Mary
In S wall, window to commemorate the ferry *Herald of Free Enterprise*, by Frederick Cole (1989).

Downe, St Mary the Virgin
Evie Hone window of the Crucifixion, 1949.

East Malling, St James
Some 14th-century glass in tracery of N aisle windows, and Coronation of the Virgin in W window.

East Sutton, St Peter and St Paul
Fragments of 14th- and 15th-century glass in S chapel.

Eastchurch, All Saints
E window by G.H. Cook, 1872. In S aisle, window by Karl Parsons (memorial to victims of the first fatal flying accident), 1912.

Elham, St Mary
15th-century heraldic glass and two 16th-century Flemish windows.

Farningham, St Peter and St Paul
NE window of nave contains some medieval glass, put together in 1832 by Charles Winston (q.v.), the man who rediscovered the recipe for pot-metal. Winston's father was incumbent here. E window of nave also by Winston.

Faversham, St Catherine
13th-century grisaille roundel in NE chancel window. S chancel windows by Clayton & Bell, *c.* 1879.

Fawkham, St Mary
In S window of chancel, 14th-century fig-

ure of St Anne teaching the Virgin to read, and other medieval fragments.

Fordwich, St Mary
14th-century glass in quatrefoils on the S side, 15th-century glass in the two on the north.

Goodnestone (near Wingham), Holy Cross
14th-century St Michael and a bishop in N window, also 15th-century bishop.

Goudhurst, St Mary
15th-century fragments in W window of S aisle.

Graveney, All Saints
14th-century glass, symbols of St Luke and St Mark, in E window of N aisle.

Great Chart, St Mary
15th-century glass, though restored, in E window – including Bishop Goldwell between two kneeling figures. 15th-century glass also in a S window, and two 16th-century female heads.

Harbledown, Hospital of St Nicholas
At top of all chancel windows, 14th-century glass including censing angels and Canterbury Bells.

Hastingleigh, St Mary
13th-century grisaille glass in its original setting.

Hever, St Peter
E window of Bullen Chapel has new glass by John Hayward.

High Halden, St Mary
Medieval fragments in a chancel window,

and 15th-century angels in tracery of a S aisle window.

Hildenborough, St John
Morris & Co. glass in W windows of transept, 1876 and 1881.

Hoo, St Werburgh
15th-century fragments in W window of S aisle, and in chancel tracery.

Horsmonden, St Margaret
E window 1946 and W window 1948 by Rosemary Everett.

Ightham Mote, chapel
16th-century glass with large figures. There is also 16th-century glass in the Hall and in a gatehouse room.

Kemsing, St Mary
Fine medieval glass: 13th-century Virgin and Child in a S window of nave, and in a S window of chancel a 15th-century figure of St Anne. W window of N aisle by Douglas Strachan, 1935.
E and W windows by Comper, 1902.

Kennington, St Mary
In a N chancel window, roundels of 13th-century grisaille.
S chapel has some 15th-century fragments.

Kilndown, Christ Church
19th-century glass by Franz Eggert of Royal Munich Works.

Kingsnorth, St Michael and All Angels
Early 15th-century figure of St Michael, also 15th-century glass in heads of nave windows.

Lamberhurst, St Mary
Window of the Annunciation to the Shepherds, designed by John Piper and made by David Wasley (1984).

Langton Green, All Saints
Much Morris & Co., glass, by Morris, Burne-Jones and Ford Madox Brown. E window by Kempe, 1904.

Leigh, St Mary
14th-century Virgin in quatrefoil at top of N aisle window.

Lullingstone, St Botolph
In E window, early 16th-century glass – also in S window of nave (Martyrdom of St Erasmus). In chapel, heraldic glass, three early 14th-century figures, and three panels of 1563. Nave N windows by Peckitt of York, 1754.

Maidstone, All Saints
19th-century glass by Wailes, Powell & Sons, Capronnier, Lavers & Westlake, Clayton & Bell.

Marden, St Michael and All Angels
The three chancel windows by Patrick Reyntiens, designed by him as well, 1962 (given by William Day, churchwarden). E window of Christ in Majesty, very dramatic though harsh, with an effective use of reds; the design sharp and angular. The two side windows more abstract – again with wonderful glowing reds, a central spiny design and green eyes peering through the dark.

Meopham, St John the Baptist
In S aisle, 15th-century fragments including a bishop and St Catherine.

Mereworth, St Laurence
16th-, 17th- and 18th-century armorial glass in E window.

Mersham, St John the Baptist
Some late 14th-century glass in W window, apostles. Music-making angels in central band of tracery lights, sleeping soldiers from a Resurrection scene above. Two symbols of the evangelists.
15th-century glass in N window of chancel, with St George (alas, headless) and a very delightful dragon – done mainly in yellow stain. Above this, smaller figures of St Christopher and St Edmund. Rich E window of Lady Chapel has old borders in the tracery heads.

Monks Horton, St Peter
15th-century fragments in NW window, including half figure of St Mary Magdalene.

Nackington, St Mary
In N window of chancel, early 13th-century glass, including (NW) top of a Jesse tree – Virgin with David and Solomon – and (NE) Marriage at Cana, St Thomas à Becket.

Nettlestead, St Mary
Notable for its medieval glass. In N window of chancel, 15th-century figures of St Laurence and St Stephen, light and silvery with yellow stain predominating, also different shades of blue.
The nave originally had glass depicting the twelve apostles; the best surviving glass is in the middle window on N side; it dates from 1425–39. (The S windows were all blown out in a storm in 1763.) The nave also contains very clever reproductions of medieval glass by Curtis

East window of Christ in Majesty by Patrick Reyntiens, 1962. Marden, Kent

(1894 and 1911). Curtis was also mainly responsible for the E window, though there is medieval glass in the tracery.

The window opposite the S door was the Becket window, now mostly fragmentary, but shows Becket's return from exile in France, and pilgrims at the shrine (note Canterbury Cathedral in the tracery, top left).

Otford, St Bartholomew
Small imported 17th-century panels in E windows.

Otterden, church (near Charing)
Fine Wilhelmina Geddes window of St Joseph of Arimathea (1933), dominated by large figure of the saint.

Patrixbourne, St Mary
17th-century Swiss glass.

Penshurst, St John the Baptist
W window has heraldic glass of 1627. 'Becket' window by Laurence Lee, 1970.

Pluckley, St Nicholas
E window and N window by Francis Stephens and John Hayward, 1954.

Ramsgate, St Augustine (RC)
Hardman glass, mid-19th century.

Ramsgate, St Lawrence College Chapel
Large E window, mainly by Patrick Reyntiens (The Firmament); Risen Christ in tracery lights by John Piper, 1981. Rose window by Reyntiens.

Reculver, St Mary
In N aisle, lancet by Laurence Lee.

Rochester, Cathedral
19th-century glass, by Clayton & Bell in N transept, by Kempe in S transept and W window of N aisle.

Sandhurst, St Nicholas
In S aisle, E window, 15th-century St Michael weighing souls. In S window, St George, a priest and an abbess, also 15th century.

Selling, St Mary
Wonderful medieval glass: a whole E window of *c.* 1300. There are five lights with panels set in grisaille, swaying figures of saints between rudimentary trees (chestnuts), and heraldic shields below. The Virgin is in the centre panel. Very fine deep blues, and coloured borders with clover leaves (see p. 39).

Also a modern (*c.* 1970) Benedicite window, with peacocks, oast-houses, horses and hops – designed by Buss for Goddard & Gibbs.

Sevenoaks, St Nicholas
Extensive 19th-century glass by Dixon, Kempe, Tower, Heaton, Butler & Bayne, and Powell & Sons. E window looks more like 16th-century glass, although dated 1881.

Shadoxhurst, St Peter and St Paul
Fragments of 14th-century glass in N nave window and in W lancet.

Speldhurst, St Mary
William Morris glass, designed by Burne-Jones, in N aisle windows – St Gregory, St Augustine, St Ursula, St Nicholas (1873), and in S aisle, the Virgin and St Elizabeth (1874).

Staplehurst, All Saints
Fragments of medieval glass. A N window by Owen Jennings, 1952.

Stodmarsh, St Mary
In chancel, a window of 13th-century grisaille. Fragments of 15th-century canopies in the nave.

Stowting, St Mary
Delightful and lively early 14th-century Virgin and Child. Also 15th-century window of three saints under canopies, with donors below (*c.* 1460).

Sutton-at-Hone, St John the Baptist
In N and S windows, 17th-century continental glass.

Temple Ewell, St Peter and St Paul
Panels of 17th-century continental glass on chancel and N chapel.

Tonbridge, St Stephen
Morris & Co. glass of 1910–11: the Maries at the Sepulchre, Road to Emmaus, Resurrection, Agony in the Garden.

Tonbridge, Tonbridge School
Windows by Martin Travers and Hugh Easton.

Trottiscliffe, St Peter and St Paul
Window of the Virgin Mary, designed and made by Keith and Judy Hill (1990).

Tudeley, All Saints
A remote church notable for its very lovely glass designed by Marc Chagall – the only other glass by this artist in the country is in Chichester Cathedral. Here the glass is far more extensive.
The earliest and most important window is the E, a memorial to Sarah d'Avigdor-Goldsmid (a girl who was drowned), and dates from 1967. It is predominantly blue with flashes of yellow and red, the watery effect is enhanced by the lozenge-shaped pieces of glass – a very moving composition (colour plate 50).
Chagall designed the rest of the glazing scheme, now installed.

Tunbridge Wells, Convent of the Sacred Heart
Glass by J. Nuttgens and Paul Quail, also a glass appliqué by Keith New.

Tunbridge Wells, King Charles the Martyr
'Ruth' window by Laurence Lee in N aisle.

Upchurch, St Mary the Virgin
Medieval glass including roundel of censing angel in a N aisle window.

Upper Hardres, St Peter and St Paul
Early 14th-century E window, brought here in 1795 from Stelling Minnis. It consists of two lights with three figures under crocketed arches, the arms of Haut and Hardres, and borders of oak leaves. (There used to be three roundels of *c.* 1200 at the W end; these were destroyed recently by fire – a very sad loss.)

West Kingsdown, St Edmund
In quatrefoils of nave N window, a 14th-century Christ in Majesty and a crowned Virgin and Child. 14th-century fragments in a S window.

Westwell, St Mary
Central lancet of E wall of chancel has a Jesse tree, of which the upper half is 13th century, the lower half extremely

cunningly made out of pieces of ancient glass in 1960. Apparently all three lancets were filled with 13th-century glass until about a hundred years ago.

In N chapel, the tracery of the E and NE windows have late 14th-century glass, mainly grisaille but including in the NE window the arms of Richard II with Anne of Bohemia and Richard's patron saint, Edward the Confessor (left), and (right) the arms of Edward the Confessor and his wife Edith. E window contains a kneeling angel.

Wickhambreaux, St Andrew
14th-century glass in S aisle, E window of Art Nouveau glass.

Willesborough, St Mary
Early 14th-century glass in chancel windows, partly re-arranged.

Woodchurch, All Saints
In S aisle, 13th-century roundel of the Death of the Virgin, dark and decayed but still glowing. Above it, a small piece of 15th-century glass with a head of Christ. 16th- and 17th-century Flemish glass in N chapel.
E window by Kempe, 1895.

Woodnesborough, St Mary
Two windows by Frederick Cole: Creation (1980) and St Francis (1992).

Wormshill, St Giles
In tracery of E window, glass of *c.* 1400 with figure of Christ, Coronation of the Virgin and two kneeling angels (recently restored by the V & A).
Fragments in NE window of N aisle, including coat of arms of Northwood impaling Gatton (Hans de Gatton, Lord of

the Manor of Wormshill, d. 1299; one of his daughters married Simon de Northwood).

Lancashire

Accrington, St John
New window by Tom Denny (1992).

Aspull, St Elizabeth
Transfiguration window in S wall by Rosemary Rutherford, 1968.

Billington, Old St Leonard
Medieval fragments in SE window.

Blackburn, Cathedral
Large near-abstract window by John Hayward in S transept. Abstract glass also in E window of S chapel.

Blackburn, Queen Elizabeth's Grammar School
Window from Wilmar Lodge, by Morris & Co., 1903.

Blackburn, St Gabriel
Baptistery window by Brian Clarke, 1977.

Burnley, All Saints, Habergham
East window by Brian Clarke (1976), near-abstract, based on the concept of creation, brilliant colour.

Halsall, St Cuthbert
14th-century fragments in E window of S aisle.

Leyland, St Ambrose
Recent glass by Jane Gray.

Leyland, St Mary (RC)
Patrick Reyntiens glass of 1964–5

Appliqué glass designed by John Hayward, 1967, for the Lantern of Blackburn Cathedral, Lancashire

throughout the whole church, using *dalle-de-verre* technique.

Longridge, St Lawrence
Gallery windows of nave by Brian Clarke, 1975, near-abstract rectilinear forms, said to have been based on the landscape around the River Ribble.

Lytham, St Cuthbert's
Burne-Jones window of the Transfiguration in the S aisle, 1875.

Morecambe, St Barnabus
Large E window, recent, by S. Waugh.

Penwortham, St Mary
New glass by Jane Gray.

St Michael's on Wyre, St Michael
In north chapel are medieval fragments, including a 14th-century shield.

Tunstall, St John the Baptist
15th- and early 16th-century Netherlandish panels in E window. Modern memorial window by Jane Gray, 1979.

Turton Tower
Swiss 16th- and 17th-century enamel-painted panels in corridor.

Upholland, St Thomas
Medieval fragments in a S window.

Leicestershire

Appleby, St Michael, Appleby Magna
Early 14th-century glass, including figures, in heads of N windows.

Ashby-de-la-Zouch, St Helen
Many imported roundels (Flemish, Swiss, German).

Ayston, St Mary (formerly Rutland)
15th-century figures in E windows of S aisle.

Bagworth, parish church
14th-century glass in tracery lights, including Virgin & Child, the Three Magi, and the Flight into Egypt.

Beeby, All Saints
19th-century glass, by Warrington (1843).

Broughton Astley, St Mary
Good, although fragmentary, early 14th-century glass.

Burrough-on-the-Hill, St Mary
19th-century glass by O'Connor in E window, E window of S aisle and N window of chancel.

Clipsham, St Mary
Finely restored 15th-century bird quarries in N aisle behind organ. Also armorial glass of later date.

Cossington, All Saints
E window by Strachan, *c.* 1918 (*cf.* Winchelsea, Sussex).

Coston, St Andrew
14th-century stained glass (Crucifixion and the Virgin).

Frolesworth, St Nicholas
15th-century glass (figures) in chancel window.

Garthorpe, St Mary
Small roundels of 14th-century glass in W and E windows of N aisle.

Hallaton, St Michael
19th-century stained glass by Kempe.

Launde, Abbey
E window has mid-15th-century glass (three large figures). Small figures in tracery of S windows also 15th century.

Leicester, Cathedral (St Martin)
E window by Christopher Whall, 1920.

Leicester, museums
Jewry Wall Museum has 29 yellow-stained panels of 15th-century date. Newarke House has early 16th-century figures of saints.

Leicester, St Andrew, Aylestone
E window by Harry A. Payne, 1930.

Leicester, St Margaret, Church Gate
Glass of 1840s by Willement.

Little Casterton, All Saints
Glass by Christopher Whall in E window of chancel and W windows of tower.

Loughborough, All Saints
E window of S transept by Holiday, 1907. W window by Hughes & Ward, 1864.

Melton Mowbray, St Mary
Fragments of medieval glass in a S aisle window.

North Luffenham, St John the Baptist (formerly Rutland)
Three good 14th-century figures under canopies in a window in the N aisle.

Noseley, St Mary
Much 14th- and 15th-century glass, although fragmentary.

Peckleton, St Martin
Early 14th-century glass in S window of chancel, including figure of St Michael.

Preston, St Peter and St Paul
Nativity window by Rosemary Rutherford in S chancel, 1962.

Saxelby, St Peter
E window of S aisle by Rosemary Rutherford, 1959.

Sheepy, All Saints
Two S windows are by Morris & Co., designed by Burne-Jones (1879), the other two S windows by Kempe (1897).

Skeffington, St Thomas à Becket
Medieval glass in E window of N chapel.

Stockerston, St Peter
In N aisle some medieval glass, fragmentary but including whole figures.

Thornton, St Peter
Early 14th-century glass in E window of S aisle: Flight into Egypt, Virgin, two of the Magi.

Twycross, St James
Superlatively good very early French glass in E window. Centre light has Presentation in the Temple, of 1140–4, originally from St Denis on the outskirts of Paris (see p. 22). Below this are panels of the Deposition and the Spies Carrying the Grapes, mid-13th century, originally from the Ste Chapelle.
The left light has: the devil with stones to throw, a kneeling monk who may be the Abbot Suger (both 1140–4, from St Denis); below these, two panels of mid-13th century from Ste Chapelle. The right

Kneeling monk, possibly the Abbot Suger of St Denis, French glass, 1140–4. Twycross, Leicestershire

light has at the top St Benedict casting the devil out of a monk (from Chapel of St Benedict, St Denis), then a kneeling woman *c*. 1224 (from Le Mans), then Moses and below that, the Emperor Domitian (both from Ste Chapelle, 1243 8). The glass was bought in Paris ahead of the French Revolution, was in royal hands from George III to William IV; presented to this church, and installed in 1840 by Willement. Restored by York Glaziers' Trust 1983–4, with replica window fitted on outside.

Uppingham, St Peter and St Paul (formerly Rutland)
E window of N aisle by Peter White, 1955.

Whitwell, St Michael (formerly Rutland)
Early 14th-century Crucifix in SW window of chancel.

Wing, St Peter and St Paul
In S aisle, window by Roger Fifield, 1971.

Withcote, private chapel
Very good early 16th-century glass, probably by Galyon Hone, the King's Glazier: eighteen standing figures of prophets and apostles. Date is probably 1536–7.

Lincolnshire

Addlethorpe, St Nicholas
15th-century glass depicting saints in four tracery lights of N nave.

Alford, St Wilfrid
N window of chancel and N window of N chapel still have 14th-century glass.

Algarkirk, St Peter and St Paul
E window by Hardman. Elsewhere, glass by Clayton & Bell.

Belton, St Peter and St Paul
S window has 19th-century heraldic glass, probably installed in 1823.

Boothby Pagnell, St Andrew
15th-century fragments in the porch windows.

Boston, St Botolph
E window by O'Connor, 1853. Others by Kempe (1891) and Hardman (1883, 1876 and 1868).

Brant Broughton, St Helen
Most of the glass designed by Canon F.H. Sutton and made by Kempe. E window by Burlison & Grylls. All 19th century.

Carlton Scroop, St Nicholas

E window has two figures of donors in the tracery, late 13th century; these are still *in situ*, except that one has a misplaced head. The figure of Christ comes from another church.

Corby, St John the Evangelist
In the N aisle window a quatrefoil with figure possibly of St John; 15th century.

Gedney, St Mary Magdalen
In E window of N aisle, substantial remains of an early 14th-century Jesse tree – one whole figure and large parts of others. 14th-century glass also in N and S windows.

Grantham, St Wulfram
19th-century glass by Clayton & Bell, Wailes, Kempe, and Tower. Modern windows by John Hayward in N and S nave.

Heydour, St Michael
In two N aisle windows 14th-century figures of Saints George, Edmund, Edward, and Laurence with St Vincent and St Stephen (latter two are 15th century). Grotesque decorations below.

Holywell, St Wilfrid
The E window is a mosaic of 15th–19th-century fragments of English and imported glass.

Leadenham, St Swithin
Tracery of E window has early 16th-century Flemish glass, Christ and angels.

Lincoln, Cathedral
Very important for its early 13th-century glass, especially the 'Dean's Eye' rose window, which is still *in situ*. (For a full analysis, see the article on 'The Stained

Glass Decoration of Lincoln Cathedral in the Thirteenth Century' by M. Jean Lafond, published in the *Archaeological Journal*, Vol. CIII, 1947; also see p. 33 of this book.)

The Dean's Eye in the N transept has tracery of 'plate' design, and dates from *c.* 1210. It is 23 ft in diameter and contains about sixty Biblical scenes, including the carrying of the bier of St Hugh, who was Bishop of Lincoln 1186–1200, into the cathedral by two kings (King John and King William of Scotland) (colour plate 11 and pp. 32, 33).

Much of the medieval stained glass was destroyed by being shot at, first by the servants of Dean George FitzHugh in 1501, and then by the Earl of Manchester's soldiers in 1644. In 1788 the fragments seem to have been collected up and installed in the S transept and the E windows of the choir aisle. The rose window of the S transept, known as the Bishop's Eye, is a fascinating mosaic of these pieces.

Lincoln Cathedral also has a very representative collection of 19th-century glass – almost everyone except Morris is there – Clayton & Bell, Ward & Hughes, Holiday, Hardman, Wailes and so forth. For further details see Peter Binnall's pamphlet *The 19th Century Stained Glass in Lincoln Minster*, published by the Friends of Lincoln Cathedral, 1966. 20th-century glass by Stammers in N transept.

Long Sutton, St Mary
Fragments of medieval glass in N and S chancel aisles and in N aisle. Figure of St George in S chancel aisle.

Manthorpe, St John
W window by Willement, mid-19th century.

Market Deeping, St Guthlac
Glass by H. Hughes, 1880.

Morton, St Paul
Morris & Co. glass – the Stoning of St Stephen (1892), also the westernmost window of the S transept (1896).

Nettleham, All Saints
New E window by John Hayward (1971).

Pinchbeck, St Mary
14th-century fragments in E window of N aisle. In other N aisle windows, many small 15th-century figures in the tracery.

Ruskington, All Saints
E window of S aisle has very good Morris glass of *c.* 1873–4: three lights, three figures, ascending Christ and two angels – background of yellow flowers.

Sleaford, St Denys
Morris & Co. glass of 1900 in S aisle S window – four angels in white and pale green.

Stamford, Brown's Hospital, chapel
Good and extensive glass of 1475.

Stamford, St George
In S window of chancel, two figures of *c.* 1450. N window contains about 200 mottos of the founder members of the Order of the Garter, assembled by a glazier called Exton in 1732.

Stamford, St John the Baptist
Mid-15th-century glass in many tracery lights.

Stamford, St Martin
Extensive mid-15th-century glass

(arranged by William Peckitt), including E window with the Deity and four saints, angels and royal arms above. Notably in the S aisle, three scenes from the Old Testament paralleled with three from the New (tough-looking David beheading Goliath with a somewhat oriental sword).

Stamford, St Mary
E window of Lady Chapel is by Christopher Whall – early, *c.* 1890.

Tattershall, Holy Trinity
The glass in the E window is original, and dates from 1481–2. It includes various scenes and saints, e.g. a Baptism, Feeding the Hungry, Clothing the Needy, various virtues, St James, St Peter, St John the Evangelist, and music-making angels. The accounts reveal the names of several glaziers: John Glazier of Stamford, Robert Power of Burton-on-Trent, John Wymondeswalde of Peterborough, Richard Twygge and Thomas Wodshawe.

Tealby, All Saints
In chancel side windows, fragments of 14th-century glass.

Thorpe Tilney, garden pavilion
Four amazing windows of Life of St Paul, John Piper 1977.

Wrangle, St Mary and St Nicholas
Much glass of 1350–70 is preserved in the N and NE windows: whole small figures and an almost complete Resurrection scene.

Greater London

Addington, St Mary
Kempe windows in S aisle, 1891 and 1898.

Battersea, Ascension, Lavender Hill
Late 19th-century glass by Kempe and W.E. Tower.

Battersea, St Mary (parish church)
Glass of E window dated almost certainly 1631, attributed to Bernard van Linge. It was commissioned by Sir John St John who became Lord of the Manor in 1630; he also had estates at Lydiard Tregoze and Purley. The glass contains royal portraits of Henry VII, Margaret Beauchamp and Elizabeth I. Restored by John Hayward in *c.* 1974 (see article in *Journal of the British Society of Master Glass Painters*, Vol. XV, no. 3, 1974–5). By him, four nave windows depicting local worthies.

Beckenham, St George
Glass by Thomas Freeth, 1963–6.

Bexleyheath, The Red House
Figures by Morris in lower corridor, also quarries with designs of birds and bushes by Burne-Jones.

Bickley, Trinity Church (Presbyterian)
Stained glass by M.C. Farrar-Bell, 1958–67.

Blackheath, Morden College Chapel
E window of *c.* 1600, rich in colour; it appears interesting, but it is impossible to see much of it since it is obscured by the reredos.

Bromley, St Mary, Downe
Crucifixion window by Evie Hone.

Camberwell, St Giles
Late 13th-century glass, possibly German, and a late 19th-century E window

designed by Edmund Oldfield and made by Ward & Nixon of Frith Street. For Ruskin's opinion of this, see p. 84. The left lancet of the E window (Old Testament themes) unique in being designed by Ruskin himself.

Camden, Christ Church, Albany Street
Notable for Victorian glass: extensive and fine work by Clayton & Bell (1867–1908), and three small windows of the Sermon on the Mount in S aisle designed by D.G. Rossetti for Morris & Co., *c.* 1870.

Camden, St Luke, Caversham Road, Kentish Town
Glass in apse is designed by H. Holiday and made by Heaton, Butler, and Bayne. Morris glass of *c.* 1910 in clerestory.

Carshalton, All Saints
Kempe glass of 1895 and 1900 in Lady Chapel.

Charing Cross Hospital, Chapel
Fine Tree of Life and River of Life windows, John Piper, 1977.

Chelsea, Holy Trinity, Sloane Street
An enormous E window of 1894–5, filled with William Morris glass.
There are 48 single-figure panels: the top row are apostles, the next Old Testament figures, and the bottom two rows mainly saints. They are set against a green foliage background. In the tracery, panels of Adam and Eve, the Crucifixion, Annunciation, angels etc., with palm-tree-like effect of green foliage.

Chelsfield, St Martin of Tours
E window of Moira Forsyth, 1948.

Chipping Barnet, St John the Baptist
Henry Holiday glass, 1887–9, in N and S windows of aisles.

Croydon, Archbishop's Palace
E window by Clayton & Bell.

Croydon, St Matthew
Modern glass by John Hayward in six windows on S side.

Deptford, St Paul
Mid-18th-century figure of a saint in NW window.

Edmonton, St Edmund
Near-abstract sanctuary window by Mark Angus, based on the theme of the Easter Candle, 1982; by the same artist, chancel window on the theme of baptism.

Enfield, Christ Church, Southgate
Good glass by Morris & Co. of 1862, designed by Burne-Jones, Ford Madox Brown, Rossetti, and Morris himself.

Finsbury, St James
E window of the Ascension by Heaton & Butler, 1863.

Greenford (near Ealing), Holy Cross
Glass, mainly heraldic, of *c.* 1500, said to have come from King's College, Cambridge: arms of Henry VIII and Catherine of Aragon in E window.

Greenwich (Charlton), St Luke, Charlton Village
Some 17th-century glass in the E window (1639), and 17th-century heraldic in a N window.

Greenwich, Trinity Hospital, chapel

Early 16th-century Flemish E window, with Agony in the Garden, Crucifixion and Ascension.

Hackney, Church of the Good Shepherd
Interesting late 19th-century glass by Walter Crane and Sylvester Sparrow.

Hammersmith, Charing Cross Hospital, chapel
Two John Piper/Patrick Reyntiens windows, also glass of 1976 by Alfred Fisher.

Hampstead, Opus Dei Hostel
Modern slab glass by David Atkins.

Hampstead, St Mary, King Henry's Road
W window by Kempe, 1896, also small window by Comper.

Hampton Court (formerly Middlesex), Hampton Court Palace
In the Great Hall, stained glass by Willement, mid-19th century, replacing the original glass by Henry VIII's glazier, Galyon Hone (see Earsdon, Tyne & Wear). The glass is mainly heraldic, it includes figures of Henry VIII and the arms of all six queens and of Wolsey (as it would never have done in Henry VIII's time). It is a pity that the original glass is no longer there, but Willement's is cheerful, well thought out, and not at all bad for its time. Glass by Willement also in the Great Watching Chamber, 1846; restored in 1979.

Haringey, St Michael
Fine E window by Evie Hone.

Harrow-on-the-Hill, Harrow School chapel

19th-century glass by Wailes (in chancel), Hardman, Clayton & Bell etc.

Harrow Weald, All Saints
S aisle windows of Faith, Hope and Charity are by Morris & Co., 1883.

Havering, St Mary, North Ockendon
Early 14th-century female saint in N chapel, and 15th-century glass in W window of the tower.

Hillingdon, Hillingdon Hospital, chapel (interdenominational)
Glazing scheme of 26 windows by Jane Gray, symbolic forms, 1965.

Hillingdon, Uxbridge, Underground Station
Unexpectedly, glass by the Hungarian artist Ervin Bossanyi (his most important work is in Canterbury Cathedral), heraldic.

Holborn, Lincoln's Inn Chapel
S windows by Bernard van Linge, 1623; they depict the Apostles. Considerably restored.

Holborn, St Pancras, Woburn Place
Clayton & Bell glass, 1860–6 and 1881–2.

Holborn, Temple Church
E windows of chancel by Carl Edwards, 1957–8, three windows of three lights each. The overall effect is of brilliant mosaic: small pieces of glass, predominantly blue, including panels showing London burning at the time of the Blitz, and the Temple Church itself. The central window was presented by the Glaziers' Company and includes their coat of arms.

Christ as Judge is shown in the top of the centre light; also included, two knights on one horse, an early symbol of the Templars. In the window to the N, the Lamb and Flag device of the Inner Temple, and figures of Henry I and Stephen. In the window to the S, Pegasus the device of the Middle Temple, and figures of Henry II and Henry III.

In S aisle, what is left of Willement's E window of 1842 (six diamond medallions).

Glass in the Round Church is Victorian, with good strong cobalt blues.

Hounslow, St Mary, Norwood Green

Panels and fragments of late 16th- and early 17th-century glass.

Islington, Emmanuel Church

Modern window by Mark Angus.

Kensington, St Barnabus, Addison Road

Glass at the W end is by O'Connor, 1852; at the E end, possibly by Morris & Co. (?), 1895.

Kensington, St Cuthbert, Philbeach Gardens

Glass mainly by W. Bainbridge Reynolds, also some by Kempe. Late 19th century.

Kensington, St Mary Abbots (parish church)

Late 19th-century glass by Clayton & Bell. Rose E window by Powell & Sons.

Kensington, St Philip, Earl's Court Road

Has some Flemish glass, 16th century.

Kensington, Victoria and Albert Museum

A great collection of glass in the galleries, also Burne-Jones glass in the *Morris Room.* Designed by Burne-Jones in collaboration with William Morris. Six panels representing the months, linked with frieze panels. (Scheme of room by Morris and Webb.)

Gamble Room: stained glass by Powell & Sons, restored by June Lennox, 1977. Mainly gold on white, with arabesques and culinary quotations.

Dutch Kitchen: glass designed by Poynter, made by Crace and Co., *c.* 1874 (Fox and Cow fable of La Fontaine).

Cole Staircase: now has Bossanyi panel of Virgin, Child, and two doves, 1946. Above this is Christ Blessing, 1953, Bossanyi.

Kingston-upon-Thames, All Saints

W window by Lavers & Barraud, *c.* 1865.

Lambeth, St Mary

Modern glass by Laurence Lee and Francis Stephens.

Lewisham, St George, Perry Hill

W rose window by Henry Holiday, *c.* 1900.

Lewisham, St Mildred, Lee

Glass of 1950s by Wilhelmina Geddes, and by Frederick Cole.

Marylebone, All Saints, Margaret Street

19th-century glass by O'Connor and Alfred Gérente.

Marylebone, St Peter's, Vere Street

E window 1881 by Morris and Co. S aisle

window of Christ's entry into Jerusalem, 1884 by Morris & Co.

Morden, St Laurence
Some 17th-century glass in the E window, also glass of 1828.

Orpington, Grammar School, chapel
Windows by Susan Ashworth, 1966–7, 'Earth', 'Air', 'Gold'.

Paddington, Christ Church, Lancaster Gate
Glass by Wailes (1856) and Powell & Sons (1892).

Paddington, St Mary Magdalene, Woodchester Street
Glass by Holiday in chancel and at west end, some glass in crypt by Comper.

Peckham, St John's
Creation window by Susan Ashworth.

Richmond, Strawberry Hill (St Mary's College)
Netherlandish roundels, 16th–18th century, from Horace Walpole's collection of early glass, set by William Peckitt in the 18th century. Richly coloured window by the Irish artist, Harry Clarke, in the little chapel in the wood.

St Pancras, Christ Church, Albany Street
Window of the Sermon on the Mount, by Rossetti, 1867.

St Pancras, St Mary Magdalene, Munster Square
Glass by Hardman, Clayton & Bell, Heaton, Butler & Bayne, Lavers & Barraud.

Southwark, Southwark Cathedral
16th-century arms are the only early glass. W window of the Creation is by Henry Holiday, 1893; E window by Ninian Comper. Modern glass by Laurence Lee in S choir. Shakespeare window in S aisle by Christopher Webb, 1954.

Stepney, St Anne
E window of Crucifixion, by Clutterbuck, 1853.

Streatham, Christ Church, Christchurch Road
Glass designed by Walter Crane, 1891, in NE and SE aisle windows. Also modern glass by John Hayward and Laurence Lee.

Twickenham, St Margaret
E and baptistery windows by Patrick Reyntiens (1969), of fine, bold design.

Twickenham, St Mary's College, Strawberry Hill
See **Richmond**.

Wandsworth, All Saints, Putney
Morris & Co. glass in many windows, largely designed by Burne-Jones.

Wandsworth, Church of the Ascension, Lavender Hill
Fine quality glass by Kempe.

Wandsworth, Our Lady of Victories (RC), Clapham Park Road
Glass by Pugin of 1850–3.

West Wickham, St John the Baptist
E window late 15th century, with St Christopher, St Anne teaching the Virgin to read, kneeling skeleton and arms of

donor (Heydon). Late 15th–early 16th-century glass also in N chapel, and N side of church.

Westminster, Abbey

Abbot Islip's Chapel & Chapel of St Benedict: glass by Hugh Easton, 1948.

S transept rose window and lancets below: by Burlison & Grylls, designed by Bodley, 1902.

Muniment Room: mid-13th-century roundel of the Resurrection (formerly in the Jerusalem Chamber, and of equal quality with the glass there).

N rose window: by Joshua Price, 1722, to designs by Sir James Thornhill.

W aisle: Bunyan window by Comper, 1915. HMS *Captain* window by Clayton & Bell, 1870.

N aisle: Seven windows by Sir Ninian Comper, 1907–26. Trevithick window by Burlison & Grylls, 1883. Sir Henry Royce window by Comper, 1962.

Under NW tower: window made up of medieval fragments of *c.* 1400.

W window: by Joshua Price, 1735.

S wall, S aisle: glass by Burlison & Grylls, 1922. glass designed by Norman Shaw and Henry Holiday, and made by Heaton, Butler & Bayne, 1869. Glass by J.D. Forsyth, 1921.

Jerusalem chamber: without a doubt the best glass in Westminster. Six medallions of superb mid-13th-century glass, showing the Ascension, the Descent of the Holy Spirit, the Martyrdom of St John the Baptist, the Stoning of St Stephen, the Massacre of the Innocents and the Miracle of St Nicholas. (Maybe by William le Verrer, who was mentioned in a charter of 1272.)

Westminster, All Saints, Margaret Street

15th-century figures of St John, Christ with a chalice, angel and Lion of St Mark in W window of S aisle. 19th-century glass by Gérente, Gibbs and O'Connor.

Westminster, Immaculate Conception (RC), Farm Street

E window, and window in the Lourdes Chapel, by Evie Hone, 1953.

Westminster, St George, Hanover Square

E window of Jesse tree, of mid-16th-century glass from Antwerp (attributed to Arnold van Nijmegen), adapted by Willement.

Westminster, St Margaret, Parliament Square

The E window of *c.* 1502 was part of the dowry of Catherine of Aragon when she was married to Prince Arthur, and contains portraits of them both. It was intended for the Henry VII Chapel in the Abbey, and has been in its present position since 1758. The subject is the Crucifixion; it is verging on the Renaissance in style, and predominantly blue in colour.

In the S aisle is glass designed by Piper and made by Reyntiens, an abstract design mainly in grey, rather chilly in effect.

Westminster, St Mark, North Audley Street

E window by N.H.J. Eastlake. A cartoon by Burne-Jones, of St Mark, on Ponsonby Memorial.

Westminster, St Michael, Chester Square

Two S windows by Morris & Co., 1882,

on either side of the Queen's Door: one of Faith and Hope, largely cobalt blue and gold (for George Berkeley Maxwell, d. 1882, and his wife), the other of Charity, against an olive green leafy ground (for Fanny Dick, d. 1882).

W window by Hugh Easton, 1951: the Agony in the Garden shown within the Crown of Thorns, set in white quarries – not wholly successful.

Westminster, St Paul, Wilton Place
Late 19th-century glass designed by Bodley for Lavers & Westlake, and mid-19th-century glass by Wailes.

Westminster, St Stephen, Rochester Row, Vincent Square
Glass by Wailes (1850), and by Burne-Jones for Morris & Co. (1890).

Wimbledon, St Mary, Arthur Road
Late 14th-century panel of a knight (St George) in S wall of Cecil Chapel; the saint is shown in white armour against a blue ground, a red cross on his shield; he seems to be standing on the dragon. Said to have come originally from the N side of the chancel, where it was placed above figures of St John the Baptist and St Christopher.

In the left light of the same window, arms of Sir Thomas Cecil, Earl of Exeter (father of Viscount Wimbledon who built the chapel in 1625–30).

14th- and 15th-century heraldic glass, reset, on either side, also in two windows in E wall, and in two in S wall of Warrior Chapel.

In S aisle a window of 1919, with Faith, Hope and Charity – not at all bad. The E window of 1944 is not of great merit.

City of London

St Andrew Undershaft (Leadenhall Street and St Mary Axe)
Late 17th-century glass in the W window – Betjeman says it was originally in the E – with standing figures of Edward VI, Elizabeth I, James I, Charles I and William III. All in strong colours.

St Andrew-by-the-Wardrobe (Queen Victoria Street)
Mid-18th-century Conversion of St Paul in W window.
S aisle windows by Carl Edwards.

Bakers Hall, Harp Lane
Three windows designed by John Piper symbolizing destruction of the Hall by fire, 1968–9.

St Bartholomew's Hospital
In the Great Hall, 17th-century window showing Henry VIII giving the Hospital Charter to the Lord Mayor of London.

St Botolph (Aldersgate)
E window by James Pearson, 1788.

St Botolph (Bishopsgate)
E window by Powell & Sons, 1869.

Dutch Church (Austin Friars)
Stained glass by Max Nauta.

St Ethelburga (Bishopsgate)
17th-century armorial glass in sanctuary and chapel. E window by Kempe, 1878.

St Giles (Cripplegate)
E window by A.K. Nicholson Studios, 1967.
W window by John Lawson, 1969.

St Katharine Cree (Leadenhall Street)
E rose window dates from 1630, abstract patterning, predominantly gold.
Restored by Pearson in 1777.
Modern window in S aisle, Christ Walking on the Waters, by M.C. Farrar-Bell, 1964 – swirling shapes compose the waters, and squarish ones denote the calm above.

St Lawrence Jewry (next to the Guildhall)
Postwar stained glass by Christopher Webb, including a figure of Sir Christopher Wren in the vestibule.

St Magnus (Lower Thames Street)
S aisle windows by Laurence Lee.
N aisle windows by A.L. Wilkinson.

Mansion House
19th-century glass by Alexander Gibbs (1868).

St Mary-le-Bow (Cheapside)
Modern stained glass, quite impressive – the city churches are depicted in the side E windows. Also etched glass screen to crypt, by John Hayward.

St Michael (Cornhill)
Clayton & Bell glass of 1858. Pevsner says it is of very good quality, and so it is, especially the W window of the S aisle showing the Magi.

St Michael, Paternoster Royal (College Street)
Modern glass by John Hayward.

Moorfields Eye Hospital, City Road
Slab glass and concrete (Celtic Cross and Angel of the Sundial) by Rosemary Rutherford, 1971.

The Three Magi, Clayton & Bell glass of 1859. St Michael, Cornhill, London

St Sepulchre-without-Newgate
Musicians' window by Gerald Smith, incorporating (incredibly) Handel, Bach, St Cecilia, and Sir Henry Wood playing the organ. In the N chapel, memorial

windows to John Ireland and Dame Nellie Melba, designed by Brian Thomas; John Smith window by Francis Skeat.

St Vedast (Foster Lane)
E windows by Brian Thomas, 1961.

Greater Manchester

Ashton-under-Lyne, Albion Congregational Church
Chancel E window, 1893, and S transept window, 1895, by Morris & Co., designed by Burne-Jones.

Ashton-under-Lyne, St Michael
Extensive medieval stained glass: 15th and early 16th century, eighteen scenes from the life of St Helena, with donors (Assheton family) and figures of kings.

Bramhall, Bramhall Hall
Three small 16th-century Crucifixion figures in E window of chapel.

Denton, St Lawrence
In N and S windows of chancel, 15th- or early 16th-century fragments.

Farnworth, St Luke
In S aisle, window by Morris & Co., 1875.

Hulme, St Mary
Window by William Peckitt, 1769 – formerly in St John's, Manchester.

Manchester Cathedral
Modern windows in W wall are by Anthony Holloway (1973, 1976, 1982 and 1983–4). They include fine St Mary window of 1982 with dominant blue circle; the theme is the Magnificat. St Denis

window of 1976, predominantly fiery red, is said to reflect St Sermin in Toulouse, with which Manchester is twinned.

Manchester (Didsbury), Emmanuel Church, Barlow Moor Road
S window of transept has very fine Morris glass of 1889 – three standing figures set against foliage scrollwork.

Manchester (Wythenshawe), St John the Divine, Brooklands Road
A N transept window by Kempe, and a S aisle window by Morris & Co., both of the 1890s.

Manchester, Whitefields Synagogue
Roy Young glass in twelve windows of the Tribes of Israel (1969–70). Window on the theme of the Warsaw Ghetto designed by R.F. Ashmead (1975).

Marple, St Martin
E window (1869–70) and two S windows of chancel are Morris glass. The W and SW windows were designed by Christopher Whall.

Middleton, St Leonard
Window of 1524 commemorating Sir Richard Assheton and his wife (kneeling), and seventeen archers who fought with him at Flodden under Sir Edward Stanley. Each archer wears a blue jerkin and carries his arrows on his back; his name appears alongside. Rather fragmentary.

Pendlebury, St Augustine
Good stained glass by Burlison & Grylls, probably designed by Bodley.

Rochdale, St Chad
W window of Faith, Hope and Charity is

Morris glass, 1873.

Swinton, St Peter
S aisle window, the Calling of St Peter, designed by J.H. Dearle, 1902.

Merseyside

Birkenhead, All Saints, Shrewsbury Road, Oxton
Morris & Co. glass in E window (1881) and later glass in S aisle and N chancel.

Birkenhead, Holy Cross, Woodchurch
15th-century glass in porch, fragmentary, and imported roundels in E window. Also some glass by Kempe.

Birkenhead, St Mark, Devonshire Road, Claughton
E window by Christopher Whall, 1906.

Birkenhead, St Saviour, Bidston Road, Oxton
Late Morris & Co. glass (1903) in N transept and W window.

Frankby, St John the Divine
Adam and Eve window designed by Burne-Jones for Morris & Co. in N aisle, 1873. Also windows of Abel and Enoch, Abraham and Moses, 1873.

Gateacre, St Stephen's
W window 1883 by Morris & Co.

Halewood, St Nicholas
Glass in the apse and S and N windows by Morris & Co. (mainly 1870s).

Heswall, St Peter
Stained glass mainly by Kempe, 19th century.

Kirkby, St Chad
Extensive stained glass by Holiday, from 1872 onwards.

Knotty Ash, St John the Evangelist
Absalom window by Morris & Co. 1872.

Liverpool, Cathedral
19th-century glass by Powell & Sons, and early 20th-century glass by Morris & Co. (Chapter House) and Kempe – nothing of great interest. Fine large Benedicite W window by Carl Edwards, 1979.

Liverpool, Cathedral of Christ the King (RC)
Very notable modern stained glass. The finest is in the lantern – abstract, the colouring yellow to the N, blue to the SE, red to the SW, designed by John Piper and made by Patrick Reyntiens. They also did the strips of blue glass between the chapels. 1965–7.
The glass in the Chapel of the Blessed Sacrament was designed by Ceri Richards. That in the Lady Chapel and the Chapel of St Paul by Margaret Traherne. Glass in St Columba's Chapel made by David Atkins.

Liverpool, All Hallows, Allerton
Remarkable for its Morris & Co. glass. Chancel E window of the Rivers of Paradise, 1875.
N transept window, 1880, S aisle second window, of the Resurrection, 1885, and S aisle easternmost window, of the Ascension, 1882.
S aisle westernmost window, Feast in the House of Simon, 1885; S aisle third window, Crucifixion, 1885.
Fourth window of N aisle, Annunciation to the Shepherds, 1883; third window of

N aisle, Nativity, 1886.
N aisle westernmost window, Baptism of Christ, 1886.
N aisle second window, Christ among the Doctors in the Temple, 1886.

Liverpool, St John the Baptist, Tue Brook
Chancel E window, chancel S window and S aisle W window are Morris glass, designed by Burne-Jones, *c.* 1868.

Liverpool, St Mary, Edgehill
Glass by Morris & Co. in W window of N aisle – St Mary, Christ and St Martha (1873), and N aisle second window (1879).

Port Sunlight, Christ Church
W window by Heaton, Butler & Bayne. Two aisle windows by Ervin Bossanyi (1950).

Prescot, St Mary
E window of S aisle by Morris, 1879.

St Helens, Pilkington Glass Museum
A good display of stained glass of various ages, the earliest being Saxon (8th–9th century), also of glazing techniques.

West Kirkby, St Bridget
Good and extensive stained glass by Kempe – from 1870 onwards.

Whiston, St Nicholas
S aisle E window, *c.* 1873, glass by Morris & Co. Also by Morris, the W windows and S chapel S window. E window by Clayton & Bell.

Woolton, St Peter's
S aisle window of Crucifixion and Ascension, 1874, designed by Burne-Jones for Morris. (Cartoon for Ascension is in the National Gallery of Victoria, Australia.)
Also baptistery window with Noah building the ark.

Norfolk

Antingham, St Mary
Chancel S window by Morris & Co., 1865. Also 19th-century glass by Powell and by Kempe.

Ashill, St Nicholas
In N nave windows, glass of Norwich School, *c.* 1460–80, with three of the Four Doctors of the Church.

Aylsham, St Michael
Much mid-19th-century glass: S chapel window of the Brazen Serpent is by Clutterbuck, 1857 – the W window of S aisle (Repton family window) probably by him as well. Also some old glass fragments and a 16th-century St John, Flemish or German, in S aisle.

Bale, All Saints
Early 14th-century glass in a S window, including two apostles holding scrolls, against dark red backgrounds. Also 15th-century glass.

Banham, St Mary
Medieval panel of Virgin and Child in N aisle, also good Victorian glass by James Powell, J.R. Clayton and Henry Holiday.

Banningham, St Botolph
14th- and 15th-century glass, including parts of a series of the Nine Orders of Angels, and a much restored Annunciation.

Bawburgh, St Mary and St Walstan
15th-century glass, including St Barbara, angel from an Annunciation, and female saint, possibly St Catherine.

Bedingham, St Andrew
E window of 14th- and 15th-century glass, rather confused, also two enamelled roundels of later date.

Booton, St Michael and All Angels
Flamboyant late 19th-century glass, mainly of angels.

Bridgham, St Mary
Early 14th-century fragments in windows of chancel.

Brundall, St Lawrence
16th-century roundel of St Lawrence, Netherlandish.

Burnham Deepdale, St Mary
Fragments of glass, mainly 15th century, leaded into six windows.

Carlton Rode, All Saints
In S window of chancel, 13th-century figure seated against dark blue background.

Chedgrave, All Saints
A mixture of 16th- and 17th-century continental glass in E window, bought by Lady Beauchamp Proctor in 1802, possibly from Rouen.

Cley-next-the-Sea, St Margaret
S aisle windows have 15th-century female saints in the tracery.

Denton, St Mary
Glass of 15th century and later, assembled by Joshua Price in 1716–19.

Earsham, All Saints
Imported 16th- and 17th-century glass.

East Barsham, All Saints
15th-century scene of Visitation.

East Carleton, St Peter
17th-century heraldic glass in S chapel.

East Harling, St Peter and St Paul
Remarkably complete E window of 15th-century glass, saved from the Parliamentarians by being hidden in an attic in East Harling Manor House. It shows:
Top Row: 1. Archangel Gabriel hails Mary. 2. The Visitation. 3. The Nativity. 4. The Shepherds. 5. The Wise Men.
Second Row: 1. Fragments. 2. Simeon receives Jesus in the Temple. 3. Jesus among the doctors. 4. Marriage at Cana. 5. Fragments.
Third Row: 1. Mary Magdalene. 2. Judas betrays and Peter defends Christ. 3. The Crucifixion. 4. The Deposition. 5. Assumpton of the Virgin Mary.
Bottom Row: 1. Sir Robert Wingfield (donor). 2. Resurrection. 3. Ascension. 4. Pentecost. 5. Sir William Chamberlain (largely responsible for the rebuilding of the church) (colour plates 29 and 30).
Colour is mainly silvery-gold, with brighter hues in the various scenes, e.g. deep wine colour of Magdalene's dress.

Elsing, St Mary
Good 14th-century glass in chancel:
of *c.* 1330, small figure of Virgin in gold and red, S window;
of *c.* 1375, three figures of Apostles under canopies, one in S window, the other two in window to W of this.

Erpingham, St Mary
In E window, 15th- and 16th-century Flemish panels, from Blickling Hall.

Felbrigg, Felbrigg Hall
In the hall windows, stained glass from St Peter Mancroft, Norwich, also Swiss 16th-century glass.

Feltwell, St Mary
19th-century glass by the French glaziers Eugène Oudinot and Adolphe Napoléon Didron.

Field Dalling, St Andrew
Late 15th-century glass, mainly in N nave windows, including apostles and female saints.

Framingham Earl, St Andrew
Two 15th-century figures: St Margaret and the dragon; St Catherine.

Gaywood, Kings Lynn, St Faith
E window of S transept (Harvest) by Rosemary Rutherford, 1966.

Geldeston, St Michael
Modern E window by Leonard Walker.

Glandford, St Martin
Glass of 1896–1906 by Kempe and his pupil Ernest Heasman.

Gooderstone, St George
14th-century pieces in S aisle.

Great Cressingham, St Michael
15th century glass in heads of N aisle windows.

Great Massingham, St Mary
15th-century glass in chancel tracery.

Great Snoring, St Mary
Remains of a 15th-century series of the Nine Orders of Angels, in chancel.

Great Walsingham, St Peter
Numerous fragments of 14th-century glass.

Great Yarmouth, Elizabethan House Museum
Various small panels and roundels, mainly 16th century. 15th-century St George and the Dragon on the staircase.

Great Yarmouth, St Nicholas
E windows and S window of S transept by Brian Thomas, 1959–60.

Guestwick, St Peter
15th-century glass, but rather jumbled, in two S aisle windows – mainly 1460–80.

Haddiscoe, St Mary
20th-century glass by Martin Travers.

Halvergate, St Peter and St Paul
In head of N window, early 14th-century St Christopher, very small.

Hardwick, St Margaret
Chancel windows have 14th- and 15th-century fragments.

Harpley, St Lawrence
Tracery of W window has 15th-century glass, fascinating in its iconography. E window of S aisle has 14th-century canopies, much restored.

Hemsby, St Mary
E window by Caroline Swash, 1980.

Hevingham, St Botolph

16th-century glass in a S nave window, originally from monastery of Steinfeld.

Hingham, St Andrew
Very extensive early 16th-century German glass, possibly from Cologne, assembled here in 1825. The enormous E window has four principal scenes: Crucifixion, Deposition, Ascension, Resurrection. The centre light in between these has: above, St Thomas with a T-square; below, a very large St Anne holding a tiny Virgin who holds an even tinier Child.

Holt, St Andrew
E window of N aisle, 1933, by F.H. Spear, depicting the Canterbury Pilgrims.

St Anne with the Virgin and Child, glass of *c.* 1500, which possibly came from Cologne. Hingham, Norfolk

Kelling, St Mary
Crowned female saints, probably mid-15th century, in S window.

Ketteringham, St Peter
15th-century glass in E window, including Coronation and Annunciation of Virgin Mary, with heraldry (arms of Sir Henry Grey).

Kimberley, St Peter
Much 14th-century glass in E window. The earliest is in the tracery – head of Christ, and sun and moon, with faces, on either side. Notable figure of St Margaret in centre left main light, elongated and elegant against red ground, with canopy above, *c.* 1375 – a lovely thing. German glass at the side, and in S window of chancel (Christ expelling the money-lenders, and General Resurrection) quarrels with it rather.

Langley, St Michael
16th-century French glass, said to have come from Rouen Cathedral and to have been imported in 1787 by Lady Beauchamp Proctor.

Letheringsett, St Andrew
15th-century fragments in S window of chancel. Late 19th-century W window by Kempe, early 20th-century glass by Heasman.

Litcham, All Saints
Early 15th-century glass in N window.

Little Walsingham
Church rebuilt after fire, with complex E window by John Hayward, 1961.

Martham, St Mary

Much 15th-century glass: E window of N aisle has Crucifixion, Presentation in the Temple, Mocking of Christ, Ascension, St Juliana with a chained devil, Edward III and Queen Philippa; E window of S aisle also has 15th-century glass, including a magnificent St Michael weighing souls, the scales on the lighter side holding grisly blue-green devils (one has fallen off); in addition, Eve spinning, St James the Great, St John, and St Margaret with a dragon (colour plate 31 and p. 51).

Merton, St Peter
Some early 14th-century glass (1320–30) mainly in NE window.

Methwold, St George
Tolerably good window by Henry Holiday, 1866.

Mileham, St John the Baptist
N window of *c.* 1350, with figures under canopies and foliage in tracery lights. Some old glass in chancel windows.

Mulbarton, St Mary Magdalen
15th-century glass in E and one S window of chancel. Originally an Old Testament series.

Nordelph, Holy Trinity
Good Heaton, Butler & Bayne E window of *c.* 1865.

North Elmham, St Mary
N and S windows have 14th-century glass, including good figures of the Virgin Mary.

North Pickenham, St Andrew
Henry Holiday W window, E window by O'Connor & Son, both of 1864.

North Tuddenham, St Mary
15th-century glass, installed in the late 19th century: three lower panels of W window, two of St Margaret, one of St George.

Norwich, Cathedral
Ambulatory: Erpingham window has 15th-century fragments, and large 16th-century figure in window of St Brice.
N transept: W window by Morris & Co., designed by Burne-Jones, 1901–2.
W window, very large, by Hedgeland, 1854.
St Andrew's Chapel: 15th–16th century panels.
Bauchun Chapel: Benedictine window by Moira Forsyth, 1964.
S transept: Barclay window, 19th-century French in 16th-century Flemish tradition.

Norwich, Christ Church, Eaton
New E window by Anthony Holloway.

Norwich, Guildhall
15th-century glass in E windows of Council Room.

Norwich, Norwich Union Building, Surrey Street
In fanlight of doorway, two oval panels of 1697 by Henry Gyles of York.

Norwich, St Peter Hungate (Church Museum)
E window has whole figures of 15th and 16th century, including priest praying; angels in tracery lights holding scrolls with quotations from 'Nunc Dimittis'.
Lighted stand with 15th-century glass, including angel in white and gold, playing cittern, against red ground, *c.* 1450 (see frontispiece).

188

Norwich, St Peter Mancroft

15th-century East Anglian glass in E window, 42 panels – the earliest is *c.* 1440. A whole Poor Man's Bible, but not *in situ*; the glass was salvaged after an explosion of gunpowder in a nearby cottage during the Civil War. The glass was re-arranged in December 1947; missing panels are at Felbrigg Hall, nr. Cromer, and one in the Burrell Museum, Glasgow. The arrangement is, briefly, donors in bottom row, next two rows show the Life of Our Lord, the next the Life of St Peter, the top two rows are mainly saints. Seven panels are modern, mainly in the centre of the window.

W window by Dennis King and Andrew Anderson, installed *c.* 1968.

Old Buckenham, All Saints

15th-century heraldic glass.

Outwell, St Clement

Some 16th-century glass in E window of S chapel.

Oxborough, Our Lady and St Margaret (RC, in grounds of Oxborough Hall)

Church built in 1835, and glass imported from various sources: includes French 13th-century roundel (left of altar), English 14th-century seated figure, kneeling king – Norwich School (?), *c.* 1400 – with sword and book, to right of altar (colour plate 22); above this, somewhat earlier figure in brown holding a fish and a book.

In S window (liturgically this is W), heraldic glass relating to Edward IV. In window to right of door, angel blowing trumpet, below this a crowned seated figure (both 14th century), and below this an archer (15th century) – in window to right

of this is St Sebastian. (Note that the whole church seems orientated to the north.)

Poringland, All Saints

14th-century glass in chancel.

Pulham St Mary, St Mary

14th-century Christ with two angels in head of NE window of nave.

Ringland, St Peter

15th-century glass, including large figures in clerestory of Annunciation, Holy Trinity, Virgin and Child, and St John the Baptist, *c.* 1460 – also donors.

Sall, St Peter and St Paul

Remarkable for its 15th-century glass: Remains of early 15th-century series of the Nine Orders of Angels in E window. Figures of prophets, patriarchs and cardinals (of 1440s) in side windows of chancel. In heads of S transept windows, figures of donors, saints and angels; 15th-century glass also in heads of N transept windows.

Saxlingham, St Mary, Saxlingham Nethergate

Great riches here, of different periods of the Middle Ages.

S window of chancel has four mid-13th-century panels (the earliest glass in Norfolk); at the top, St John and St James to left, beheading of unknown saint to right; below these are maple-leaf grisaille panels of later date; below, to left, Martyrdom of St Edmund (he was shot with bow and arrows), oddly restored, the assassin's head replaced with foliage pattern; below, to right, St Edmund offering up the arrows of his martyrdom to heaven (marvellous panel).

Possibly these came originally from Saxlingham Thorpe.

SW window of chancel has figures of St Philip and St James the Less, *c.* 1350–90 (Pevsner says it is the best preserved 14th-century glass in Norfolk).

Small window to W of this has little roundel, *c.* 1500, of Virgin, Child and St Anne; below this, Resurrection and Nativity scenes.

E window of chancel has some original 14th-century glass in tracery lights. In main lights, three large shields of *c.* 1400.

N window of chancel has 15th-century panels, silver-stained mostly, including a delightfully rustic St Jerome in a bright red cardinal's hat.

Oddments in E window of N aisle, date *c.* 1400, origin unknown, include attractive little figure of St Edward the Confessor, also bishop and archbishop – St Edward flanked by music-making angels of 15th century.

Glass restored in 1959 with grant from the Pilgrim Trust. Could the 13th-century glass now do with further attention?

Scole, St Andrew

Fine E window of the Brazen Serpent, by Patrick Reyntiens, 1965.

Sculthorpe, St Mary and All Saints

19th-century glass, early Morris & Co.: E window of S aisle, Faith, Hope and Charity, designed by Burne-Jones. S window of chancel, Christ walking on the Water, designed by Madox Brown.

Shelton, St Mary

15th- or early 16th-century glass in aisle windows, including two kneeling donors (John Shelton and his wife Anne Boleyn) – the Queen's aunt – or so the heraldry suggests, but the heraldry may be earlier than the figures).

In E window, Sir Ralph Shelton (the builder of the church) and his wife.

Shotesham, St Mary

E window of N chapel has 15th-century angel in gold and white playing a cittern, against red background, and other fragments done in silver stain, with crowned monogram MR (Maria Regina).

South Acre, St George

13th-century grisaille glass in E window of N chapel.

N window has late 14th-century fragments.

South Creake, St Mary

14th- and 15th-century glass, rather fragmentary.

South Walsham, St Mary

1907 window by R.O. Pearson in S aisle, depicting astronomy.

Stody, St Mary

15th-century glass in N nave windows.

Stradsett, St Mary

16th-century German glass.

Stratton Strawless, St Margaret

15th-century glass including the Evangelists, and fragments of a Coronation of the Virgin.

Sustead, St Peter and St Paul

15th-century fragments including music-making angels, one of whom plays the bagpipes.

St Jerome; fifteenth-century glass from Saxlingham Nethergate, Norfolk

Swannington, Swannington Manor

15th-century English glass, said to have come from Heydon Church; also foreign glass.

Thursford, St Andrew

Remarkable E window designed by Revd Arthur Moore, 1862. Pevsner says it is 'one of the most beautiful of its time in

England, or indeed Europe'.

Thurton, St Ethelbert
Foreign glass of 16th–18th centuries, also English 15th-century Trinity.

Warham St Mary, St Mary
16th-century foreign glass, including French Entombment of Christ, and much German work. Seems to have been brought in by the rector W.H. Langton in the early 19th century.

West Rudham, St Peter
Very good glass of 1430–40 in a N nave window: Christ displaying the wounds, seated Christ with crown of thorns, Coronation of the Virgin, Gabriel from an Annunciation, and St Mark with his lion.

West Tofts, St Mary
19th-century glass designed by Pugin, made by Hardman.

Weston Longville, All Saints
Small figures of saints in heads of S aisle windows, *c.* 1460.

Wiggenhall, St Mary Magdalene
15th-century figures in five windows of N aisle, including an unusual assortment of saints.

Wighton, All Saints
14th-century glass, some of it heavily restored.

Northamptonshire

Abington, St Peter and St Paul
Annunciation by John Piper/Patrick Reyntiens in E window of N aisle, 1982. In S aisle, St Elizabeth with infant

St John, Monastery Glass, 1991.

Aldwinkle, All Saints
Late 15th-century glass in the Chambre Chapel, and two 14th-century donors in tracery of chancel E window.

Aldwinkle, St Peter
Some 14th-century glass in a S window, including figures of St George and St Christopher.

Apethorpe, St Leonard
Early 17th-century glass in Mildmay Chapel, probably Flemish; E window has painting of Last Supper on glass by John Rowell, 1732.

Ashby St Ledgers, St Leodegarius
Some 14th–15th-century heraldic glass, and figure of a bishop (15th century) in a S window of nave.

Aynho, St Michael
Victorian glass by Willement (E window 1857) and Kempe.

Barnwell, St Andrew
Early 15th-century glass in S window of chancel.

Braybrooke, All Saints
Fragments of medieval glass, including Trinity Shield, in S window of nave. E window of N aisle by Alan Younger, 1967.

Brockhall, St Peter and St Paul
Two late 14th-century roundels in N window of nave.

Byfield, Holy Cross
Much stained glass by Kempe.

Catesby, St Mary
Fragmentary, 14th- and 15th-century glass in W window.

Corby, St John the Baptist
Some 14th-century glass, fragmentary, in chancel and S aisle of nave. Also late (20th century) Morris & Co. glass.

Cranford, St John
E window has Flemish fragments and roundels.

Cranford St Andrew, St Andrew
In E window, 15th-century figure of donor. Also Netherlandish glass, fragmentary. Church is now redundant, but E window has been restored by Graham Pentelow.

Cransley, St Andrew
Windows contain 14th-century cranes (birds) from which the village takes its name.

Croughton, All Saints
Early 14th-century heraldic glass (arms of England) in E window, also fragments in E window of S aisle.

Denford, Holy Trinity
16th- and 17th-century Flemish roundels in E window of S aisle.

Fawsley, St Mary
A number of Flemish roundels.

Grafton Underwood, St James
American War Memorial window by Brian Thomas (E window of S aisle), 1979.

Great Addington, All Saints
Late 15th-century glass in N chapel (Virgin and arms of the Vere family). Some 13th-century grisaille in the nave.

Great Brington, St Mary
16th-century glass in S window of chancel (including St John the Baptist), c. 1532. Spencer Chapel has glass by Ward and by Morris & Co.

Great Weldon, St Mary
Early 16th-century Flemish W window (Adoration of the Magi), installed 1897, restored 1977 by York Glaziers' Trust – said to have been a gift from Nelson to Sir William Hamilton (was probably in Kirby Hall at some time). Mid-14th-century heads and early 16th-century figure in N aisle, and lozenge-shaped yellow-stained panel. Stained glass also in tracery lights: armorial bearings (arms of Bassett, Lord of the Manor). Fine abstract window in N aisle by Alan Younger, 1992.

Adoration of the Magi; early sixteenth-century Flemish window, said to have been given by Nelson to Sir William Hamilton. Great Weldon, Northamptonshire

Guilsborough, St Etheldreda
Morris & Co. glass in the chancel, Crucifixion with Virgin and St John in E window, also Lazarus, and Rachel and Jacob windows: designed by Burne-Jones, date 1877–8. Morris & Co. glass also in S aisle, but late, and suffers by comparison.

Harringworth, St John the Baptist
In chancel, 15th-century angel's head and 14th-century fragments.

Haselbech, St Michael
E window, 1966, by Alan Younger.

Helmdon, St Mary Magdalene
14th-century glass, fragmentary, in tracery (including figure of a stonemason).

Hinton-in-the-Hedges, Holy Trinity
Early 15th-century Coronation of the Virgin in S window of chancel.

Holdenby, All Saints
Late 13th-century Coronation of the Virgin in S window of chancel.

Kelmarsh, St Dionysius
Hugh Easton window of 1947.

Lamport, All Saints
E window of the Resurrection by Warrington, 1847.

Litchborough, St Martin
14th-century Annunciation and Trinity Shield in nave windows, and 14th-century foliage designs in N window of chancel.

Loddington, St Leonard
S window of chancel has Morris & Co. glass, 1893.

Lowick, St Peter
Early 14th-century figures, sixteen of them in N aisle window, originally from a Jesse tree. Also donor knight.

Maidwell, St Mary
Stained glass by Kempe.

Marston Trussell, St Nicholas
Some 14th-century glass in clerestory (S), including figure of St Peter.

Mears Ashby, All Saints
Stained glass is mainly 19th century. Clayton & Bell glass in E and W windows, French glass by A. Lusson in S chancel. In N aisle, Laurence Lee window of 1970.

Middleton Cheney, All Saints
Very notable for the Morris & Co. stained glass. E window of 1865, memorial to William Croome, designed by Burne-Jones (ther Fathers of the Church), Morris (Eve and the Virgin), Webb (some of the angels and the banners), and probably, Simeon Solomon (the Twelve Tribes, David, Isaiah, Abraham and Moses).
Chancel S window, 1866–70, by F.M. Brown and Webb. W window of 1870 (The Fiery Furnace) designed by Burne-Jones, very dramatic, with Dove designed by Webb. N aisle E window of the Annunciation, 1880, designed by Burne-Jones (St Mary) and by Morris (St Elizabeth and St Anne). N aisle NE window, 1880, designed by Burne-Jones (Samuel) and Morris (Elijah) (colour plates 43 and 45).

Newton Bromswold, St Peter
Some good 15th-century heads, one said to be of Henry Chichele, Archbishop of Canterbury.

Northampton, St Matthew, Kettering Road
19th-century glass by Clayton & Bell (apse), Burlison & Grylls, Powell & Sons, Alexander Hymers, Kempe.

Norton, All Saints
E window by Willement, 1847; the rest of the glass also by him.

Old, St Andrew
Fragments of medieval glass in a S aisle window, including a man ridden by the devil.

Oundle, Oundle School Chapel
Apse has stained glass by John Piper and Patrick Reyntiens, 1955–6: nine great majestic single figures. The forerunner of modern design in the medium.

Overstone, St Nicholas
16th-century French glass in E window.

Raunds, St Mary
15th-century St Elizabeth in N window of chancel. In a S aisle window, fragments of 14th-century glass. E window by Kempe, 1907.

Rockingham, St Leonard
Ascension window of 1853 by George Hedgeland. Stained glass also by Powell and by Herbert Bryans.

Rushden, St Mary
15th-century stained glass in E window tracery lights: figures from a Jesse tree against a blue ground; four angels in the centre, mostly in yellow stain on white, and four more at the sides appear generally 19th century. Tracery lights of one window of N aisle have figures of the

apostles, again in yellow stain. More apostles in tracery lights of E window of N chapel.

Stanford, St Nicholas
Wonderfully rich in stained glass; the best church for this in Northamptonshire: from 14th century to 16th century.
Of the first quarter of the 14th century: the E window – Virgin and Child in centre lancet, two abbots in tracery, seated Christ. In side windows of chancel – ten apostles and two saints under canopies; in NE window of chancel – Crucifixion; in NW window of chancel – Virgin, with below a female donor.
Of the second quarter of the 14th century: in E window of N aisle – Resurrection with angels; in tracery, Crucifixion with Virgin and St John, and below that, St Anne, Virgin, a Bishop and four canopies. In E window of S aisle – two female saints, canopies, and tracery heads with Crucifixion, Virgin, St John and angels. In SE window – figures in tracery (angels). In NW window – a kneeling female figure and heraldic panels. Next to this to the E – an Agnus Dei (damaged).
Of c. 1500: SE window – the Virgin, Assumption, St John the Evangelist. Next window to W: St George, the Visitation. Next window to W again – heraldic glass with donors. Early 16th-century donors also in S aisle windows.
Of c. 1558: members of the Cave family in E window. The large panels at the bottom of this window have (from left to right): Henry VII, red dragon, royal coat of arms, greyhound, Elizabeth of York. Henry VII and Elizabeth of York probably come from Stanford Hall; it has been suggested that they are 19th century, but they may be restored 16th-century work.

At the time of writing the revised edition, all the glass is out of the church, being restored by the York Glaziers' Trust; it should be back in place not long after publication date.

Stoke Albany, St Botolph
Late 13th-century heraldic and grisaille work in chancel.

Sywell, St Peter and St Paul
E window by Willement, apparently made up of 16th-century glass.

Thenford, St Mary
Early 15th-century glass of St Anne with Virgin, and St Christopher, in E window of N aisle.

Wellingborough, All Hallows
Remarkable for its modern glass.
W window of S aisle by Evie Hone, 1955 (apparently her last window): Christian symbols of the Loaves and Fishes, the Lamb, the Ark, the Flames and Dove of the Holy Spirit, the Ten Commandments, the Seven-branched Candlestick, the Keys of St Peter, the Crown of Martyrdom, the Chalice, the Star of David (see p. 96).
W tower rose window designed by John Piper, made by Reyntiens, 1964: red star and crystal shape against a blue background.
W window of N aisle also designed by Piper, made by Reyntiens, 1961: emblems of the prophets Moses, Judah, Aaron, Elijah, and over them the symbols of the four evangelists Matthew, Mark, Luke, John. Brilliant colour, but with rather a lovely watery effect.
W window of S chapel is also by Piper and Reyntiens: a more or less abstract window, predominantly blue, with panel

of red; it may symbolize the creation of the sun, moon and planets, 1969.
S chapel, second window from E, by Jean Barillet, 1962: St Crispin and St Crispinian, with the Virgin and Child to the right of them.

Wellingborough, St Mary
Entire glazing scheme by Sir Ninian Comper.

Woodford, St Mary
Early 15th-century figures of apostles and prophets in N window of chancel.

Northumberland

Alnwick, St Michael
W window of N aisle has 15th-century roundel of pelican. A good deal of Victorian glass: Clayton & Bell; Bagulay; Lavers, Barraud & Westlake; Powell.

Bamburgh, St Aidan
Twelve windows in this church are 19th-century Dutch. Memorial window to Grace Darling by A.K. Nicholson in N transept. Memorial window to Betty and Andrew Jameson (d. 1915 and 1916), with St Frideswide and St Cuthbert, is in the style of Christopher Whall.

Berwick-upon-Tweed, Church of the Holy Trinity
A large number of Netherlandish roundels, ovals and panels in the 3-light W window.

Blanchland, Abbey Church
Some 15th-century glass: abbot/donors, quarries with emblems of the Passion. Windows by L.C. Evetts in nave, 1976–7.

Allegory of Fortune. The winged nymph showers coins into the rich man's basket, but stones are dropped on to the head of the poor peasant. Church of the Holy Trinity, Berwick-upon-Tweed, Northumberland (*RCHME*)

Bothal, St Andrew
Fragmentary, late 14th-century glass in tracery heads, including bits of Coronation of the Virgin, Annunciation, and Instruments of the Passion.

Corbridge, St Andrew
Most of the glass is 19th century (unusually, one stained glass window is hinged to open); in N wall of nave, window of St Christopher by L.C. Evetts.

Cresswell, St Barthlomew
The two E windows are by Willement,

1836; the six medallions in each window are based on themes from the Life of Christ.

Embleton, Holy Trinity
E window by Kempe, 1884.

Haltwhistle, Holy Cross
E window of the Passion designed by Madox Brown for Morris & Co., 1872.

Haydon Bridge, parish church
Window on S wall of chancel based on Life of St Cuthbert MS of *c.* 1200, by L.C. Evetts, 1984–5.

Hexham, Priory Church
1901 Barker memorial window by Henry Holiday, in S transept.

Holy Island, St Mary the Virgin
Two memorial windows by L.C. Evetts, 1970 and 1987, in W wall.

Morpeth, St Mary
E window a Jesse tree, 14th century; though much tampered with by Wailes in the 19th century, still very fine. 14th-century glass also in E window of S aisle.

Ponteland, St Mary
Heads of a S window in chancel have medieval glass, including small figure of a donor priest.

Rothbury, Cragside Mansion
Morris & Co. glass depicting eminent writers in bay window of library in this Norman Shaw house.

Wylam, parish church
Three-light window of the Creation by L.C. Evetts on N wall, 1990–1.

Nottinghamshire

Averham, St Michael
In a N window, fragments of medieval glass, including 15th-century figures. In S window early 19th-century copies of Italian paintings.

Babworth, All Saints
Resurrection window by Francis Egington, late 18th century.

Balderton, St Giles
Fragments in chancel windows, 14th–16th

century, including St Michael, feathered angel and saints.

Coddington, All Saints
Early Morris & Co. glass, including E window of Crucifixion, 1865.

East Retford, St Swithin
Victorian glass by O'Connor, Clayton & Bell, Kempe, Wailes and Hardman.

Edwinstowe, St Mary
Foljambe memorial window in the Arts and Crafts style by C.G. Savile Foljambe, 1873.

Egmanton, St Mary
14th-century figures of St George and St Richard, also fragments, in S transept.

Farnsfield, St Michael
Glass by Mrs E.M. Everett, in the Arts and Crafts style, 1904.

Fledborough, St Gregory
Very fine mid-14th-century glass, though rather restored, mainly in E window of N aisle.

Holme, St Giles
E window largely the original late 15th-century glass, but also includes two early 14th-century quatrefoils of the Coronation of the Virgin (from Annesley), 12th-century grisaille (from Salisbury), and 16th-century figures (from Beauvais).

Hucknall Torkard, St Mary Magdalene
Twenty-five windows by Kempe, early 1880s and of good quality: 'Victorian stained glass at its most competent', says Pevsner.

Lambley, Holy Trinity
14th-century glass in E window (Crucifixion, Virgin, Virgin and Child).

Linby, St Michael
E window S aisle partly 14th century.

Low Marnham, St Wilfrid
15th-century St James in a N window.

Misterton, All Saints
N aisle E window, foliate Cross with symbols of Stigmata, by John Piper, 1966.

Newark, St Mary Magdalene
Extensive medieval glass: 14th-century panels the Creation, Expulsion from Eden (Adam delves, Eve spins), the Adoration of the Magi, the Last Supper, the Scourging, the Three Maries at the Tomb. Of the 15th century there are: Suitors of the Virgin attacking Joseph held back by a Rabbi, panel showing either a Corpus Christi procession or a *Te Deum*, Massacre of the Innocents. All in S chapel.
Glass in S aisle by Gérente of Paris, and by Wailes, mid-19th century.

Nottingham, All Hallows
Semi-circular window of St Giles and Our Lady, by Michael Stokes, *c.* 1992.

Nottingham, St Mary
S chancel aisle has 15th-century fragments; otherwise much Victorian glass by Clayton & Bell, Burlison & Grylls, Hardman etc.
High Pavement Chapel has David and Jonathan window by Morris & Co., 1907.

Nuthall, St Patrick
In E window a 15th-century Crucifixion.

Armorial glass in a S window.

Papplewick, St James
Four panels of 15th-century glass, kneeling knight, family of donors, St Peter and St Stephen.
E window by Egington – a misguided copy of Reynolds's painting.

Southwell, Southwell Minster
In the E window, the four lower panels are 16th-century Flemish glass (from the Temple Prison, Paris); they show the Baptism of Christ, the Raising of Lazarus, the Entry into Jerusalem, and the Mocking of Christ.
In the Chapter House, an Adoration of the Magi, and a Visitation, both of *c.* 1300. Apart from this, the rest of the glass is 19th century, including much by Kempe, and some by O'Connor (two of the latter were shown in the Great Exhibition of 1851).

Strelley, All Saints
N windows contain 14th-century figure of St Ugbertus and 16th–17th-century continental glass.

Tuxford, St Nicholas
In S aisle, E window a figure of St Lawrence, *c.* 1500.

Whatton, St John of Beverley
S aisle E window with figures of St Peter, St John and Christ, by Morris & Co., 1878.

Oxfordshire

Abingdon, St Helen
Three windows by Kempe: N of 1889, W of N inner aisle 1914, outer S aisle 1893.

Also window by M.C. Farrar-Bell.

Alkerton, St Michael
In tracery of N nave window, a lily-pot from an Annunciation, 15th century.

Asthall, St Nicholas
In N window of the Cornwall Chapel, glass of *c.* 1320 – Virgin, Crucifixion, St John the Evangelist under canopies, with heraldic glass in tracery heads.

Aston Rowant, St Peter and St Paul
E window of N aisle has mid-14th-century glass, including two female heads and part of a Christ in Majesty.
In tracery of next window of N aisle, 15th-century glass including music-making angel and Christ in Majesty.
E window of 1903 by Clayton & Bell.

Beckley, St Mary
14th-century glass in tracery of chancel windows: Assumption of the Virgin (S), Coronation of the Virgin (E), and St Edmund (N). Remnants of 14th- and 15th-century glass also in N windows of nave.

Begbroke, St Michael
Numerous fragments dating from the 15th to 18th centuries, mainly Flemish. Also heraldic glass by Willement, 1827.

Bicester, St Eadburg
Morris & Co. glass – Faith, Hope and Charity (early 1866) – in E window of S chapel.

Binsey, St Margaret
In E window, interesting 15th-century fragments including a sensitively drawn female head, and bits of knights from a panel of the murder of St Thomas à Becket.

Bloxham, St Mary
14th-century glass in N window of nave, including heads of St Peter and St Paul. E window by Morris & Co. (angels, saints and archangels), designed by Burne-Jones, with sky by Philip Webb, 1869.

Bodicote, St John the Baptist
E window by W. Holland of Warwick, 1847. Modern glass by A. Fisher (Chapel Studio) and M.C. Farrar-Bell.

Brightwell Baldwin, St Bartholomew
Much 15th-century glass: various figures and scenes, including St John the Evangelist, an Annunciation and several shields. S aisle window has some 14th-century fragments.
In the Stone Chapel, early 15th-century St Paul and Virgin of the Annunciation, 14th-century St Peter and St Paul (faces much corroded), and pair of scales with small soul being weighed against vigorous-looking devil, who is trying to pull down the balance (colour plate 32). Charming 14th-century figure of a saint in a S tracery light.

Broadwell, St Mary
In the tracery, chancel S window has a 14th-century lion's head, *in situ*, with background of oak leaves and acorns.

Broughton, Broughton Castle
In the chapel, 14th-century heraldic roundels; below, royal arms flanked by greyhounds. Panels of heraldic glass also in the gallery.

Broughton, St Mary
Three circular heraldic panels in S window, 16th century.

Burford, St John the Baptist

15th-century glass in tracery of nave windows, including St George and the Dragon, St Mary Magdalene, the Bull of St Luke, St Barbara, St Margaret and other female saints and seraphim.

In N window of N transept, 15th- and 16th-century fragments including the arms of Edward the Confessor, head of St James the Greater, and a female saint wearing white coif.

E window of chancel has 15th-century glass in tracery, including St John the Baptist, St Barbara, Archangel Gabriel, St Christopher and roundels with IHS and M (for Maria).

Much 19th-century glass by Kempe, including fine Jesse tree, 1869, and window by Christopher Whall (1907) in S transept.

Nativity window, Iffley, St Mary. John Piper/David Wasley.

Buscot, St Mary

Morris & Co. E window of the Good Shepherd, designed by Burne-Jones, 1891, also S window of chancel, c. 1895.

Childrey, St Mary

Some 15th-century glass, N transept.

Chinnor, St Andrew

In chancel, fine mid 14th-century glass from Acts of Mercy Series: to S, St Laurence (colour plate 17), St Alban, and Clothing the Naked; to N, bishop and archbishop, and Giving Drink to the Thirsty. In N aisle tracery, Christ in Majesty with angels, and arms of Zouche of Dene. E window by Clayton & Bell, 1865.

Coleshill, All Saints

Early 16th-century glass from Angers in E window of chancel.

Combe, St Laurence

15th-century angels in many tracery lights, figure of St James in nave.

Compton Beauchamp, St Swithun

E window by Martin Travers, with 14th-century glass in tracery.

Cuddesdon, Ripon Theological College

In Chapel, small Tree of Life window, by Piper, 1964.

Dorchester, Abbey of St Peter and St Paul

All the glass except two panels dates from 1290–1320, and is associated with the rebuilding of the chancel and the making of a new shrine to St Birinus in c. 1320.

Chancel N: A Jesse window showing glass and architecture combined, Jesse on the sill and the tracery in the form of a tree.

Chancel E: c. 1320 glass mixed with 19th century. Bottom two tiers are 19th century; then in the 3rd tier, St Lawrence and a crowned head, St Michael, head of St Edmund, the donor Radulphus de Tiwe and the head of a man, St Birinus preaching. In the 4th tier, Virgin and Child, Christ in Majesty, Trinity, Agnus Dei and fragments. In the 5th tier, Annunciation, the head of a queen, the figure of a king, a large head of a queen, and a figure of a bishop.

Chancel NE: fragments of *c.* 1320, a Jesse tree: sixteen heads of kings and prophets, with fragments of inscriptions.

Chancel SE: Coats of arms of *c.* 1300–20: from left to right: Bigod Earl of Norfolk, part of a 14th-century Jonah and the Whale, Foliot (restored), Tyes (restored), Seagrave (restored), Edward Prince of Wales, Geneville (restored), Edmund Earl of Cornwall, Léon and Castille (restored), Grey of Rotherfield (restored), Fitz Alan, de Vere, Ferrers, Bigod (restored), Fitz Walter, Toni (restored), Ferrers, Hastings, Wake, Latimer (restored), Toni.

E window: in head of sedilia, mid-14th-century scene of the Mass, roundel with bishop (late 13th–early 14th century), roundel with pope, foliage.

N chancel chapel, E window: in centre light, St Birinus sent as a bishop to England by Pope Honorius, mid-13th-century.

Nave, N, first window from E: 14th-century fragments. Three early coats of arms – England, Earl of Cornwall, Earl of Lancaster.

There is also Victorian glass: by Hardman, O'Connor and Mayer of Munich.

Drayton St Leonard, St Leonard
Mid-14th-century figure of St Leonard in N window of chancel (restored).

East Hagbourne, St Andrew
In a N window, 14th-century Virgin and a Nativity, very fine.

Eaton Hastings, St Michael
Morris & Co. windows of Risen Christ and St Matthew, designed by Burne-Jones, 1872–4.

Enstone, St Kenelm
E window of S aisle has 17th- or 18th-century Crucifixion and Nativity.

Ewelme, St Mary
Many 15th-century fragments in E window of S chancel chapel, including St Andrew, St Mark and other saints, angels and heraldic glass.

Eynsham, St Leonard
Early 15th-century figure of St Thomas, also fragments, in a S aisle window.

Fifield, St John the Baptist
13th-century heraldic glass, 14th-century foliage, and 15th-century quarries in SW window of chancel.

Finstock and Fawler, Holy Trinity
E window by Kempe.

Forest Hill, St Nicholas
Chancel windows by Willement, *c.* 1847.

Fulbrooke, St James

15th-century tracery lights in S window, including an eagle and a peacock.

Great Coxwell, St Giles
Heraldic glass by Egington, 1792, in E window.

Great Milton, St Mary
In lower tracery lights of E window of N aisle, two 14th-century scenes, probably relating to Lazarus. E window by Willement, 1850.

Great Rollright, St Andrew
A S aisle window has 15th-century roundels: eagle of St John, two crowns, star and rose.

Hampton Poyle, St Mary
Early 15th century glass in tracery lights of N window of chancel.

Harpsden, St Margaret
15th-century heraldic glass in N window of nave.

Headington Quarry, Holy Trinity
Engraved glass window by Sally Scott, on the theme of C.S. Lewis's 'Narnia' stories, c. 1991.

Henley-on-Thames, St Mary
Good 19th-century glass by Hardman in N chapel.

Heythrop, St Nicholas
Early 16th-century glass in E window: Virgin, St John, St Christopher, with above, the Four Evangelists and St Paul. Donors in S windows – John Ashfield and family, 1522.

Horley, St Ethelreda

15th-century donor figures in tracery of two N aisle windows – Henry Rumworth and Robert Gilbert.

Horspath, St Giles
Chancel contains much medieval glass: on S side, (i) figures of the Virgin and St John the Evangelist, c. 1300, and (ii) 15th-century fragments including an archbishop, incomplete. On N side, (i) Crucifixion of c. 1500 (the Temptation of Adam is 19th century), and (ii) 15th-century fragments including head of Virgin and head of a female saint. 18th-century figure of saint in enamelled glass.

Iffley, St Mary
Superb window of Nativity symbolized by animals, designed by John Piper, now a memorial to him. Made (by David Wasley) 1982, installed 1995.

Kelmscott, St George
E window has 15th-century St George.

Kidlington, St Mary
Fragments of medieval glass assembled in 1829 into the E and S chancel windows; restored in 1951. Mainly 15th century, including St Frideswide, Virgin and Child, figures from a Jesse tree, St Anne teaching the Virgin to read, and a good deal of armorial glass.
Interesting panel of St Frideswide restoring the sight of a messenger from Prince Algar. E window also has some earlier pieces: a 14th-century archbishop, and a rather darkened king from a 13th-century Jesse tree. In the S window, heraldic glass. The 'Parry' window is a 19th-century copy from the Reynolds designs for New College, Oxford.
W window by O'Connor, 1857.

Lewknor, St Margaret
NE and SE windows of chancel are Morris glass.

Little Faringdon, church (dedication not known)
A S window of nave contains medieval glass including a 13th-century roundel which may have come from Salisbury Cathedral.

Little Milton, St James
Glass by Willement in E, SE and NE windows.

Littlemore, St Mary and St Nicholas
Glass is largely by Willement and dates from 1840s.

Lower Heyford, St Mary
W window of S aisle has 14th-century glass in tracery, part of a Christ in Majesty, and late 15th-century heraldic glass (Achard, and Achard quartering De la Mare).

Mapledurham, St Margaret
In E window of chancel, a good deal of late 15th-century glass, including figures of St Stephen, St Zita of Lucca, St Mary Magdalene, also 14th- and 15th-century heraldic glass in tracery lights.
Some 16th- and 17th-century fragments in window at E of the Bardolf aisle.

Milton, Manor House
Six panels of 14th-century glass set in grisaille in apse window of first-floor chapel; it is said to have come from Steventon Church.

Minster Lovell, St Kenelm
In tracery lights of chancel E window,

15th-century figures of Isaac and David. 15th-century glass also in two N and one S windows of chancel, and in nave windows, both N and S, nearest to E. In the W window, one angel remains from a series of the Nine Orders of Angels.

Mongewell, synagogue
Architectural use of chunks of coloured glass, making in effect three glass walls to the wedge-shaped building: by Nehemiah Azaz, 1963.

Nettlebed, St Bartholomew
Two windows by John Piper/Patrick Reyntiens. E window (1970) shows Symbols of the Resurrection: a Tree of Life with fish against a red ground on one side, butterflies against blue-green on the other. S (memorial) window also designed by Piper: tree with birds (colour plate 51).

Newington, St Giles
Late 15th-century glass in a N window of chancel: Assumption of the Virgin, and Trinity, with donor priests below.
S window has a Virgin Annunciate, mid-15th century.

North Aston, St Mary
Fragments of late 15th-century glass in chancel S chapel.

North Leigh, St Mary
Stained glass of c. 1440, original although fragmentary, in the Wilcote Chantry.

North Moreton, All Saints
Very fine late 13th- or early 14th-century glass in E window of S chapel; fifteen scenes from the lives of Christ, the Virgin, St Peter, St Paul, St Nicholas.

Over Worton, Holy Trinity
The chancel windows were designed by C. Clutterbuck, 1845.

OXFORD*
Cathedral and Colleges
Oxford, Christ Church Cathedral
E window, Chapel of St Lucy: the original early 14th-century glass survives in the tracery lights, very rich in colour and amazingly mixed in subject (colour plate 12). It includes the Martyrdom of St Thomas à Becket, St Martin dividing his cloak, St Cuthbert, St Augustine, heraldry, censing angels, a Christ in Majesty, and various grotesque men and fabulous beasts. *Latin Chapel:* the glass here dates from *c.* 1360 in three windows on the N side, fine quality standing figures under canopies. First window from W has St Catherine, Virgin and Child, St Hilda; second has Archangel Gabriel and Virgin Annunciate with archbishop or male saint between them; third has Saints Margaret, Frideswide and Catherine. Note a very early use of perspective in the canopy designs. The Virgin Annunciate is especially lovely, in white and yellow against a green ground.

The St Frideswide window to the E was designed by Burne-Jones for Powell & Sons (1859), a somewhat crowded composition but fine colour.

17th-century enamelled glass in the window of Jonah before Nineveh to W of N aisle, by Abraham van Linge, *c.* 1630 (colour plate 39). Fragmentary 17th-century glass in the clerestory.

Large dramatic window of St Michael in N transept, by Clayton & Bell, 1872.

Good Morris & Co. glass, designed by Burne-Jones, in the St Cecilia, St Catherine and Vyner memorial windows; it dates from the 1870s.

The Chapter House has 15th- and 16th-century panels, also 17th-century heraldic glass.

Oxford, All Souls College Chapel
Much of the glass dates from the 1440s and is by John Glazier of Oxford; some restoration was done by Clayton & Bell in 1876–9. The E windows either side of the screen have apostles in the upper lights and the holy women in the lower, the holy women, e.g. St Anne, in very stylish wimples. The figures are under elaborate canopies; the colouring has much white and gold (silver nitrate), apart from that, predominantly red and deep blue.

The W windows were much restored by Betton & Evans. The Royal Window to the S contains the figures of various kings from Constantine to Henry V; to the N are Bishops and Doctors of the Church – in the tracery are half-figures of saints by Clayton & Bell.

The Doom window (W window of main chapel) is by Hardman, 1861, somewhat garish. Inside the chapel, Clayton & Bell glass, graphic scenes including Samson pulling down the temple and Noah building the Ark.

Oxford, Balliol College Chapel
The present chapel dates from 1856–7, but much of the glass came from the original chapel and dates from 1529.
E window: Passion and Ascension subjects, including scenes of the Agony in the Garden and the Ecce Homo which are derived from Dürer's Engraved Passion.

---

*The pre-1540 glass of Oxford has been the subject of careful analysis by the late Dr Peter Newton for the *Corpus Vitrearum Medii Aevi.* A briefer account of the ancient glass, also by Peter Newton, will be found in the Oxfordshire volume of Pevsner's *Buildings of England.* There is also an informative handbook by Paul & Paula San Casciani, *The Stained Glass of Oxford,* which covers 19th-century and modern glass as well.

S window: six subjects from the Life of St Catherine (1529).

Antechapel windows and two windows on the N side by Abraham van Linge, given in 1637.

Antechapel: (S) St Philip and the Eunuch, (N) Sickness and Recovery of King Hezekiah.

Upper Library: mostly heraldic glass relating to benefactors, mainly 15th century.

Oxford, Brasenose College

W window of antechapel has Christ and the Four Evangelists, by J. Pearson, 1776. 19th-century glass in main chapel, by Wailes, Clayton & Bell, and Kempe.

Oxford, Corpus Christi College

E window of St Christopher is by H.A. Payne, 1931.

Oxford, Exeter College, chapel

Clayton & Bell glass of 1859–80 in Scott's Sainte-Chapelle-inspired building, rich if slightly overwhelming. W window over S door is by Powell & Sons, 1914, rather lighter in effect.

Oxford, Jesus College

Victorian glass: E window is by Hedgeland, 1856, scenes under rustic canopies. Other windows by Westlake & Lavers *c.* 1893, Clayton & Bell of 1870s, and Kempe, 1897.

Oxford, Keble College

Stained glass and mosaic by A. Gibbs, complementing Butterworth's Gothic chapel. Late 19th century.

Oxford, Lincoln College Chapel

Windows of 1629–30, probably by Bernard van Linge. The E window is espe-cially interesting for its iconography: from left to right: the Nativity above, the Creation of Adam below (Adam looks remarkably like Charles I), the Baptism of Christ above, the Crossing of the Red Sea below, the Last Supper above, the Passover below, the Crucifixion above, the Brazen Serpent below, the Resurrection above, Jonah below (being spewed up by the whale), the Ascension above, Elijah and the Chariot of Fire below.

The N windows have figures of Prophets, the S windows have Apostles.

Oxford, Magdalen College

The antechapel has greyish, almost monochrome figures by R. Greenbury, in eight windows, 1633. Glazing scheme of main chapel is by Hardman, 1857–60.

The dining hall has 17th-century portraits in glass of Charles I and Henrietta Maria.

Oxford, Manchester College

Chapel has complete scheme of Morris glass, designed by Burne-Jones, 1893–8. Especially original is the Creation series of windows on the S side, fine colour too (memorial to an undergraduate of Brasenose College).

In the library, 19th-century glass by Heaton, Butler & Bayne.

Oxford, Mansfield College

Glazing scheme mainly by Powell & Sons, 1909.

Oxford, Merton College Chapel

In the E window, late 14th-century glass (panels of the Crucifixion with the Virgin and St John, Virgin and Child, two Benedictine Abbess Saints, Virgin possibly from a Visitation scene, and seraphim), leaded together with

East window of St Christopher by Henry Payne, 1931. Corpus Christi College, Oxford (*reproduced by permission*)

15th–16th-century heraldic glass. In the tracery the original late 13th-century glass, including an Annunciation.

In the N and S windows of the choir, more 13th-century glass *in situ*, figures under canopies, set in grisaille. In N and S windows of nave, figure panels with – many times repeated – the kneeling figure of the donor, Henry de Mamesfield (d. 1328), and the inscription 'Henricus de Mamesfield me fecit'. They date from *c.* 1295.

W window of transept has many 15th-century figures and fragments.

Some 15th-century glass also in the old library, with German panels of the late 16th century.

Oxford, New College Chapel

In the antechapel, important windows dating from 1380–6, almost certainly by Thomas Glazier of Oxford: large majestic figures under canopies.

Below the figures is the repeated exhortation to pray for the soul of William of Wykeham, founder of the college. Among the Old Testament figures are Adam and Eve, fully clothed in 14th-century costume. Figures of the Virgin and St John are repeated, using the same design.

E window on N side has been restored recently, revealing much clearer colour. This is the original glass, mostly *in situ* although reset in 1899.

The technically brilliant but rather deplorable W window was designed by Sir Joshua Reynolds, and painted in 1778–85 by Thomas Jervais; there are seven vaporous ladies representing the Virtues. Above is a Nativity, after Correggio.

The S windows of the chapel are mainly by William Price junior, executed 1735–40 but containing some 14th-century

glass, as do the N windows by William Peckitt of York.

14th–16th-century glass in the Hall staircase, heraldic.

Oxford, Nuffield College

Chapel in the roof has near-abstract glass by Piper/Reyntiens (1965–6).

Oxford, Oriel College

Antechapel has early 16th-century figure of St Margaret and the dragon, also fragments, in NW window. The chapel also contains two late 15th-century Becket panels, SW window by Peckitt of York (1767), and much glass by Powell & Sons (1885).

Oxford, The Queen's College

Chapel has eight large enamelled windows by Abraham van Linge, scenes with smallish figures dominated by lavish landscape or architectural backgrounds, 1635. Two windows to the W date from 1518; the rest is mainly by Joshua Price (*c.* 1715), who restored and reset the rest of the glass (which came from the earlier chapel) when the present chapel was built. In the dining hall, portraits of Charles I and Henrietta Maria, as at Magdalen.

Oxford, St Edmund Hall

Chapel has Morris & Co. glass of 1865, designed by Burne-Jones, the earliest Morris glass in Oxford.

Oxford, St John's College

Rather dark E window by Kempe, 1892. In a S window, two very striking panels by Ervin Bossanyi on the theme of St Francis, *c.* 1944, given by the artist's son (who was an undergraduate here) in memory of his father in 1977.

Oxford, St Peter's College

Chapel contains fine E window by John Hayward, 1964, its theme the life of St Peter.

Oxford, Trinity College, Old Library

Glass of early–mid-15th century in four windows of E wall, mainly saints and evangelists, including St Frideswide, St Swithin, St John the Baptist, St Benedict, St Augustine, St Dunstan, St Gregory, St Thomas à Becket, Matthew, Mark, Luke and John – some of the figures much restored and the inscriptions modern.

In the S window, 15th-, 16th- and 17th-century glass, largely heraldic. In the tracery above, the arms of Thomas Hatfield (Bishop of Durham in 1345–81) supported by three angels; this is original and *in situ*.

Chapel has glazing scheme by Powell & Sons, 1885.

In the dining hall, interesting 15th- and 16th-century roundels and Swiss panels, which came from Basel Cathedral.

Oxford, University College

The chapel has glass in eight windows by Abraham van Linge, 1641. Also 19th-century glass by O'Connor.

Oxford, Wadham College

The E window of the chapel is by Bernard van Linge, 1622.

Oxford, Worcester College Chapel

The glass is all by Henry Holiday, 1864–5.

Rich colour and fine bold designs, breaking away from medievalism.

Oxford, Bodleian Library

Contains a great many roundels and panels, dating from 15th–18th century. They include an early 15th-century marriage scene from Seven Sacraments series (once in Great Rollright Church), also 15th-century St Thomas à Becket at the French court, and Henry II penitent at Becket's shrine (originally these were at St Mary's, Woodstock).

Oxford, Headington Hall

The large window of Samson at the landing of the hall staircase was made by an Israeli artist, Azaz. Commissioned by Robert Maxwell, the artist chose the theme. Interesting if fragile technique: coloured pieces of glass contained between sheets of clear glass, no leading, glittering colour. Piece of actual chain round Samson's neck – a mistake?

Oxford, Magdalen College School

The glass in the Assembly Hall is by Laurence Lee, 1966. Nine panels set horizontally, bold abstract design.

Oxford, Pusey House Chapel

E window is Jesse tree by Comper, 1913.

Oxford, St Ebbe

In the S aisle there is medieval glass, mainly 15th century and mainly heraldic, but including female saint, presumably St Ebbe.

Oxford, St Mary (University Church)

Late 19th-century Jesse window by Kempe.

Mid-19th-century glass by Clayton & Bell in S aisle, and by Pugin and Hardman in both N and S aisles.

Samson window, modern glass by Nehemiah Azaz. Headington Hall, Oxford

Oxford, St Michael at the North Gate

Four small panels of late 13th-century glass in E window: figures of saints (Michael, Nicholas and Edmund of Abingdon) and Virgin and Child. In panels set against NE window of N aisle, 15th-century seraphim on wheels, and Christ crucified set against the lily (the lily symbolic of the Annunciation) *cf.* Long Melford, Suffolk.

Oxford, St Peter-in-the-East
(St Edmund Hall Library)

E window has 17th-century figures of the Four Evangelists, and in the tracery 15th-century saints, Crucifixion, Virgin and Child, some of this fragmentary, some over-restored.

Pishill, St Paul

Piper window of emblems of St Paul, 1969.

Radley, St James

16th-century heraldic glass, restored by Willement. Foreign 16th-century glass in E window; 16th-century glass also in W window.

Sandford St Martin, St Martin

14th-century fragments in tracery lights, S Chapel. Lancet window of symbols of St Martin, John Piper, 1974.

Shillingford, St Faith

Medieval glass including crowned female heads in E window. Fragments elsewhere in chancel and in S window of nave.

Shiplake, St Peter and St Paul

Extensive 15th-century glass imported in 1825 and 1830 from Saint-Omer in France.

E window of chancel has (from left to right, beginning at the bottom): St Anthony Abbot, Vision of the Cross by the Blessed Peter of Luxembourg (unique subject), St John the Evangelist, St Barbara, St Peter, St Catherine, Coronation of the Virgin, St Omer, Christ blessing, seraphim, St Andrew, seraphim, St John the Baptist.

More 15th-century glass in E window of S aisle, first window from E in S aisle, and in W window.

An expressive head in French glass of *c.* 1500. Shiplake, Oxfordshire

Shipton-under-Wychwood, St Mary
E window by Hardman, 1874, S window of chancel by O'Connor, 1852. Two Morris & Co. windows (late); modern memorial window to Derek Cooke (*c.* 1960). Most interesting is W window of S aisle, memorial to Baron Latymer (d. 1949), richly coloured roundels in 13th-century style.

Sibford Gower, Holy Trinity
19th-century glass including E window by Thomas Willement.

South Leigh, St James
15th-century glass in E window of chancel N chapel; also in first window to E, second from E in N aisle, and W window of tower.

South Newington, St Peter ad Vincula
In tracery of chancel side windows, fragments of symbols of the Evangelists (emblems of St Luke and St John). Tracery of E window contains dragons, birds and heads.

South Stoke, St Andrew
13th-century Virgin and Child in E window of S aisle.

Standlake, St Giles
Medieval fragments in W window of S transept.

Stanford-in-the-Vale, St Denys
14th-century figures in heads of chancel and S windows.

Stanton Harcourt, St Michael
Fragments of 13th-century glass in S

13th-century grisaille glass at Stanton St John, Oxfordshire

chancel lancets, including figure of St James the Greater, and heraldic glass in the Harcourt Chapel.

Stanton St John, St John the Baptist
Interesting 13th-century glass including Funeral of the Virgin, where a Jew attempts to overturn the bier. Above are censing angels and arms of Clare. A delightful 14th-century roundel of a man scaring birds. Late 13th-century geometric grisaille in a N chancel window.

Stonesfield, St James
Fragments of 14th- and 15th-century glass in E window of chancel. 16th-century heraldic glass in a S chancel window; more 15th-century glass in W window of tower.

Stratton Audley, St Mary and St Edburga
Original 14th-century glass in tracery of E window of N aisle. 14th-century heraldic glass in W window of S aisle, 15th century lion's head in S chancel window.

Sunningwell, St Leonard
Good quality E window by J.P. Seddon, c. 1877 – he was a friend of Morris's and the glass is much in his style.

Tubney, St Laurence
The church is said to be the only Anglican one designed by Pugin. New W windows by D. Wasley in memory of Richard Blackwell: angel blowing trumpet (1991), and God the Father (1992); fused layers of glass, painterly in effect.

Waterperry, St Mary
In tracery light on N side a fine late 13th- or early 14th-century Christ in Majesty. Donors below, male and female, 14th century, set against quarries. 15th-century donor figures of Robert Fitz-Ellis and his wife Margaret in fashionable head-dress and small daughter Margaret (or grand-daughter Sybil), on N side of chancel. On the S side, early 16th-century donor groups of the Curzon family (whose heraldry is also displayed): Walter Curzon and sons, Isobel Curzon and daughters.
A pair of modern roundels by Dennis King of Norwich on the theme 'As pants the hart for cooling streams'.

Waterstock, St Leonard

15th-century donor figures in N aisle tracery: John Brown, rector 1469–1500, and his father, Thomas. Also good though incomplete 14th-century figure of an archbishop. Late 15th-century figures of Virgin and Child between St Ignatius and St Swithin. Heraldic shields of the Ashurst family in N aisle. E window by Willement, 1850–60; more interesting is E aisle window of 1861, good bold design – who did it?

Westwell, St Mary

In a S window of nave, remains of medieval glass: Crucifixion and donors.

Wiggington, St Giles

14th-century dragon and lion's head in tracery of a S window.

Wolvercote, St Peter

Recent John Piper window on the theme of Palm Sunday, with many large hands reaching for waving palm branches.

Wroxton, Abbey, private chapel

E window of four lights by Bernard van Linge. Painted in enamels. The subject-matter is intricate, but includes four of the Apostles with sentences from the Apostles' Creed, the Sibyls, scenes from the Passion, and birds.

Wytham, All Saints

Fragmentary 15th-century glass in N window of nave. Continental roundels in S window of chancel. E window of chancel is 18th century (Adoration of the Shepherds).

Yarnton, St Bartholomew

Extensive medieval and later glass, 14th–17th century – some of it Flemish, mostly assembled by Alderman Fletcher and installed in 1813–16.

Panels include mid-15th-century St Christopher, St John the Baptist, St Thomas, Crucifixion, cherubim, a 16th-century roundel of the Prodigal Son in a brothel, and some delightful bird quarries with inscriptions, *c*. 1500, from the Funeral of Reynard the Fox. Early 15th-century Virgin suckling Child, and two angels balanced on wheels (*cf*. St Michael's, Oxford) (colour plates 24 and 36).

In the Spencer Chapel, very fine armorial glass of the 17th century.

Shropshire

Alderbury, St Michael

S window of 1897, memorial to Sir Baldwin Leighton, designed by his daughter Mrs Sotherby rather in the manner of Burne-Jones.

Astley Abbots, St Calixtus

Figure of *c*. 1300 in E window.

Atcham, St Eata

In E window, three large late 15th-century figures (from Bacton, Herefordshire).

Badger, St Giles

Netherlandish roundels in tracery.

Battlefield, St Mary Magdalene

Early 16th-century French glass in vestry.

Bromfield, St Mary

16th-century Flemish roundels in vestry. Otherwise much glass by Kempe.

Calverhall, Holy Trinity
Morris glass, designed by Burne-Jones, in
S window of chancel.

Cheswardine, St Swithin
Extensive early glass by Kempe (from
1890s).

Church Stretton, St Lawrence
16th- and 17th-century Flemish roundels
in N and S windows of chancel.

Cleobury Mortimer, St Mary
E window of chancel designed by Powell,
1875 (of Piers Plowman).

Cound, St Peter
14th-century figure in E window of S
aisle. Also head of Christ with red and
green nimbus.

Cressage, Christ Church
Early 19th-century E window by David
Evans.

Donington, St Cuthbert
In a N window of chancel 14th-century
glass, fragmentary but including figures
of the Virgin and Christ.

Edgmond, St Peter
S window of chancel 1876 by Morris &
Co. Also glass by Kempe (E and N win-
dows of chancel).

Edstaston, St Mary
Fragments of 15th-century glass in a S
window of nave.

Hughley, St John the Baptist
14th-century glass in E and N windows of
chancel.

Ludlow, St Laurence
Much 14th-century glass, though heavily
restored by Evans of Shrewsbury in
c. 1828.
W window has 27 scenes from the life of
St Laurence, a little congested yet dramatic.
Jesse window has fairly original-looking
heads in tracery.

St Catherine, fifteenth-century glass at Ludlow,
Shropshire

St Katherine's Chapel has 14th-century glass, but fragmentary.

Some early glass, though much restored, in St John's Chapel.

Chancel windows seem by now mainly 19th century. Panels from St Leonard's, Ludlow installed in NW corner of nave, by Hobbs of Hereford (1990).

For further detail see *Ludlow Stained and Painted Glass* by E.W. Ganderton and J. Lafond, 1961.

Market Drayton, St Mary

19th-century glass largely by Kempe (E window 1895, S aisle windows 1901 and 1903, N aisle 1904). W window by Shrigley & Hunt.

Meole Brace, Holy Trinity

Very remarkable Morris glass here, especially the apse windows of 1870–2, designed by Burne-Jones. In the centre apse window, the Crucifixion, Virgin, Christ and angels; in the left window, scenes from the Old Testament (Temptation, Expulsion, Moses and the Burning Bush, Finding of Moses, Worship of Golden Calf, Samuel and Eli, Building of the Temple, Sacrifice of Zacharias), in the right window, New Testament scenes.

The aisle windows are also Morris & Co. glass, and apart from one in the S aisle of *c.* 1870, are of later date, 1890s onwards.

Moreton Corbet, St Bartholomew

E window of 1905 by Sir Ninian Comper.

Morville, St Gregory

Early 14th-century figure of the crucified Christ in chancel.

Munslow, St Michael

15th- and 16th-century fragments in a S window, including two seated Virgins.

Newport, St Nicholas

Early Morris & Co. glass in S window of chancel, designed by Burne-Jones, 1872.

Prees, St Chad

Early 15th-century glass, fragmentary, in a N window.

Shawbury, St Mary

Fragments of 15th-century glass in S window of chancel, including Virgin Annunciate.

Shrewsbury, Holy Cross (Abbey)

E window of *c.* 1887 designed by Pearson for Jackson of London.

Shrewsbury, St Alkmund

Late 18th-century enamelled glass by Francis Egington in E window (the Virgin of the Assumption is based on a painting by Guido Reni).

Shrewsbury, St Chad

Rather dreadful pictorial glass by Evans, mid-19th century.

Shrewsbury, St George, Drinkwater Street

Stained glass by David Evans, also later 19th-century glass by Ward & Hughes.

Shrewsbury, St Julian

16th-century French glass in S window of chancel, other glass by David Evans.

Shrewsbury, St Mary

Important Jesse window (E window of chancel), richly coloured though rather restored. It dates from between 1327 and

1553; the donors were Sir John de Charlton and his wife. Placed here in 1792, it probably originated from the Franciscan church at Shrewsbury (colour plate 19).

Chancel N window and S aisle central window are imported early 16th-century German glass from the abbey at Altenberg near Cologne: scenes from the life of St Bernard of Clairvaux. It was bought by the vicar, W.G. Rowland, for £425 in 1845.

More 15th-century German glass from Trier and elsewhere, which was bought by Sir Brooke Boothby for £200 in 1801; some of this is in the N aisle (some went to Lichfield Cathedral).

A good deal more 15th- and 16th-century glass throughout the church; also windows by David Evans of Shrewsbury, who was responsible for much of the restoration.

Sir John de Charlton, donor of the Jesse window, c. 1340. St Mary's, Shrewsbury

Stanton Lacy, St Peter
Early 19th-century copy of the Reynolds' Faith, Hope and Charity windows of New College, Oxford, but the virtues are here joined by the Hon. R.H. Clive MP.

Stoke-upon-Tern, St Peter
Good early Kempe glass in E window and E window of S aisle (1876).

Stottesdon, St Mary
Fragments of 14th-century glass in a S window.

Tong, St Bartholomew
15th-century glass in W window.

Whitton, St Mary
Late 19th-century and early 20th-century glass by Morris & Co., including E window.

Somerset

Babington, Babington House
15th-century glass, four saints, in staircase window.

Cheddar, St Andrew
Fragments of 15th-century glass, including St Barbara and an Annunciation, in outer S chapel.

Cheddon Fitzpaine, St Mary
Recent glass by Mark Angus, The Four Seasons (1990).

Compton Bishop, St Andrew
Original late 14th-century glass in tracery of E window, also in N aisle.

East Brent, St Mary
Three 15th-century figures in E window of N aisle.

East Chinnock, St Mary
Complete modern glazing scheme by Gunther Anton (he donated the windows, having been a German prisoner of war in this area).

Exford, Methodist chapel
Morris glass.

Farleigh Hungerford, St Leonard
Fragments of 15th- and 16th-century glass in E window, including Virgin and Child and St Leonard; Flemish roundels in a N lancet.

Frome, Holy Trinity
N and S windows by Morris & Co., from 1880 onwards.

Frome, St John
Armorial glass, fragmentary, in baptistery; it dates from 1517.
Glass to commemorate foundation in AD 900, by Mark Angus, 1990.

Glastonbury, St John the Baptist
15th-century fragments in N and S windows of the Sanctuary. Much 19th-century glass by Clayton & Bell; E window by Westlake.

Hardington Mandeville, St Mary the Virgin
Two recent windows by Gunther Anton (1988 and 1989).

Horton (near Ilminster)
Memorial window N side of nave by David Gubbin, 1990.

Kilmersdown, parish church
Impressive glass by Henry Holiday (1878). E window of chapel by L.F. Day (1912).

Langport, All Saints
In E window, good 15th-century glass (ten figures of saints), assembled by Clayton & Bell in 1857.

Mark, St Mark
15th-century glass, eight figures set in pairs, in W window of N aisle.

Marston Bigott, St Leonard
E window has Flemish and German glass of the early 16th century.

Mells, St Andrew
In a N aisle window a 15th-century figure. 15th-century glass also in the vestry.

Nettlecombe, St Mary
Late 16th-century glass in two N windows.

North Cadbury, St Michael
15th-century figures of saints in W window of tower. E window by Clayton & Bell.

Norton sub Hamdon, St Mary
15th-century fragments in all the tracery lights. E window by Wailes, S window of chancel by Heaton, Butler & Bayne.

Orchardleigh, St Mary
Mid-15th-century glass in the chancel: E window has saints and angels, N and S windows have saints. 15th-century glass also in the W window: angels and half-figures of kings.

Over Stowey, St Peter and St Paul
Morris glass of 1873: St Mary Magdalene at the Sepulchre.

Pitminster, St Andrew and St Mary
E window by Jane Gray, 1988.

Priddy (near Wells)
S transept memorial window by Fran Davies (1990).

Trull, All Saints
15th-century glass including E window of the Crucifixion.

Wells, Cathedral
Lady Chapel: early 14th-century glass, especially in the SE window; some fragmentary, but including a panel with two of the three Magi, also a trumpeting angel. An early use of the silver stain technique. E window by Willement, 1843.
In E chapels, E transept and retrochoir: more early 14th-century glass – including in SE chapel a Christ in Majesty and a Christ from a Coronation of the Virgin. S window of SE transept is early 16th-century work from Rouen.
S chancel aisle: lovely early 14th-century glass in tracery heads (Crucifixion, St Michael, Virgin Mary with angels).
N chancel aisle: 14th-century glass in tracery (St Michael, Crucifixion and St John the Baptist).
Chancel E window: Jesse tree, very fine work of the mid-14th century.
N transept: in the clerestory to the E, a Beheading of St John the Baptist, dated 1507 and probably by Arnold of Nijmegen.
Nave W window: dates from 1670.

Wells, St Cuthbert
19th-century glass by Wailes and by Bell of Bristol.

West Pennard, St Nicholas

15th-century figures in E window of N aisle.

Staffordshire

Alrewas, All Saints
Good E window by Holiday, 1877. Glass by Kempe in E window of N aisle.

Amington, St Editha
Excellent early Morris glass (1864), designed by Burne-Jones, in E window, mainly Crucifixion with Nativity and Adoration of the Shepherds and Magi below. Window of St Editha in chancel also designed by Burne-Jones.

Armitage, Hawkesyard Priory
Spode House Chapel has St Martin de Porres window designed by Gonril and Philip Brown.

Broughton, St Peter
Extensive and assorted early glass, ranging from 14th to 17th century. Four 15th-century figures in E window, elsewhere saints, coats of arms and fragments.

Brown Edge, St Anne
E window has Morris & Co. glass of 1874.

Checkley, St Mary
14th-century glass in E, SE and NE windows, including Henry II being scourged at Becket's tomb, Stoning of Stephen, Crucifixion, Sacrifice of Isaac, and St Margaret and the Dragon – also heraldic glass.

Cheddleton, St Edward the Confessor
Morris & Co. glass; by Ford Madox Brown in the chancel (1864) and in the

W window of S aisle, Baptism of Christ (1865). S aisle window by Burne-Jones (1869), with three golden angels blowing trumpets, against a background mainly red.

E window of N aisle (1866) and NE window of N aisle also by Burne-Jones.

Church Leigh, All Saints
In E window of chancel, early 14th-century glass: Coronation of the Virgin, and Crucifixion with saints. Fragments of medieval glass elsewhere.

Elford, St Peter
S aisle W window of the Presentation of Mary at the Temple, *c.* 1525, probably Netherlandish. W window by Wailes, 1841.

Endon, St Luke
E window with three figures, by Morris & Co., 1893.

Enville, St Mary
Early 14th-century glass in S aisle E window, also 14th-century heraldic glass on S side of chancel.

Hamstall Ridware, St Michael and All Angels
16th-century figures of nine apostles in the N aisle. In the S chapel, 14th-century heraldic glass, also crowned saint of slightly later date, and Virgin of *c.* 1500.

Hanbury, St Werburgh
Medieval glass (a Crucifixion) in SE window of S aisle.

Ingestre, St Mary
N window of nave has Morris glass, two angels, 1890.

N window of chancel by Willement.

Leek, St Edward the Confessor
Much glass by Morris & Co., but late.

Leigh, All Saints
14th-century glass in SE and NE windows of chancel, including a Crucifixion.

Lichfield, Cathedral
Several windows of glass imported from Herckenrode, dating from *c.* 1540 – in Lady Chapel, S choir aisle and N choir aisle. Also 19th-century glass by Kempe.

Lichfield, St John's Hospital
Magnificent E window of Chapel, Christ in Glory, by John Piper, 1984.

Madeley, All Saints
W window of S aisle is Morris glass *c.* 1873, with Noah (by Ford Madox Brown), St Philip (also by Madox Brown) and St Peter (by Morris), and a Crucifixion designed by Burne-Jones.

Okeover, All Saints
14th-century fragments in chancel.

Rocester, St Michael
19th-century E window designed by de Morgan – better known for his pottery.

Rolleston, St Mary
15th-century roundels in S aisle E window, and below them signs of the zodiac; 14th-century heraldic glass in tracery.

Sandon, All Saints
Fragment of 14th-century glass in W window, rest by Wailes. 17th-century armorial glass in E window.

Seighford, St Chad
15th-century glass in S window of chancel.

Sheen, St Luke
Glass of 1854 by O'Connor.

Swynnerton, St Mary
Good E window of 1864 by Powell & Sons.

Tamworth, St Editha
Excellent glass by Morris & Co. in several windows: that in the chancel clerestory (1873) designed by Ford Madox Brown, and that in the E window of the N chapel (1874) by Burne-Jones.
E window is by Wailes (1870), aisle windows designed by Henry Holland for Powell & Sons. W window of five lights is modern: 'Revelation of the Holy City' by Alan Younger (1974).

Trysull, All Saints
Some 14th-century glass (two figures) in E window.

Weston-under-Lizard, St Andrew
E window by Hardman, 1874, incorporating 14th-century fragments.

Wombourne, St Benedict Biscop
The stained glass is largely by Kempe.

Suffolk

Aldeburgh, St Peter and St Paul
Window designed by John Piper in memory of Benjamin Britten depicting the Prodigal Son and the Burning Fiery Furnace, separated by the Curlew River (1979).

Bardwell, St Peter and St Paul
Three early 15th-century kneeling figures, one being the donor William Berdewell; also 15th-century German Pietà. The windows of the chancel are by O'Connor.

Barton Mills, St Mary
Original 14th-century glass, fragmentary, in S aisle.

Blaxhall, St Peter
Early 20th-century glass in porch by Ellen Mary Rope, and in E window by Margaret Rope.

Blythburgh, Holy Trinity
In N and S aisles, 15th-century figures and fragments.

Boxford, St Mary
E window of the Transfiguration designed by Rosemary Rutherford, 1972.

Bradfield, St George
In S chancel window, lower part of a knight, c. 1500.

Brantham, St Michael
In S window of chancel, 15th-century glass, fragmentary.

Bures, St Stephen's Chapel
13th-century fragments, possibly from Earls Colne Priory.

Bury St Edmunds, Cathedral (St James)
One window in S aisle is 16th century Flemish (the Story of Susanna, and the Jesse tree).
The rest is 19th-century glass, including W window of the Last Judgement and E

window of the Transfiguration by Hardman, Clayton & Bell. Jesse tree in W window of N aisle.

Bury St Edmunds, St Mary
Much 19th-century glass by Heaton, Butler & Bayne, Willement, Ward & Hughes etc.

Cavendish, St Mary
Original 14th-century fragments in various windows.

Chelsworth, All Saints
Early 16th-century glass in S porch.

Chilsford, St Peter
E window of the Ascension by Surinder Warboys, 1990.

Clare, St Peter and St Paul
Heraldic glass in E window, 1617.

Cockfield, St Peter
14th–15th-century glass (four heads) in a S aisle window.

Combs, St Mary
Late 15th-century glass, including Seven Works of Mercy, part of a life of St Margaret, and fragments of a Jesse tree.

Debenham, St Mary Magdalene
Tree of Life window in N chancel by Surinder Warboys, 1992.

Dennington, St Mary
Early 14th-century glass in N and S windows of chancel.

Denston, St Nicholas
In E window, fragments of medieval glass.

Depden, St Mary
16th-century scenes, mainly from the Old Testament, under 14th-century canopies.

Drinkstone, All Saints
14th-century glass, fragmentary, in chancel, but whole figures in S window and seated Virgin in N window.

Easton, All Saints
In heads of windows some 14th-century glass.

Elveden, St Andrew and St Patrick
Some remarkable glass here: E window by Kempe, a 1927 window designed by Frank Brangwyn (rich and busy), and a fine SW window by Laurence Lee, 1971.

Fressingfield, St Peter and St Paul
19th-century glass: SE window of 1895 by Holiday.

Gipping, chapel
15th-century glass in E window, largely restored.

Gislingham, St Mary
Fragments of medieval glass in N and S windows (Crucifixion, King, Coronation of the Virgin).

Great Ashfield, All Saints
Memorial window to US airmen, 1991.

Great Bricett, St Mary and St Laurence
Early 14th-century glass: the four Evangelists.

Great Saxham, St Andrew
Early 16th-century German glass in E window, also Netherlandish and Swiss.

GAZETTEER

Hadleigh, St Mary
N window designed by John O'Connor, made by Alfred Fisher, Chapel Studios, 1985.

Harkstead, All Saints
Rainbow memorial window by Ann Gray, modern.

Hawstead, All Saints
15th-century glass in SW window of chancel and N window of nave.

Hengrave Hall, chapel
Early 16th-century glass possibly by Robert Wright, glazier (he was paid £4 in 1527), possibly by Galyon Hone the King's Glazier: scenes from Genesis and Life of Christ, *c.* 1525 (colour plate 35).

Herringfleet, St Margaret
Fragments of English 15th-century and German 16th-century glass in E window.

Hessett, St Ethelbert
15th-century glass in aisle windows, including St Nicholas blessing little boys.

Hopton, St Margaret
Burne-Jones/Morris window *c.* 1881.

Icklingham, All Saints
Medieval bits in chancel and S aisle.

Ipswich School Library
Four striking circular windows of foliate heads, by John Piper, 1981. Rosemary Rutherford Tree of Life in Chapel, 1970.

Ipswich, St Matthew
19th-century glass mainly by Hedgeland.

Lavenham, St Peter and St Paul
Some medieval glass in N aisle window; the rest is 19th century, mainly by Lavers & Barraud.

Leiston, St Margaret
Two windows in N transept by M. Aldrich Rope; one of 1927, the other from the 1940s.

Little Thurlow, St Peter
W window of the Soame Chapel has early 17th-century glass.

Long Melford, Holy Trinity
Very fine late 15th-century glass, especially the row of kneeling donors in the windows of the N wall (quite large figures: the ladies in butterfly head-dresses). E window also 15th century, and has a Pietà with St Andrew, St Edmund, two other saints and kneeling donors.
In the Clopton Chantry Chapel, a Lily Crucifix panel in the E window; this seems of earlier date. The glass was possibly made at Norwich (colour plate 18).

Lowestoft, St Margaret
S chancel window has early 19th-century painted glass by Robert Allen. E window by Heaton, Butler & Bayne, W window by Christopher Whall.

Mellis, St Mary
15th-century figures in tracery of a S window.

Norton, St Andrew
Medieval glass including whole figures in S window of chancel.

Nowton, St Peter
About 75 roundels of Flemish glass, 16th

Richard Pigot, judge, figure in fifteenth-century glass at Long Melford, Suffolk

Risby, St Giles
Fragments of 14th-century glass in SE window of chancel.

Rushbrooke, St Nicholas
Medieval glass in E window, also S and N windows – mainly fragmentary.

Saxmundham, St John the Baptist
Flemish 16th- and 17th-century roundels in E window of S aisle.

Sotterley, St Margaret
In W window, two small 15th-century figures.

Stoke-by-Clare, St John the Baptist
15th-century fragments in S transept.

Stoke-by-Nayland, St Mary
19th-century glass by O'Connor (W window), and Capronnier of Brussels.

Sweffling, St Mary
Modern S window, The Call of the Disciples, by Paul Quail.

Thorndon, All Saints
Medieval glass, fragmentary, in NW window of chancel. Also 16th-century Flemish glass.

Thwaite, St George
14th-century fragments in several windows.

and 17th centuries, said to have come from monasteries in Brussels.

Parham, St Mary
Fragments of 14th-century glass in E window, including whole figures.

Peasenhall, St Michael
E window by Willement, 1861.

Walsham-le-Willows
Medieval fragments in E window. Fine N chancel window a memorial to Rosemary Rutherford, Virgin with flowers, from her designs, executed by Kent Blaxill, Colchester, 1973.

GAZETTEER

Westerfield, St Mary Magdalene
W window of *c.* 1875 by Morris & Co.

Westhall, St Andrew
14th-century glass in E window, fragmentary.

Woodbridge, St Mary
E window by Martin Travers, 1909 (Adoration of the Magi).

Worlingworth, St Mary
Fragments of 14th-century glass in heads of nave and chancel windows.

Wortham, St Mary
N window of the Four Seasons by Dennis King of Norwich, 1980.

Yaxley, St Mary
Fragments of medieval glass of various periods leaded together.

Surrey

Abinger, St James
E window of modern glass by Laurence Lee (the Living Cross), 1967; most interesting.

Ashtead, St Giles
16th-century Netherlandish glass in E window, came from Herck near Maastricht – Crucifixion with interesting architectural details.

Buckland, St Mary
Good 14th-century glass in one of the nave windows (St Peter and St Paul). Windows in chancel are 19th century, by Hardman.

Busbridge, St John the Baptist
Late Morris & Co. glass of 1905 in S windows of chancel.

Byfleet
E window of organ chamber on the theme of Music, by Laurence Lee.

Chiddingfold, St Mary
Chiddingfold was an ancient medieval centre of glass-making.
In W window of S aisle are leaded-up fragments of glass from local furnaces. 19th-century E window by Warrington.

Chipstead, St Margaret
Round window in S transept has 13th- and 14th-century fragments. 15th-century fragments incorporated in otherwise mid-19th-century E window.

Compton, St Nicholas
Tiny panel of Virgin and Child in E window of lower chancel, 12th century or perhaps even earlier; very dark, the drawing has almost disappeared.
16th-century Flemish window in baptistery. Christ is shown knee-deep in Jordan, with a red robe around Him, John, with right hand upraised, trickles water down on His head; above flies the Dove in a sky of horizontal flakes of blue (colour plate 38).

Crowhurst, St George
15th-century glass in tracery of E window (angels).

Dorking, St Martin
19th-century stained glass by Powell etc.

East Molesey, St Paul
N aisle window, 1899, and baptistery window, 1891, by Kempe.

Farnham, St Andrew
E window designed by Pugin, unexciting but it was shown in the 1851 Exhbition.

Gatton, St Andrew
16th-century glass, possibly Flemish, in E window and in E window of N transept, German glass of *c.* 1600 in S nave window.
W window has arms of Henry VII, but Pevsner suggests a date of *c.* 1830.

Great Bookham, St Nicholas
15th-century German or Flemish glass in E window – six scenes from a Life of Christ. It came from Costessey Hall, Norfolk.

Guildford, Cathedral
Engraved glass by John Hutton in W and S transept doors, and several windows by Moira Forsyth, including the rose window of 1940. N window of E chancel, Carterhouse window, by Rosemary Rutherford, 1960.

Haslemere, St Bartholomew
In W window, two 17th-century panels, Flemish. Tennyson memorial window in N aisle by Morris & Co., designed by Burne-Jones.

Holmbury St Mary, Pasture Wood (Beatrix Webb's house)
Window reputedly designed by George Bernard Shaw, showing himself and other members of the Fabian Society.

Laleham, All Saints
Stained glass in N window is by W.M. Geddes, 1926, a dramatic St Christopher.

Leatherhead, St Mary and St Nicholas
Medieval fragments in N aisle, leaded together in 1940s by Wall & Wall.

Leigh, St Bartholomew
E window by Kempe, 1890.

Long Ditton, St Mary
Interesting modern glass of the Sower (N aisle) and the Annunciation (S aisle).

Lowfield Heath, St Michael
Two lancets and rose window at E end – are they by Morris & Co.?

Merstham, St Katharine
Glass of 1877 in E window, probably by Selwyn Image. Similar glass in N chapel window.

Mickleham, St Michael
Early 16th-century Netherlandish glass in W window.

Milford, St John
In N aisle two windows by Morris & Co., 1897 and 1907.

Nutfield, St Peter and St Paul
Morris & Co. glass in E window, designed by Burne-Jones, *c.* 1890.

Ockham, All Saints
In tracery lights of chancel, 15th-century figures. 18th-century German glass in S windows of nave. E window by Powell & Sons, 1875, designed by Sir T.G. Jackson. Recent window by Laurence Lee to commemorate 700th anniversary of the birth of William of Occam (1985).

Oxted, St Mary
14th-century glass (figures of evangelists) in tracery of E window. Late Morris &

Co. glass in aisle windows.

Peper Harow, St Nicholas
Glass by Pugin; the church was very largely designed by him.

Pyrford, St Nicholas
14th-century glass (Trinity) in tracery of E window.

Shere, St James
Good 14th-century glass, although fragmentary, in E window of aisle and in other windows.

Stoke D'Abernon, St Mary
Extensive 15th-century and early 16th-century glass. In the E window, 15th-century German glass in centre light, originally from Costessey Hall in Norfolk. 15th-century glass in heads of chancel windows, and in some nave lancets. French glass of *c.* 1510 (roundel of the Virgin) in the most easterly nave lancet. 15th- and 16th-century glass also in N transept and baptistery.

Thorpe, St Mary
Fine modern E window by Laurence Lee.

Thursley, St Michael
15th-century Flemish glass in N aisle, originally from Costessey Hall, Norfolk (*cf.* Great Bookham, Surrey and Stoke D'Abernon, Surrey).

Titsey, St James
Good 19th-century glass by Clayton & Bell.

Walton-on-the-Hill, St Peter
17th-century Netherlandish fragments in SE window of nave.

West Clandon, St Peter and St Paul
Glass is mainly 19th century but includes 17th-century medallions.

West Horsley, St Mary
Good 13th-century panels in two lancets of E window, one of St Catherine and the other of St Mary Magdalene annointing Christ's feet. 14th-century figure of Sir James Berners in a N window.
Douglas Strachan glass in apse windows.

Worplesdon, St Mary
14th-century glass, formerly in the E window, distributed into the four windows of the nave in 1887 (to make room for Clayton & Bell window). Includes delightful Annunciation in N side of nave, angel in green and Virgin in gold against deep red grounds, under canopies. To the W of this, roundel with head of a bishop,

Arms of Henry VIII and Anne Boleyn; sixteenth-century glass at Worplesdon, Surrey kneeling monk on chequered ground, two armorial shields, two gold crowns. More armorial glass in S nave windows.

Sussex

(WS) = West Sussex
(ES) = East Sussex

Arundel (WS), Arundel Castle
In the Barons' Hall, heraldic glass by John Hardman & Co. of Birmingham; also pictorial glass showing episodes in the history of the castle.

Battle (ES), St Mary
15th-century fragments and figures of saints, mainly in tracery lights.

Bersted (WS), St Mary Magdalene
E window by Powell & Sons, 1880.

Bexhill (ES), St Augustine
Benedicite window, by Marguerite Douglas-Thompson, 1979.

Bexhill (ES), St Peter
15th-century figures, N aisle W window.

Bosham (WS), Holy Trinity
In S aisle, four medieval roundels.

Boxgrove (WS), St Mary and St Blaise
E window by O'Connor, 1862.

Brede (ES), St George
Window above porch has medieval glass.

Brighton (ES), Church of the Annunciation
E window of the Annunciation, 1866, has Morris glass.

Brighton (ES), St Michael and All Angels
Interesting for its Morris glass in the S aisle (originally the nave) of the church; the E window has the Three Maries at the Sepulchre (1862), precise but brilliant. The W window of this aisle has glass designed by Burne-Jones, including rose window of Virgin and Child surrounded by angels; below this are the archangels Michael, Raphael, Uriel, Gabriel. To the S of this in the corner, a Morris window of 1855 of the Baptism of Christ.
In the E chapel, the S window is Morris's design, well-fitted to shape of window, Flight into Egypt (1862).

Brighton (ES), St Paul
Two very large windows by Pugin, recently restored by David and Meg Lawrence of Canterbury.

Chichester (WS), Cathedral
The stained glass is mainly 19th century. E window of retrochoir is by Kempe, rather sombre, also S aisle and SE chapel of retrochoir.
Clayton & Bell glass in the Lady Chapel, brilliant although perhaps rather lacking in cohesion.
Christopher Webb glass in N aisle, 1949. But the most interesting window now is the Chagall window to the N (designed by Marc Chagall, made by Charles Marq) on theme of Psalm 150, 'O praise God in His Holiness'; predominantly red, David near the top, riding and playing his harp, and many small figures of musicians playing instruments – all very joyous. Commissioned by Dr Walter Hussey shortly before he retired as Dean. (Note the memorial to Kempe in S transept.)

Chichester (WS), St Richard (RC)
The glazing scheme, dating from
c. 1970, uses the *dalle-de-verre* technique, and was designed by Gabriel
Loire.

Cowfold (WS), St Peter
14th- or 15th-century Crucifixion, very
small, in chancel.

Eastbourne (ES), St Mary
E window of S chapel is by Douglas
Strachan, his last work.

**Etchingham (ES), The Assumption and
St Nicholas**
Late 14th-century glass in many tracery
heads.

Firle (ES), St Peter
Fine window by John Piper based on
Blake's Book of Job, 1985.

**Fletching (ES), St Mary and St
Andrew**
Much glass by Kempe, note particularly
the E window of chancel, 1898.

Forest Row (ES), Ashdown Park Hotel
13 jewel-like windows on the Life of the
Virgin, by Harry Clarke (1924–5).

Framfield (ES), St Thomas Becket
Modern (1962) window of Christ and the
Children, by Jane Ross.

Frant (ES), St Alban
15th-century glass in N and S windows.

Friston (ES), St Mary
1959 window in N chapel by Margaret
Thompson.

**Groombridge (ES), St John the
Evangelist**
Panel of armorial glass of 1625 in E win-
dow. Much 19th-century glass by Kempe.

Haywards Heath (WS), St Wilfrid
Baptistery window, c. 1868, by Morris & Co.

Henfield (WS), St Peter
Stained glass mainly by Kempe (1875,
1905), but lancet in S chancel chapel by
Lowndes & Drury, 1901, with inscription
'She hath done what she could'.

Hooe (ES), St Oswald
14th-century figures of Christ and the
Virgin Mary, also (incomplete) figures of
Edward III and Philippa of Hainault.

Horsham (WS), St Mary
19th-century glass, including O'Connor,
Wailes, Clayton & Bell, Heaton & Co.

Hurstpierpoint (WS), Holy Trinity
15th–17th-century medallions in E window of S aisle.
E window by Kempe.

Isfield (ES), St Margaret
14th-century fragments in a S window.

Kirdford (WS), St John the Baptist
N aisle window has medieval glass, reputedly from local furnaces.

Lancing (WS), Lancing College chapel
Enormous heraldic rose window by
Goddard & Gibbs, of recent date.

Lodsworth (WS), St Peter
Unexpected and delightful modern glass in
S chapel: St Nicholas, done in *dalle-de-
verre*.

North Stoke (WS), parish church
In E window small early 14th-century Coronation of the Virgin; also early 14th-century glass in E window of S transept.

Northchapel (WS), parish church
W.M. Geddes window of St Francis (1930).

Oving (WS), St Andrew
19th-century E window by Powell & Sons, S transept glass by Kempe.

Pagham (WS), St Thomas Becket
16th-century Flemish glass in E window – otherwise heraldic glass by William Miller of 1837 – Adoration of the Child, Adoration of the Magi, Presentation in the Temple.

Poynings (ES), Holy Trinity
Several windows have 15th-century glass, e.g. Annunication in E window of N transept.

Rottingdean (ES), St Margaret
Good Morris & Co. glass: E window, designed by Burne-Jones, 1893; chancel N window (St Margaret) 1894; chancel S window (Virgin Mary) 1894; N and S windows of the tower (Jesse tree and Jacob's Ladder) 1897; also later Morris glass in the nave.

Rye (ES), St Mary
Two colourful windows by E. Nottbeck for Powell's glass (1929 and 1937). N aisle window by Morris & Co., 1897.

Salehurst (ES), St Mary
Tiny birds, 14th century, drawn in brown on the glass of tracery in SE and SW windows.

Stanstead (WS), chapel
Early 19th-century glass in E window, with Jewish Old Testament themes (the donor having a preoccupation about the conversion of the Jews); its consecration in 1819 was attended by the poet Keats.

Stopham (WS), St Mary
Early 17th-century glass in N aisle, signed 'Roelant', commemorates Brian Stopham (d. 1273) – he is the kneeling knight in medieval costume in the left light, below is another kneeling figure of (?) 1638. In the right-hand light is a kneeling donor in 16th-century dress, and below that three female donors in Elizabethan costume. Most of the window is enamelled, but the 17th-century figure is pot-metal.
E window of armorial glass, 1638, has six shields set in quarries decorated in silver stain with plants and flowers.

Ticehurst (ES), St Mary
14th-century glass in N side of chancel, also in NW window of N aisle.

Uckfield (ES), Holy Cross
Modern glass, c. 1960, by Alexander Klecki.

Warbleton (ES), St Mary
13th-century fragments in a N aisle window and in E window of chapel. W window is by Kempe.

West Firle (ES), St Peter
Some 13th-century glass in E window of S aisle.

West Grinstead (WS), St George
In W aisle window, 14th-century fragments.
E window of chancel is by Kempe, also N

window.
War memorial window by Walter Camm, *c.* 1925.

Westham (ES), St Mary
15th-century glass in tracery of E window.

Winchelsea (ES), St Thomas
Nearly all the glass by Douglas Strachan, 1928–33, characteristically expressive.

Woolbeding (WS), All Hallows
16th-century continental glass of scenes from the Passion, originally from the chapel of the Holy Ghost, Basingstoke (taken out during the Civil War). The glass is in the N window of the chancel (angel in left panel, with below, Judas and soldiers; in right panel, soldiers with instruments of Passion, and below, Peter cutting off ear – lovely blue-greens in angel panel), and W window of S nave (on left, kneeling St John and another figure with a book, below a sleeping disciple; on right, part of a Deposition, below a sorrowing Madonna with book, also another figure in green with book).

Worth (WS), St Nicholas
Window in S transept by Willement, 1849.

Tyne and Wear

Earsdon, St Alban
Very extraordinary, but some of the glass made for Hampton Court Palace by Galyon Hone, King's Glazier to Henry VIII, is here in this 19th-century church. It is secular heraldic glass: coats of arms, portcullises and Tudor roses, and lion, greyhound and bear supporters. Probably

Heraldic glass by Galyon Hone, King's Glazier to Henry VIII, originally at Hampton Court Palace. Earsdon, Tyne & Wear

it was removed from the palace when Willement's glass was installed; Lord Hastings had it and gave it to Earsdon in 1874.

Gateshead, St Mary
In the S aisle 13th-century French panel of Pilate washing his hands; installed 1937.

Gosforth, Sacred Heart
Glass by Morris & Co., *c.* 1875.
In chancel E window, Crucifixion. In chancel N window, St Matthew and St Mark.
In S aisle window, Virgin Mary and Joseph.

Jarrow, Bede Monastery Museum
Three panels have been leaded up from the 7th-century glass excavated from the devastated Guest-house of the Saxon monastery at Jarrow, and are displayed in light-boxes:

1. A number of diamond-shaped quarries, slightly varying in size.
2. Nine coloured square quarries leaded up in cruciform pattern.
3. Most interestingly, carefully shaped pieces which appear to constitute a standing figure, and have been leaded up as such. A good range of colour; against a white ground, the figure is predominantly blue, with some gold, red, and tawny glass (colour plate 1).

Jarrow, St Paul

In a S window of the chancel (which was part of the Saxon monastery), a tiny roundel of 7th-century glass. Non-representational, with a wide range of colour, it is claimed to be the earliest glass church window in Europe (see reference to Saxon glass on p. 15).
E window by L.C. Evetts, 1950.
Modern window by John Piper commemorating Benedict Biscop, who founded the monastery in AD 682.

Long Benton, St Bartholomew

N and S windows of chancel by John Hardman, 1856.

Monkwearmouth, St Peter

Fragments of Saxon glass, late 7th century (see pp. 14–15).

Newcastle, Cathedral of St Nicholas

In St Margaret's Chapel, upper half of a Virgin and Child, late 14th century.
S window of chancel by Wailes, E window by A. Dunn, 1859.
Modern abstract window by Stan Scott on N side.

Newcastle, RC Cathedral (St Mary)

E window and side chapel windows by Wailes, but it is likely that Pugin, who was responsible for the architecture, designed these windows also.

Newcastle, Gosforth parish church

Chancel window by L.C. Evetts, 1976–7.

Newcastle, St Andrew

Memorial window by Wailes to four of his children, c. 1850.
Five windows in nave by L.C. Evetts, 1976–7.

Newcastle, St John

Fragments of 14th- and 15th-century glass. E window of N transept has heraldic glass of the late 17th century.

Newcastle, St Joseph (RC), Banwell

Abstract screen over entire chancel opening, by L.C. Evetts, 1981–2.

Roker, St Andrew

E window in the Arts and Crafts style by H.A. Payne of Birmingham.

Sunderland, Christ Church, Ryhope Road

Good stained glass by Morris & Co. in E window – early, probably 1860s.

Sunderland, Sunderland Museum

Fragments of 7th-century Saxon glass, leaded up. They came from Benedict Biscop's monastery at Monkwearmouth (see pp. 14–15).

Wallsend, St Luke

Very fine stained glass of 1922 by the Irish glazier Wilhelmina Geddes, depicting the Crucifixion and Deposition.

GAZETTEER

Warwickshire

Ansley, St Lawrence
Fragments of medieval glass in N window of chancel.

Astley, St Mary
Remnants of medieval glass in two windows of chancel, also in heads of windows in nave.

Aston Cantlow, St John the Baptist
Glass by Kempe in E window, also in E window of N aisle. In NE window of N aisle, medieval fragments.

Atherstone, St Mary
Late 19th-century glass by Kempe (E, SE and NE windows).

Atherstone-on-Stour, St Mary
E window by Kempe.

Austrey, St Nicholas
Early 14th-century glass in SE window of S aisle, fragmentary.

Baddesley Clinton, St Michael
E window is early 16th century, heavily restored.

Barton-on-the-Heath, St Lawrence
In N window of chancel, early 14th-century fragments.
In N window of nave, 15th-century falcons drawn in yellow.

Beaudesert, St Nicholas
see Henley-in-Arden

Bilton, St Mark
In N window of chancel and E window of N aisle, fragments of 14th-century glass.

Bishop's Tachbrook, St Chad's
E window of N aisle by Morris & Co., designed by Morris and Philip Webb, *c.* 1863, depicts Presentation in the Temple.

Brinklow, St John the Baptist
In N and S aisle windows, 15th-century fragments: birds including peacock.

Chadshunt, All Saints
Some 16th-century Italian glass in N transept (1558).

Charlecote, St Leonard
19th-century glass by Kempe, Willement and O'Connor.

Cherington, St John the Baptist
Fragments of medieval glass installed in 1750–60.

Chesterton, St Giles
Medieval fragments in a N window. E window by O'Connor, 1862.

Claverdon, St Michael
E window by Kempe, *c.* 1890.

Coughton, St Peter
Late 15th- and early 16th-century glass, especially in heads of S and N chapel windows, possibly Flemish. W window by Powell.

Ettington, Holy Trinity (St Nicholas)
E window by Evie Hone, also S window, 1948–9 (colour plate 46). (This replaced the glass from Winchester College when it was returned to Winchester.) Note that what survives of the church is in the grounds of the Ettington Park Hotel.

Fillongley, St Mary and All Saints
A N window has 14th-century fragments. In N chapel, 15th-century donor and Netherlandish panels.

Hampton Lucy, St Peter
Large E window by Willement, 1837. Shows figure of St Peter, over coat of arms and surrounded by 24 scenes of the Life of St Peter; commissioned by the rector, John Lucy (This window was the frontispiece to Willement's book *Stained Glass* of 1840).

Haseley, St Mary
In W window of tower, interesting fragments of 15th-century glass, still *in situ*.

Hatton, Holy Trinity
German early 16th-century figures from Jesse tree in W windows – heavily restored.

Henley-in-Arden, St Nicholas, Beaudesert
Early Morris & Co. glass; nave windows have the Virgin, St Michael, St Nicholas and St George, 1865.

Kenilworth, St Nicholas
Heraldic glass by David Evans, 1832, in S window of S transept.

Kinwarton, St Mary
Delightful early 14th-century Virgin with donors in a quatrefoil at head of a S window in chancel, inscribed underneath 'Wili atte ye wode' (William at Wood; his brother was priest here when the church was consecrated in 1316).

Lighthorne, St Lawrence
Heraldic glass of 17th century in NE window.

Little Packington, St Bartholomew
Some medieval glass in E window.

Mancetter, St Peter
14th-century glass in E window (figures from Merevale Jesse tree) and a N window in chancel.

Merevale, Our Lady
In E window, early 14th-century Jesse tree, five lights, probably from the abbey – delightful, although restored.
Late 14th-century heads and two 15th-century figures in tracery. More 14th-century glass in two S windows and in tracery of a N aisle window.

Nether Whitacre, St Giles
S chancel window has early 14th-century kneeling angel.

Newton Regis, St Mary
14th-century fragments mainly in W window.

Packwood, St Giles
Early 14th-century Crucifixion in N transept.

Radway, St Peter
In N window of chancel, 17th-century Netherlandish glass.

Rowington, St Lawrence
Some late 13th-century glass in E window and in a S window of chancel.

Rugby, Rugby School chapel
E window and E window of N aisle are 16th-century glass from Aerschot near

Louvain, installed in 1834 (Adoration of the Magi).

In S transept, glass said to have come from Rouen. 19th-century glass in the same style, by Willement, in N transept and S aisle.

W window (Last Judgement) by Morris & Co., designed by Dearle, 1902, also S window of the chancel and aisle windows. In both transepts, impressive large windows by Gibbs, *c.* 1866.

Spernall, St Leonard

Medieval fragments in a N window.

Detail of west window designed by Dearle for Morris & Co., 1902. Rugby School chapel, Warwickshire

Stretton-on-Dunsmore, All Saints
S window of chancel has 17th-century Christ at Emmaus.

Upper Shuckburgh, St John the Baptist
Late 16th-century armorial glass in SW window.

Warwick, St Mary
The Beauchamp Chapel: the glass was made by John Prudde of Westminster in 1440–62; the will of Richard Beauchamp stipulated that he should use only the best foreign glass. Original glass of high quality survives in E window, including richly ornamented figures of Saints Thomas à Becket, Alban (colour plate 25), Winifred and John of Bridlington. In the heads of side windows, music in plainsong is displayed, together with music-making angels, some of them playing on a fascinating assortment of medieval instruments.
There is also some medieval glass, and Flemish roundels, in N vestries and Chapter House.

Whichford, St Michael
Early 14th-century glass in E window and E window of S chapel.

Wixford, St Milburga
Fragments of 14th-century glass, including small figures, in E window of S chapel.

Wolverton, St Mary
Fragments of medieval glass, in a N window especially.
Chancel S window by Morris & Co.

Wootton Wawen, St Peter
Medieval fragments in E window and in N window of chancel.
Modern glass (1958) in Yorke memorial window, by Margaret Traherne.

Wroxall, Wroxall Abbey
Extensive medieval glass, much early 14th-century work (*c.* 1315) in the N windows, also 15th-century, especially in the E window.

Angel Musicians in the tracery lights, *c.* 1450. Beauchamp Chapel, St Mary's, Warwick

West Midlands

Binley, St Bartholomew
18th-century E window by William Peckitt: Virgin and Child with angels.

Birmingham, Cathedral of St Philip
Highly dramatic stained glass by Morris & Co., designed by Burne-Jones, who came from Birmingham. The Morris windows are: Ascension, 1884; Crucifixion, 1887; Nativity, 1887; Last Judgement, 1897 (in W tower).

Birmingham, RC Cathedral of St Chad
Tolerably good 19th-century glass by Hardman & Co., and by W. Warrington to Pugin's designs.

Birmingham, Chapel of St Mary's College (RC), New Oscott, Perry Barr
E window and first S window by Warrington, from designs by Pugin (who was largely responsible for the architecture): *c.* 1838, in the 14th-century manner.

Birmingham, Holy Trinity, Camp Hill, Bordesley (Greek Orthodox)
Good 19th-century glass by A. Gérente in SE and NE windows (1855).

Birmingham, St Martin, Bull Ring
Morris glass, designed by Burne-Jones, in S transept window, 1875–80.

Birmingham, St Peter, Highfield Road, Hall Green
Modern stained glass (1960s), set in concrete: E window and windows in upper octagon by Tristan Ruhlmann.

Birmingham, St Peter and St Paul, Witton Lane, Aston
18th-century memorial window by Francis Egington, the N window in N chancel (1793).

Coventry, Cathedral
West Screen of engraved glass by John Hutton, *c.* 1961.
Very effective abstract Baptistery window designed by John Piper, made by Patrick Reyntiens, with symbolic use of colour (colour plate 49).
Nave windows by Laurence Lee, Keith New and Geoffrey Clarke, 1957–60.
Five windows designed by Einar Forseth, *c.* 1960.
In the Chapel of Unity, abstract glass by Margaret Traherne.
Fragments of medieval glass in St Michael's Hall.

Coventry, St Mary's Hall
In the N window, richly coloured figures of kings of England, with Arthur and Constantine, also heraldry, dating from *c.* 1500. In oriel window, fragments include a roundel of a man threshing corn.

Coventry, St Michael, Stoke
15th-century fragments, heraldic glass and figures.

Elmdon, St Nicholas
In a S window, Netherlandish roundels.

Wednesbury, St Bartholomew
Much stained glass by Kempe.

West Bromwich, All Saints
Stained glass by Powell & Sons, of the 1870s.

Wightwick, Wightwick Manor
Stained glass by Morris & Co. in entrance

hall and drawing-room – also some glass by Kempe.

Wolverhampton, St Andrew
Wide W window by John Piper, 1973–4, symbolic blue seascape.

Wiltshire

All Cannings, All Saints
Fragments of 14th-century glass. In chancel 19th-century glass by Lavers & Barraud.

Alton Barnes, St Mary
18th-century heraldic glass, memorial to W. Lamplugh, d. 1737.

Amesbury, Church of Christ the King
Modern window by Henry Haig.

Amesbury, St Mary and St Melor
In a N window, 13th-century quarries and part of a medieval saint.

Bemerton, St Andrew
Kempe window of 1878 in N aisle.

Berwick St John, St John the Baptist
Good glass by Hardman of *c.* 1862 in W, E and S transept window.

Blunsdon St Andrew, St Andrew
19th-century glass: E window and E window of S aisle by Lavers & Barraud, and a N window by Kempe, *c.* 1896.

Boscombe, St Andrews
15th-century fragments in E and W windows.

Boyton, St Mary
E window has 13th-century fragments, some probably from Salisbury Cathedral, E window of S chapel has 16th- and 17th-century fragments. S windows have 15th-century German glass.

Bradford-on-Avon, Holy Trinity
Flemish roundels of 16th and 17th centuries in a S window.

Bromham, St Nicholas
Morris E window of Crucifixion, *c.* 1870, designed by Burne-Jones.

Burbage, All Saints
In S aisle, stained glass by Powell of 1859 and 1863.

Calne, St Mary
E window of S chapel by O'Connor, 1866.

Castle Combe, St Andrew
Much 19th-century glass by Ward & Nixon, also by Gibbs.

Chippenham, St Andrew
1918 window in S chapel by Christopher Whall – interesting.

Chirton, St John the Baptist
Much 19th-century glass by Wailes, but some 15th-century glass in porch window.

Christian Malford, All Saints
15th-century fragments in N aisle and N chancel windows, also in SW windows of S aisle.

Chute, St Nicholas
19th-century E window by Clayton & Bell.

Clyffe Pypard, St Peter
16th- and 17th-century Netherlandish and Swiss panels, also fragments of medieval glass in heads of N and S windows.

Colerne, St John the Baptist
Medieval grisaille glass in a N window.

Corsham, Corsham Court
Fragments of 15th-century glass.

Corsham, St Bartholomew
E window, and E window of Methuen Chapel by Kempe (1892 and 1899).

Crudwell, All Saints
Late 15th-century glass: five out of the Seven Sacraments in a N window, and in the centre a figure of Christ displaying the wounds of the Crucifixion.

Dauntsey, St James
15th- and 16th-century fragments in chancel windows.

Devizes, St James
Glass by Wailes (E window of 1849), and Kempe (NE window of N aisle).

Dinton, St Mary
Early 14th-century glass in SE window of chancel, including two angels in main lights, heads of two bishops and another tonsured head in tracery. NE window of chancel has bishop and tonsured head (medieval) and (?) 17th-century head above – all in tracery.

Downton, St Lawrence
Two 15th-century figures in a N aisle window.

Edington, St Mary, St Katherine and

All Saints (priory church)
14th-century Crucifixion between Virgin and St John in E window; it was donated by William Edington, Bishop of Winchester. Other 14th-century glass includes St William of York, St Paul, St Christopher, St Cuthbert, St Aidan and Leodgar, in the N clerestory of the nave. Two tracery lights have music-making angels.

Ford, St John the Evangelist
E window by Morris & Co., 1913, from Burne-Jones designs.

Grafton, St Nicholas
19th-century glass – W window by Willement.

Great Chalfield, All Saints
W window has some 15th-century glass.

Inglesham, St John the Baptist
Fragments of medieval glass in several windows, 13th century and later.

Lacock, St Cyriac
Medieval glass in E window of NE chapel, fragmentary.
18th-century glass in W window of N aisle.

Littlecote, Littlecote House
Great Hall has 16th- and 17th-century glass, German or Netherlandish.

Luckington, St Mary and St Ethelbert
E window by Kempe, 1881.

Lydiard Park
17th-century window by Abraham van Linge, comprising quarries with subjects from natural history painted on each, in an ante-room.

Lydiard Tregoze, St Mary
John Aubrey said of its stained glass, 'In this it exceeds all churches in this countie' – perhaps he was right.
It is 17th-century glass: a central E window in chancel of three lights. The main subjects are St John the Baptist (N light), an olive tree with shields (centre light) and St John the Divine (S light) – possibly a rebus on name Oliver St John. Below are three armorial bearings; above four cherubs hold shields bearing signs of the evangelists. A rich and fascinating mixture of the religious and the secular.
Rather unpleasant *c.* 1900 glass on either side.
Also remnants of 15th-century glass: crowned female head in N side of chancel, in N aisle Virgin and Child (to W) and three angels (to E).

Maiden Bradley, All Saints
14th- and 16th-century fragments in SE window of S aisle.

Marden, All Saints
Modern glass: a N window by J. and M. Kettlewell, 1958.

Marlborough, Marlborough College
Morris & Co. window in nave of chapel, designed by Burne-Jones. Two archangels by S. Image, 1913.

Marlborough, St Peter and St Paul.
E window by Lavers & Barraud, 1862–3. Most of the glazing scheme is by this firm and by Westlake.

Melksham, St Michael
SE window by Kempe, 1897. SW window of S chapel by Ward & Hughes, 1884.

Mere, St Michael
14th-century glass in SW window of S chapel – three large figures strongly coloured.
W window of N aisle designed by Holiday for Powell & Sons, 1865.

Mildenhall, St John the Baptist
15th-century fragments in heads of chancel windows.

Minety, St Leonard
15th-century glass in head of W window, also in door of vestry.

Oaksey, All Saints
15th-century glass in a N window, quite extensive, probably remains of a Seven Sacraments series.

Pitton, St Peter
E window by Kempe, 1886.

Poulshot, St Peter
Medieval quarries in a S window of chancel.

Purton, St Mary
Fragments of 14th-century glass, mainly in S window of S chapel.

Rodbourne, Holy Rood
E window of chancel by Morris & Co., 1862–3, with Adam and Eve designed by Madox Brown and Annunciation by Rossetti.

Rollestone, St Andrew
Some 17th-century heraldic glass.

Rushall, St Matthew
In SE window of chancel, two 15th-century panels.

Salisbury, Cathedral

Much of the cathedral's ancient glass was destroyed in the 18th century by order of James Wyatt. (Fragments of it still survive in the churches of Boyton in Wiltshire, and East Tytherley, Grately and Headley in Hampshire).

In the Cathedral there remains:

A good deal of 13th-century grisaille. Most of the best medieval figurative glass is now installed in the SE transept; varying much in date and subject, it includes at the top a 13th-century Risen Christ between the Virgin and St John.

Otherwise, much 19th-century glass: Clayton & Bell in retrochoir, S and N choir aisles, SE transept; Morris & Co. in window of S choir aisle; Holiday for Powell & Sons in E part of S choir aisle. E window of choir is 18th century, designed by Mortimer for Pearson.

Lancets by Gabriel Loire on the theme of 'Prisoners of Conscience in the 20th century' were installed in 1980 in the E window of the Trinity Chapel, where the rest of the glass is by Clayton & Bell.

By the N porch, a nave window by Harry Stammers of Elisha and Elijah; next to it, window of the Archangel Gabriel and St George by Christopher Webb.

Glass in the cloisters: 19th-century copies by Ward of 13th-century grisaille.

Salisbury, St Edmund, Bedwin Street

17th-century Swiss glass in vestry, stories from Genesis.

Salisbury, St Osmund (RC), Exeter Street

Mid-19th-century glass designed by Pugin for Hardman in E and two S windows.

Salisbury, St Thomas of Canterbury, St Thomas Square

In E and S windows of S chapel, and in N chapel, 15th-century fragments.

Shalbourne, St Michael

E window by Kempe.

Sopworth, St Mary

Glass of 1873 by Morris & Co. – the Three Maries, designed by Burne-Jones and by Morris.

Stanton Fitzwarren, St Leonard

Glass of 1896 and 1907 by Kempe.

Detail of 'Prisoners of Conscience' window by Gabriel Loire of Chartres, installed 1980. Salisbury Cathedral, Wiltshire

Stourhead
In Library of House, lunette by F. Egington, 'School of Athens'.

Swindon, Holy Rood (RC), Groundwell Road
19th-century glass by Hardman, and modern glass by the Revd Mr Norris of Buckfast Abbey.

Swindon, St Mark, Church Place
Kempe glass in E window of S chapel (1897) and in one N aisle window.

Teffont Evias, St Michael and All Angels
Many 17th-century roundels and panels of different shapes, appear to be Netherlandish. Many are in monochrome but some coloured in enamels, e.g. Dutch barge in E window of N chapel.
Bishop in window of N aisle done in pot-metal glass – perhaps 16th century.

Trowbridge, St James
Glass mainly 19th century, by Powell, Bell, Burlison & Grylls, Warrington, Hardman etc.

Upavon, St Mary
E window designed by Henry Holiday, for Powell & Sons.

West Lavington, All Saints
In chancel, two windows by Kempe (1892 and 1907).

Westwood, St Mary
15th-century glass in chancel, including E window of Crucifixion, angels and Instruments of the Passion.

Wilsford, St Michael
In a S window, 15th-century Crucifixion.

Wilton, St Mary and St Nicholas
Remarkable and unexpectedly rich collection of glass, all brought into this church of the 1840s. The best and earliest of the glass is French, some of it came from St Denis just outside Paris, and from the Ste Chapelle. It is concentrated in the windows at the E end of the church, and includes:
The seven windows of the central apse containing a wonderful assortment of French glass of the 12th and 13th centuries. The scenes are mainly set in lozenge-shapes, and since their recent

The Marriage at Cana; French glass of c. 1230, originally from Rouen. Wilton, Wiltshire

cleaning and restoration, their superb quality and colour is revealed; the panels include: (working from S to N)
1st light: angel *c.* 1250 (Île de France) Prodigal Son returns, *c.* 1144 (St Denis).
2nd light: Story of a king, *c.* 1250 (St Germain des Près, Paris), Virgin and Child, *c.* 1150 (St Denis).
3rd light: Raising of Tobias, *c.* 1250 (Ste Chapelle), Flight into Egypt, *c.* 1150 (St Denis), cherubs, *c.* 1250 (Ste Chapelle).
4th light: Prodigal Son, *c.* 1220 (northern France), an especially impressive beardless saint or Christ with folded arms and scarlet halo, 1180–1200 (St Denis ?) (colour plate 5), Cleansing the Temple, 1230 (Rouen).
5th light: Christ, Mary and the Apostles, *c.* 1230 (Rouen).
6th light: Wedding at Cana, *c.* 1230 (Rouen), scene from mass, *c.* 1225 (Compiègne, Île de France), Nathan or Balaam from a Jesse tree, *c.* 1150 (St Denis).
7th light: St Stephen (?), Martyrdom of St Catherine, 1220–5 (Compiègne, Île de France), Prodigal Son and demons, *c.* 1220 (northern France).
In N chapel, more 13th-century French glass, including Magdalen in left window, and 16th-century Swiss glass including two more decapitated saints (Regula's brother and friend).
In SW window, 16th-century glass: the male members of the Pembroke family as donors, and the arms of Mary I and Philip of Spain.

Winterbourne Bassett, St Katherine
Fragments of 14th-century glass in head of N window in chancel.

Wootton Bassett, St Bartholomew and All Saints
19th-century glass, largely by Hardman.

Yorkshire

(NY) = **North Yorkshire**
(SY) = **South Yorkshire**
(WY) = **West Yorkshire**

Acaster Malbis (NY), Holy Trinity
Early 14th-century glass in E window, mainly yellow and green, also in a chancel S window: Christ in Majesty, St Peter, St Alban, St Julia, St James of Compostella, and St Bartholomew with his skin. Also heraldic glass.

Adwick-le-Street (SY), St Lawrence
E window of N chapel by F.E. Nuttgens: stories of St Francis, 1943.

Allerton Mauleverer (NY), St Martin
Some 18th-century glass in the E window, including the Mauleverer coat of arms by William Peckitt of York, 1756.

Almondbury (WY), All Hallows
Some 15th-century glass in N (Kaye) chapel: family of donors, Saints Elizabeth, Helena, John the Baptist, Barbara, Margaret, and St Anne teaching the Virgin to read.

Ampleforth (NY), St Hilda
Window in Lady Chapel by Patrick Reyntiens, 1961.

Austerfield (SY), St Helen
Much stained glass by Kempe.

Aysgarth (NY), St Andrew
E window of N chapel (Good Samaritan) of 1860, commissioned to commemorate the parson's escape from burglars.

Baldersby (NY), St James

19th-century glass by Wailes, O'Connor, and Preedy.

Barnsley (SY), St Mary, St Mary's Gate
Glass of 1821 in N chapel N window, formerly in the E window.

Bingley (NY), All Saints
E window by Henry Holiday, 1890. In N chancel chapel window, Morris & Co. glass of 1873, designed by Burne-Jones.

Birkin (NY), St Mary
14th-century glass, fragmentary, in E window of S aisle. Also Morris window of three angels, designed by Burne-Jones.

Bolton Percy (NY), All Saints
Original 15th-century glass, though restored, in E window: ten life-size figures of saints and archbishops, with angels, cherubs and shields in the tracery.

Bradfield (SY), St Nicholas
15th- and 16th-century glass in N windows.

Bradford (WY), Cathedral (St Peter)
Very good early Morris glass (1862), notably in the E window. Designed by Burne-Jones, Rossetti, Ford Madox Brown.
Also glass by Moira Forsyth, dating from 1956–69.

Bradford (WY), Cartwright Hall (art gallery)
Stained glass windows illustrating Malory's story of Tristram and Isolde, designed by Morris, Burne-Jones, Ford Madox Brown, Rossetti, Val Prinsep and Arthur Hughes. Originally intended for Harden Grange, near Bingley.

Bramley (WY), St Peter
N aisle window by Morris & Co., 1882.

Brighouse (WY), St James
Chancel N window is glass by Morris & Co., also the E window, 1870–1. Designed by Burne-Jones, Rossetti, Madox Brown.

Brighouse (WY), St Martin
Good early Morris glass in a N window, 1872.

Brompton by Sawdon (NY), All Saints
Bird window in N wall by Rosemary Rutherford, 1970.

Calverley (WY), church
Fragmentary medieval glass in E window, including Crucifixion and heraldic shields.

Cawthorne (SY), All Saints
A N chapel window of 1867 could well be Morris glass.

Church Fenton (NY), All Saints
E window of chancel and N window of N transept have 14th-century fragments.

Clifford (WY), St Edward (RC)
Mid-19th-century glass mainly designed by Pugin.

Conisbrough (SY), St Peter
Fragments of 15th-century glass in S window of chancel: a saint and bishop.

Coxwold (NY), St Michael
In tracery of N and S windows, original 15th-century figures.

Darton (SY), All Saints
Glass of 1526, showing Mary Magdalene, in a window in N chapel.

Dewsbury (WY), All Saints
Three 13th-century medallions in a N transept; they show the labours of the months – harvesting, threshing, pig-killing.
Above are 14th-century fragments, including headless figures of St Thomas à Becket and St Jude.

Doncaster (SY), St George
19th-century glass, including enormous E window designed by Pugin and made by Hardman – it was exhibited in the 1862 exhibition.
Jesse tree W window by Ward & Hughes, 1873, based on medieval one at Merevale, Warwickshire.
Also work by Wailes, O'Connor and Capronnier.

Easby (NY), St Agatha
Two small 14th-century figures in the E window.

East Rounton (NY), St Lawrence
S window of *c.* 1884 by Morris & Co. (Virgin and angels).

Ecclesfield (SY), St Mary
Late medieval glass in a N window, apparently came from a monastery at Coventry. Also 19th-century glass by Hedgeland (E window of 1855), Hardman, Wailes, Heaton, Butler & Bayne, and Kempe.

Elland (WY), St Mary
In E window, 21 panels illustrating the life of the Virgin, largely mid-15th century.

Ellerton (NY), St Mary
14th-century heraldic glass in tracery of nave windows.

Emley (WY), St Michael
15th-century glass in E window (Crucifixion, with Virgin and St John – unfortunately headless), and in S window of chancel (St Michael and another angel).

Felixkirk (NY), St Felix
A window in the apse has glass of *c.* 1300.

Flockton (WY), St James
William Morris windows of the Good Shepherd and St Anne, *c.* 1872.

Folkton (NY), St John the Evangelist
Fragments of 14th-century glass in a N window.

Gilling (NY), Holy Cross
Some 14th- and 15th-century fragments in chancel.

Goldsborough (NY), St Mary
E window of S aisle is of 1696 – heraldic work, with inscription *Foyal et Loyal*.

Harrogate (NY), St Wilfred
A new series of windows is being commissioned for this church from Harry Harvey of York.

High Melton (SY), St James
15th-century figures in N window of chancel. Heraldic glass of *c.* 1800 in a S aisle is possibly by William Peckitt.

Howsham (NY), St John
All the glass is by Clayton & Bell, and rather good.

Huddersfield (WY), St Peter
Stained glass by Willement (1852), and by Sir Ninian Comper (E window, 1921).

Kirk Sandall (SY), St Oswald
Extensive early 16th-century glass, including St Margaret and the Dragon, other female saints, St Oswald, the Ascension.

Kirkby Wharfe (NY), St John
In a N window, medieval heraldic glass. Old glass also in chancel S windows (15th century and 16th–17th century) and E window of S aisle. Subjects include Descent from the Cross, Flight into Egypt, Abraham and Isaac, the Virgin, Jesus and the Doctors, the Agony in the Garden. The glass derives largely from Austria (six panels) and Switzerland (ten panels).

Kirklington (NY), St Michael
Three 15th-century heads in N window of vestry.

Knaresborough (NY), St John the Baptist
19th-century glass, including Morris & Co. windows, S in chancel and W in S aisle. Designed by Ford Madox Brown, 1872–4.

Leeds (WY), Mill Hill Unitarian Chapel
Morris & Co. glass in S aisle window.

Leeds (WY), St John the Baptist, Adel
SW window of chancel is by Henry Gyles of York, 1706. Also by him, heraldic glass in vestry window, 1681, formerly in the E window.

Leeds (WY), St Peter, Kirkgate (parish church)
Early continental glass in E window. The rest is 19th century: by Wilmshurst, Wailes, Warrington, Evans of Shrewsbury, and Thomas Wright of Leeds.

Leeds (WY), St Saviour, Ellerby Road
Good glass by O'Connor, designed by Pugin, 1840s.

Malsis School, Chapel (NY)
17 memorial windows, mainly abstract. Piper/Reyntiens, 1966–7.

Methley (WY), St Oswald
15th-century glass in E window of S chapel – eight figures, and eight little angels over them.

Middleham (NY), St Mary and St Alkelda
15th-century fragments in W window of N aisle.

More Monkton (NY), Red House School chapel
Late 16th-century heraldic glass by Dinnickhoff of York.

Normanton (WY), All Saints
Extensive glass of varied date, the earliest being 13th century, given by Thomas Ward (of Ward & Hughes) in the 19th century. Now cleaned and restored by the York Glaziers' Trust.

Ripon (NY), Cathedral
Medallions of 14th-century glass in S aisle. The rest is 19th century, mainly by Wailes.

Scarborough (NY), St Martin's-on-the-Hill

Much glass by Morris & Co. The E window, including the Crucifixion; the W window with Adam and Eve (1862); the W rose window of 1862 designed by Burne-Jones; window with Joshua, Michael and Gideon; window of St John the Baptist and King David – all these date from *c.* 1862, and are very early Morris glass.

Also S aisle and W window of St Martin dividing his cloak and St Martin being received into heaven – designed by Ford Madox Brown, 1864.

Selby (NY), Selby Abbey

The E window is a Jesse tree of *c.* 1330, although very restored: it contains 68 figures. The chancel N window and the sacristy E window also have medieval glass.

Sheffield (SY), Cathedral

Fine Jesse tree in N transept, by Alfred Gérente. Window of History of Sheffield by C. Webb, lantern by Keith New, 1962.

Sheffield (SY), St Mark, Broomhill

W window 'Flames' by Piper/Reyntiens, 1963–4. E window by Harry Stammers.

Studley Royal (NY), St Mary

Very fine 19th-century glass by Saunders & Co., designed by F. Weeks.

Tadcaster (NY), St Mary, Kirkgate

Fragmentary 15th-century glass and 16th-century roundels in W window of S aisle. Morris glass of 1875–80 in E window.

Thirsk (NY), St Mary

15th-century glass in E window of S aisle, including figures of St Anne, Cleophas, St Leonard; St Giles in the tracery lights. SE window of S aisle by Henry Holiday, 1875.

Thornhill (WY), St Michael and All Angels

Late 15th-century Jesse tree in E window, very fine though restored; the donor was Robert Frost. Last Judgement E window of the Saville Chapel dating from 1493. This chapel also has two Crucifixion windows, that in the N window dating from the 14th century.

Thorpe Bassett (NY), All Saints

Part of a 14th-century Crucifixion in tracery of E window, also heraldic glass.

Thrybergh (SY), St Leonard

15th-century glass, though restored in E window of S aisle, with kneeling donors.

Topcliffe (NY), St Columba

The three-light S window of chancel was made by Lavers & Barraud, 1860. The Visitation and Nativity were designed by Michael Halliday, the Annunciation by Burne-Jones.

Ugthorpe (NY), St Anne (RC)

Glass by Hardman, much in the style of Pugin, 1855–7.

Wakefield (WY), Cathedral (All Saints)

The stained glass is mainly by Kempe.

Wath (SY), St Mary

Crucifixion, *c.* 1300, in head of E window of S transept.

West Heslerton (NY), All Saints

W window of flowers, by Rosemary Rutherford, 1966.

246

West Tanfield (NY), St Nicholas

15th-century fragments in E window of N aisle (Crucifixion, Virgin annunciate, angels and saints).

Wetherby (WY), St James

Recent window by Harry Harvey of York.

Whorlton (NY), Holy Cross

Good glass by Kempe: window of the Passion in the chancel (1879), and of the Two Josephs in the nave (1902). W window by Heaton, Butler & Bayne.

Wragby (WY), St Michael

Numerous small panels of Swiss glass, dating from 16th–18th century, throughout the church. Also some English glass in E window.

York (NY), Minster

Supremely important for its medieval glass. See Peter Gibson's section on this subject in *The Noble City of York*, ed. A. Stacpoole. For a handy but detailed list, see B. Johnson's section on Stained Glass (pp. 58–67) in the *Yorkshire: York and the East Riding* volume of Nikolaus Pevsner's *Buildings of England*. There is also a booklet *The Stained Glass of York* by A.L. Laishley, generally available at the Minster. For a definitive study of the W windows of the nave, see Thomas French and David O'Connor's Volume III of the *Corpus Vitrearum Medii Aevi*.

The Five Sisters window: N wall of N transept, five lancets of grisaille glass of c. 1250–75 – mellow and subtle patterning, not by any means all grey; a panel of Habakkuk visiting Daniel in the Lions' Den at the bottom of the central light.

St William's window: the life of St William shown in a hundred panels, with the donors (the Ros or Roos family of Helmsley Castle) kneeling below, 1422.

The Great East window: by John Thornton of Coventry, 1405–8 (colour plate 20).

St Cuthbert's window: given by Thomas Langley, Bishop of Durham (d. 1437). It contains 55 episodes from the life of St Cuthbert; the donor appears in a panel below, next to Cardinal John Kemp.

Jesse window: in S wall of nave, 14th century. It came from New College, Oxford, and was given to William Peckitt, glazier of York, in 1765. Restored and sorted out in 1950.

Great West window: of 1338, given by Archbishop Melton; impressive rows of figures, with curvilinear tracery above including a heart-shape ('The Heart of Yorkshire').

Bellfounders' window: 2nd from W in the N aisle (see p. 38).

Rose window: S transept; early 16th century, may have commemorated the marriage of Henry VII to Elizabeth of York.

The 12th-century panel of a king from a Jesse tree, once thought to be the oldest stained glass in England – but no longer – is now restored (given a face), and displayed in a light-box in the Foundations Museum (see p. 21).

York (NY), All Saints, North Street

Very fine glass, mainly of the early 15th century.

E window: canopied figures of St John the Baptist, St Anne teaching the Virgin, St Christopher; below are the donors the Blackburns, senior and junior, both called Nicholas, with wives, both called Margaret. Probably between 1412 and 1428.

N aisle E window: early 14th-century

Adoration of the Magi, Crucifixion, Coronation of the Virgin; underneath, an Annunciation, Nativity, Resurrection.

Prykke of Conscience window: E end of N aisle, *c.* 1410. Possibly by John Thornton. It shows the last fifteen days at the end of the world: 1. the sea rises, 2. the sea falls, 3. the sea resumes its normal level, 4. sea-monsters appear, 5. the sea on fire, 6. trees catch fire, 7. earthquakes, 8. rocks and stones burn, 9. men hide in holes in the earth, 10. sky and earth alone to be seen, 11. men emerge from holes to pray,

12. human bones come to life, 13. stars fall from heaven, 14. men die, 15. fire destroys the world (colour plate 21).

Corporal Acts of Mercy window: N aisle, next to Prykke of Conscience window. Early 15th century. The Corporal Acts of Mercy are: feeding the hungry, giving drink to the thirsty and hospitality to the stranger, clothing the naked, tending the sick, and visiting prisoners. The same bearded benefactor appears in each scene (see p. 53 and colour plate 26).

N aisle to W: St Thomas, Christ crowned

Detail depicting sea monsters appearing, from the 'Prykke of Conscience' window, early fifteenth century. All Saints, North Street, York

with thorns, another saint who may be St Thomas of Canterbury, all under canopies.

S aisle, first from E: of *c.* 1440. St Michael, with three kneeling donors below, and St John the Evangelist with three kneeling donors below.

S aisle, third from E: window of the Nine Orders of Angels. First half of the 15th century (a man wearing spectacles).

S aisle, fourth from E: St James, the Virgin and Child, and an archbishop, all under canopies, *c.* 1440.

York (NY), All Saints, Pavement

The W window has glass of *c.* 1370, formerly in St Saviour's Church; it was restored and installed by the Minster Glass Workshops in 1955–7. A fine window showing scenes of the Passion.

York (NY), Guildhall, St Helen's Square (behind Mansion House)

The W window by H.W. Harvey of York, modern glass. (The 15th-century Guildhall was burnt in 1942, rebuilt and opened in 1960.) The window depicts the history of York: showing from left to right: York's architectural significance, York's military significance, York's coat of arms and below, a miracle play, York's trade and transport, education and social life in York.

In the tracery, people connected with York's history, together with the guild badges of the Glaziers and the Merchant Adventurers.

York (NY), Holy Trinity, Goodramgate

E window contains glass of *c.* 1470–80. In the five main lights are St George and the Dragon, St John the Baptist, the Trinity (the dead Christ supported by God the Father, with the Dove of the Holy Spirit above), St John the Divine, and St Christopher. Below are small scenes of the Holy Family, the Coronation of the Virgin, and St Ursula.

In the S aisle, 14th-century armorial glass.

York (NY), St Denys, Walmgate

The glass mainly dates from the third quarter of the 14th century. In the N aisle, scenes from the life of St John the Baptist; but incorporated are two roundels of very early date (12th century?) which seem to depict the Virgin and St Michael. Borders of gold lions on red ground and gold crowns on blue.

York (NY), St Helen, St Helen's Square

This was the parish church of the York glass painters. Note the shield with their coat of arms in the W window of the S aisle. There are fragments of 14th- and 15th-century glass, chiefly in the W window over the door; they include an archbishop, a king, a crowned Virgin, a kneeling donor with wife and five children.

E window, 19th century, by Hardman and Wailes.

York (NY), St Martin-cum-Gregory, Micklegate

Contains 14th- and 15th-century glass, mainly in S aisle E window, with St Martin sharing his cloak, saints on either side, donors below. Also 16th-century panels. William Peckitt's window of 1796 to two members of his family; he was buried here, and his memorial was painted by his wife.

York (NY), St Martin-le-Grand, Coney Street

Opposite the S door, a fine window of

c. 1437 with the life of St Martin. More 15th-century glass in the S aisle.

York (NY), St Michael, Spurrierate

The glass is mainly of the mid-15th century. It includes St John the Baptist, the Fall of Lucifer, the Woman Clothed with the Sun, the Nine Orders of Angels, and a somewhat fragmented Jesse tree. It was restored and re-inserted in 1948.

York (NY), St Michael-le-Belfry, Minster Yard

14th-century glass in the E window: saints, Annunciation, Nativity, Resurrection, Coronation of the Virgin.

In the rest of the church, good glass of the 16th century, including scenes from the life of St Thomas à Becket.

Glossary
of Technical Terms

Abrading	Scraping away the surface of the glass.
Aciding	Part-removal of a layer of flashed glass by using hydrofluoric acid.
Agnus Dei	Symbol of St John the Baptist, a lamb carrying a flag.
Aisle	Part of a church parallel to nave, choir or transept, from which it is separated by piers or columns.
'Antique' glass	Glass made by blowing an elongated bubble, cutting off the end, and splitting it.
Appliqué	Smaller pieces of glass stuck on to a sheet of glass, generally with epoxy resin.
Apse	Semicircular or polygonal termination of a chancel or chapel.
Armature	A metal framework, traditionally of iron, supporting the glass within a geometrical composition.
Back-painting	Additional iron-oxide painting on the outside of the glass to suggest a three-dimensional effect.
Biblia Pauperum	Poor Man's Bible. Properly refers to a book of illustrations, first in manuscript, later printed, forming a very important source of images for medieval glass; loosely used to refer to the glass itself.
Black Letter	Gothic script in use from *c.* 1380.
Calms or *Cames*	Leads, H-shaped in section, used for holding together separate pieces of glass.
Canopy	Representation of an architectural hood or niche, framing the upper part of a figure.

Cartoon	Full-scale drawing laying out the composition to be completed.
Censer	A small vessel containing incense.
Chancel	The part of the east end of a church that contains the main altar.
Choir	The part of the church where divine service is sung.
Cinquefoil	Five-cusped design, generally an opening in tracery.
Clerestory	The upper part of a church, pierced by windows.
Corrosion	Flaking off or pitting of the surface of glass.
Crown glass	Circular disc shape made by spinning the liquid glass on a heated rod.
Cut-line	Full-scale pattern from which the glass is cut.
Dalle-de-verre *technique*	Slabs or tiles of glass, made in a mould, and usually fixed in epoxy resin or concrete.
Diaper	Patterning of small squares or diamond-shapes.
Enamelling	The surface of the glass is painted with a mixture of ground coloured glass and a medium, and is subsequently fired in a hot kiln, to fix it.
Flashing	Alternating layers of coloured and clear glass; some colours, especially red derived from copper, need to be flashed in order not to be opaque.
Fused glass	A modern technique of fusing together two plates of coloured glass.
Golden Legend	Book on the lives of the saints, written by Jacobus da Voragine in *c.* 1275.
Grisaille	Glass in clear or muted colours (literally, greyish), often with foliage or other linear designs, but without pictorial theme (see p. 212).
Grozing iron	A metal tool for nibbling or chipping off the edges of glass in order to shape it.
Halation	The fusing of colour which is the effect of putting opposing colours next to each other.
Jesse tree	The genealogical tree of Christ.
Jewelling	Chips of coloured glass fixed on to the surface of the main piece and fired.

GLOSSARY OF TECHNICAL TERMS

Lancet	Narrow window with a pointed arch.
Lights	Openings between the mullions (stone divisions) of a window.
Lombardic script	Lettering of great clarity in use before *c.* 1380 when Black Letter became common.
Mandorla	Almond-shaped frame in which saintly figures are placed, the shape denoting their holiness.
Metal	A term for glass, particularly glass in its liquid form.
Mouchette	Dagger-shaped opening in tracery.
Muff glass	Glass formed by being blown into an iron cylinder or muff, later being cut and flattened.
Norman slab	Rectangular slabs made by blowing a bubble of glass into a square mould and afterwards cutting at the corners.
Pot-metal	Glass coloured while in the liquid state.
Quarry	Small piece of glass, generally diamond-shaped; often a number of quarries are leaded up together to make a neutral ground. Some quarries have been painted with designs of birds, flowers or leaf forms.
Quatrefoil	Four-cusped shape, generally an opening in tracery.
Rebus	The visual pun of making a name into an image.
Rood	The Crucifixion, usually accompanied by the Virgin and St John.
Rose window	Large circular window with tracery.
Roundel	A circle of glass, whether of one or several pieces; later roundels were often silver-stained or enamelled.
Ruby glass	Red glass, which was usually flashed or laminated.
Saddle-bar	Horizontal metal bar, traditionally of iron, supporting the glass panel within the window embrasure.
Silver stain	Use of silver nitrate to turn the surface of a piece of glass yellow or gold in colour.
Transom	Horizontal division in the tracery.
Trefoil	Opening formed by the meeting of three cusps.
Typology	The belief that the events in the New Testament were pre-figured by events in the Old.
Yellow stain	See *Silver stain*.
'White' glass	Uncoloured or clear glass.

Bibliography

Alexander, J. and Binski, P. (ed.), *Age of Chivalry* (Catalogue to 1987 Royal Academy Exhibition). Weidenfeld & Nicolson, 1987.

Angus, M., *Modern Stained Glass in British Churches*. 1984.

Archer, M., *An Introduction to English Stained Glass*. HMSO, 1985.

Armitage, E.L., *Stained Glass, History, Technology & Practice*. 1959.

Arnold, H., *Stained Glass of the Middle Ages in England & France*. 1913.

Aston, M., *The 15th Century. The Prospect of Europe*. Thames & Hudson, 1968.

Baker, J., *English Stained Glass*. 1960.
   English Stained Glass of the Medieval Period. 1978.

Binnal, P., *The 19th Century Stained Glass in Lincoln Minster. Friends of Lincoln Cathedral, 1966*.

British Society of Master Glass Painters – *Journals*.

Brooke, C., *The 12th Century Renaissance*. Thames & Hudson, 1969.

Brown, S. and O'Connor, D., *Glass Painters* (in series, *Medieval Craftsmen*). British Museum Press, 1991.

Caviness, M.H., *The Windows of Christ Church Cathedral, Canterbury*. British Academy, 1981.
   Stained Glass Before 1540. 1983.

Cennini, C. d'A., *Il Libro dell'Arte*. Translated by Daniel V. Thompson Jr. as *The Craftsman's Handbook*. Dover Publications, New York, 1954.

Cowen, Painton, *A Guide to Stained Glass in Britain*. Michael Joseph, 1985.

Crewe, S., *Stained Glass in England, 1180–1540* (Royal Commission on Historic Monuments). HMSO, 1987.

Day, L.F., *Windows: a Book about Stained & Painted Glass*. Batsford, 1909.

Drake, M., *A History of English Glass-Painting*. T. Werner Laurie, 1912.

French, T. and O'Connor, D., *York Minster, A Catalogue of Medieval Stained Glass*. 1987.

Gibson, P., *The Stained & Painted Glass of York Minster*. 1979.
   'The Stained & Painted Glass of York'. In: *The Noble City of York*, ed. A. Stacpoole. 1972.

BIBLIOGRAPHY

Harrison, F., *The Painted Glass of York*. 1927.

Harrison, K.P., *The Windows of King's College Chapel, Cambridge*. 1952.

Harrison, M., *Victorian Stained Glass*. Barrie & Jenkins, 1980.

Harvey, J., *Medieval Craftsmen*. Batsford, 1975.

Hayes, D., *Ervin Bossanyi: the Splendour of Stained Glass*. Friends of Canterbury Cathedral, 1965.

Holiday, H., *Stained Glass as an Art*. Macmillan, 1896.

Hutchinson, F.E., *Medieval Glass at All Souls College*. 1949.

Ingram Hill, Revd D., *The Stained Glass of Canterbury Cathedral*.

Knowles, J.A., 'Essays in the History of the York School of Glass Painting', *The Stained Glass of York Minster* (3 vols). 1936.

Laishley, A.L., *The Stained Glass of York*.

Le Couteur, J.D., *Ancient Glass in Winchester*. 1920.

Lee, L., *The Appreciation of Stained Glass*. OUP, 1977.

Stained Glass. Oxford Paperbacks, 1967.

Stained Glass (by Lee, L., Seddon, G. and Stephens, F. Photographs by Halliday, S. and Lushington, L.). Mitchell Beazley, 1976.

Marteau, R., *Stained Glass Windows of Chagall 1957–1970*.

Morgan, F.C., *Hereford Cathedral Church Glass*. 1967.

Morgan, N.J., *The Medieval Painted Glass of Lincoln Cathedral*. 1983.

Newton, P., *The County of Oxford* [stained glass] (*Corpus Vitrearum Medii Aevi*). 1979.

O'Connor, D. and Haselock, J., *Stained and Painted Glass* (in History of York Minster). OUP, 1977.

Pevsner, N., (and others). All volumes of *The Buildings of England*. Penguin.

Piper, J., *Stained Glass: Art or Anti-art*.

Rackham, B., *The Stained Glass Windows of Canterbury Cathedral*. SPCK, 1957.

Read, Sir H., *English Stained Glass*. 1926.

Read, H. and Baker, J., *English Stained Glass*. 1960.

Reyntiens, P., *Technique of Stained Glass*. 1977.

Rushforth, G., *Medieval Christian Imagery as Illustrated by the Painted Windows of Great Malvern Priory Church*. 1936.

Sewter, A.C., *The Stained Glass of William Morris & his Circle*.

Smith, M.Q., *The Stained Glass of Bristol Cathedral*. 1983.

Sowers, R., *The Lost Art*. 1954.

Spring, R.O.C., *The Stained Glass of Salisbury Cathedral*. 1979.

Theophilus, *On Divers Arts (Diversarum Artium Schedula)*. Trans. 1963, J.G. Hawthorn and C.S. Smith. Univ. of Chicago Press.

Thomas, B. and Richardson, E., *Directory of Master Glass Painters*.

Toy, J., *A Guide and Index to the Windows of York Minster*. 1985.

Wayment, H., *The Windows of King's College Chapel, Cambridge*. 1972.

Welander, D., *Stained Glass of Gloucester Cathedral*. 1985.

Westlake, N.H.J., *A History of Design in Painted Glass*. (3 vols. 1881–94).

Whall, C., *Stained Glass Work*. 1920.

Willement, T., *A Concise Account of the Principal Works in Stained Glass*. 1840.

Winston, C., 'On the Painted Glass in the Cathedral & Churches of York'. Printed in: Proceedings of the Archaeological Institute, 1846. Reprinted in: *Memoires Illustrative of the Art of Glass*. 1865.

Woodforde, C., *English Stained & Painted Glass*. Clarendon Press, Oxford, 1954.

Stained Glass in Somerset, 1250–1830.

The Norwich School of Glass Painting in the 15th Century. 1950.

WORKS NOT LISTED IN EARLIER EDITIONS

Bowe, N. Gordon., *The Life and Work of Harry Clarke*. Irish Academic Press, 1989.

French, T., *York Minster: The Great East Window*. British Academy, 1995.

Marks, R., *Stained Glass in England during the Middle Ages*. Routledge, 1993.

Osborne. J., *John Piper and Stained Glass*. Sutton Publishing, 1997.

Index

INDEX

INDEX